PLATO ON PARTS AND WHOLES

PLATO ON PARTS AND WHOLES

THE METAPHYSICS OF STRUCTURE

Verity Harte

CLARENDON PRESS · OXFORD

OXFORD
UNIVERSITY PRESS

Great Clarendon Street, Oxford OX2 6DP

Oxford University Press is a department of the University of Oxford.
It furthers the University's objective of excellence in research, scholarship,
and education by publishing worldwide in

Oxford New York

Auckland Cape Town Dar es Salaam Hong Kong Karachi
Kuala Lumpur Madrid Melbourne Mexico City Nairobi
New Delhi Shanghai Taipei Toronto

With offices in

Argentina Austria Brazil Chile Czech Republic France Greece
Guatemala Hungary Italy Japan South Korea Poland Portugal
Singapore Switzerland Thailand Turkey Ukraine Vietnam

Oxford is a registered trade mark of Oxford University Press
in the UK and in certain other countries

Published in the United States
by Oxford University Press Inc., New York

First published 2002
First published in paperback 2005

British Library Cataloguing in Publication Data

Data available

Library of Congress Cataloging in Publication Data

Data available

ISBN 0–19–823675–1
ISBN 0–19–927844–X (Pbk.)

1 3 5 7 9 10 8 6 4 2

Typeset by Hope Services (Abingdon) Ltd.
Printed in Great Britain
on acid-free paper by
Biddles Ltd.,
King's Lynn, Norfolk

For Iain

PREFACE

This book has its origins in my doctoral work at Cambridge University. For their wise counsel during this early stage in the development of my ideas I am grateful to my supervisors, Myles Burnyeat, Nicholas Denyer, and Malcolm Schofield; to my fellow graduate students, especially Mary Hannah Jones and Melissa Lane; and to my examiners, David Bostock and David Sedley.

In writing the book, I have chosen not to revise my doctoral thesis, but to write from scratch. I hope that this has made it a better book; it has certainly delayed its completion. In the meantime, I have again been fortunate in my intellectual environment. After a brief and enjoyable sojourn at St Hilda's College, Oxford, I joined the Philosophy Department at King's College London in 1996. To all my colleagues I am indebted for their contribution to my continuing philosophical education and for the supportive and invigorating community they help to create. Special thanks are due to the members, past and present, of the KCL Thursday reading group in ancient philosophy, in particular those who attended our reading of the *Timaeus*; our discussions were of considerable importance in the development of the material on the *Timaeus* presented here.

Papers based on early drafts of chapters of this book have been presented to the B-Club in Cambridge; to Philosophy Departments at Bristol, Harvard, King's College London, Ohio State, Sheffield, and Sussex; and to the Classics Department at Pittsburgh. I have been fortunate in my audience on all these occasions. In a form close to the present one, the material in Chapter 1 was given as a paper to the Boston Area Colloquium in Ancient Philosophy, at Harvard University, in October 2000. It is to be published in volume 17 of the *Proceedings of the Boston Area Colloquium in Ancient Philosophy* (Leiden: Brill, 2002). I am grateful to the editors and to Brill for permission to reuse this material here.

A number of people gave generously of their time and wisdom to read part or all of a draft of this book, and I am especially grateful to them: to Lesley Brown, Myles Burnyeat, Ursula Coope, Chris Hughes, Melissa Lane, M. M. McCabe, and Allan Silverman; to Kathrin Koslicki, who used an early draft in a seminar at Tufts University and was kind enough to relay to me both her own and the seminar's comments; as well as to two anonymous readers for Oxford University Press. This book has been much improved by their efforts. Naturally, I alone am responsible for any inadequacies that remain.

The book's eventual completion was greatly assisted by the timely gift of a sabbatical term by King's College London and the generous award of a second term of leave, supported by the Arts and Humanities Research Board. To my editor at the Press, Peter Momtchiloff, I am grateful for his early interest in the project, for his always sane advice, and for his patience in awaiting a manuscript originally promised for 1997. My thanks also to Laurien Berkeley for copy-editing in a sympathetic and helpful fashion.

Last, but by no means least, thanks of a different sort are due to my parents, Anne and Harry Harte, who have been ever supportive of my intellectual endeavours; and to my husband, Iain Petrie, for more than I can say. This book is dedicated to him with love.

V. A. H.

CONTENTS

Introduction

THIS book is an examination of Plato's treatment of the relation between a whole and its parts. It is focused on discussion of relevant passages from a group of Plato's later works: (in roughly the order of my discussion) *Theaetetus*, *Parmenides*, *Sophist*, *Philebus*, and *Timaeus*. By 'later' I mean no more than after the *Republic*, which I take to be uncontroversial, if anything is uncontroversial as regards Platonic chronology. Of the works I shall consider, there is—or has been—considerable controversy surrounding the dating of the *Timaeus* within the post-*Republic* period.[1] I myself find it more natural to take the *Timaeus* together with the *Philebus*, in some order or other, and to take them both to post-date the *Parmenides*.[2] However, since I am not proposing a developmental story about Plato's views of part and whole (on which, see further below), nothing in what I say depends on any particular chronology for the works I discuss.

While these are by no means the only works of Plato in which there is talk of part and whole, they are those in which there is actual theorizing of the relation between a whole and its parts as such, or of composition in general. What I mean by this may be illustrated, by contrast, through consideration of the following examples. In *Republic* IV Socrates famously proposes that a human soul is divided into three distinct parts. But there is here no discussion of what is involved in one thing being part of another, nor of the nature of the relation between the parts and the whole. The passage does propose a general principle which grounds the conclusion that the soul has parts; the 'principle of opposition' at 436b8–c1. However, this is, at most, a sufficient,

---

[1] Compare Owen (1953) with Cherniss (1957).

[2] But: contrast Waterfield (1980).

and not necessary, condition on something having parts. Thus it cannot be used to establish general claims about parts. Nor is it so used in the passage in question.

Or consider *Protagoras* 329d3–8, where Socrates and Protagoras discuss the proposition that virtue is a whole of which justice, temperance, and piety are parts; and consider whether these parts are comparable to the parts of a face or to the parts of gold. This latter distinction is certainly of interest, anticipating, as it does, Aristotle's distinction between anhomoeomerous and homoeomerous parts. However, beyond this distinction (which is not further discussed), there is here no discussion of the nature of parts or of the relation between parts and whole. In both the *Republic* and the *Protagoras* what we have are (undoubtedly interesting) examples of wholes of parts. However, in both works the focus of discussion is the examples themselves (the soul; the virtues) and not wholes of parts as such.

Of the works I shall discuss, none could be described as being devoted to the relation between parts and whole. Plato wrote no such work. Indeed, only of the *Parmenides* could one say that the discussion of part and whole therein has some claim to be among the dialogue's dominant themes. In general, discussion of part and whole is a theme which recurs in individual passages of the works I shall discuss, in ways which are often resonant of each other in terms of both language and content. The aim of this book is to make philosophical sense of these disparate discussions, both individually and in relation to each other.

In my view—a view for which the book as a whole constitutes a defence—Plato's discussions of part and whole in the works I shall consider may be divided into two distinct groups: those in which Plato explores a model of composition which he does not endorse; and those which work towards building an alternative to the rejected model. This book is organized around discussion of these two groups. §1.6 to Chapter 2 examine the discussions of the first group, Chapters 3 and 4 those of the second.

The division between these two groups does not coincide with the division between different works. To the first group—those which focus on the model which Plato does not endorse—belong passages of the *Parmenides*, the *Theaetetus*, and a passage of the

Sophist. To the second group—those which develop an alternative to the rejected model—belong other passages of the *Parmenides* and of the *Sophist*, and passages of the *Philebus* and *Timaeus*. The *Parmenides* as a whole enacts the contrast between the two groups and provides an illustration of the framework I propose for understanding their relation. Over the course of the *Parmenides* arguments involving the rejected model of composition are used to expose the problems that arise from its adoption; problems to which the alternative model of composition is framed as a solution.

In Plato, as we shall see, puzzles about composition are closely related to puzzles about one and many. In the discussions of composition in the first of my two groups Plato will be seen to be identifying and exploring the problems that arise from adopting a model of composition according to which a whole is identical to its collective parts. This model is shown to have the (paradoxical) consequence that the same thing(s) is (or are) both one thing and many things. The model depends—or so it emerges—on taking composition, the relation of many parts to one whole, to be identity, the relation of one thing to itself. But the claim that composition is identity, Plato argues, cannot support an adequate account of composition.

The discussions of this—as it proves to be—inadequate model of composition form the philosophical backdrop against which, in the discussions of the second group, Plato will be seen to be offering an alternative to this rejected model. The outlines of such an alternative are found in the *Parmenides*. But the development of the alternative is found in the discussions of the *Sophist*, *Philebus*, and *Timaeus*. Central to this alternative, I argue, is the view that wholes are structures, the identity of whose parts is determined only in the context of the whole they compose. The makings of a Platonic metaphysics of structure are put together through an examination of passages of the *Sophist*, *Philebus*, and *Timaeus*.

The discussions of part and whole in the two groups I consider are somewhat different in character. The discussions of the first group, without exception, talk directly—and at a level of considerable abstraction—about parts and wholes. In contrast, the discussions of the second group, save for those of the *Parmenides*, do not in general talk directly of part and whole, but of relations such as mixing and combining and of examples of the same. The rationale for my inclusion of these passages from the second group is, first, that relations such as mixing and combining are themselves relations of composition; and, second, that I take the discussion of these relations to have as its object the development of a general theory of composition.

Plato's discussions of mixing and combining provide both a range of diverse examples of composition and considerable direct theorizing of the relations concerned. Of the works I shall discuss, both the *Sophist* and *Philebus* contain a mix of theory and examples. The *Timaeus* offers no direct theorizing about composition, but it provides by far the most elaborate example of composition. In addition, discussion of the *Timaeus* proves to be in various ways complementary to the theorizing of the *Sophist* and *Philebus*.

The diversity of the examples involved in these various discussions of mixing and combining, together with the general theorizing of their mode of composition, show that Plato is not here concerned solely with particular examples of composition, considered as such. Rather, terms such as 'mixing' and 'combining' are used as general terms for composition in the development of the alternative model of composition on which Plato is here at work. Indeed, the use of these terms is itself part and parcel of Plato's development of a general model of composition which responds to the problems of the inadequate model discussed in the first of my groups. Especially in the *Philebus*, the general theorizing of these relations of composition is framed in ways which make clear its connection to the problems explored through the discussions of the first group.

Note that, in distinguishing Plato's discussions of composition in the works I consider into two groups, I am not proposing a developmental story, such that the rejected model of the first group is one to which Plato once found himself attracted and which he later gave up. At least for the passages I examine as members of the first group, I take it already to be true that the model of composition explored is there to be problematized, not endorsed. In this, I assume that Plato could spend considerable time discussing, and allow principal speakers of his works to spend time developing, a position which he takes to be false, but whose problems he is concerned to explore. For the passages in question, such an assumption must be defended by the merits of the resulting interpretation in each case. Outside of the passages which I discuss, my position leaves it open whether there ever was a time at which Plato endorsed such a model of composition; and I am content to leave this open. I stress only that I am not myself advocating that he once did.

Rather than view the contrast between the two groups of discussions of part and whole developmentally, I view them as complementary. Each, in different ways, is concerned with the nature of the composition of a whole from its parts. Each, in different ways, is concerned with the same problem. Roughly speaking, this might be put as the problem of how to give an account of the composition of a whole from its parts such that a whole is an individual rather than a mere collection. The discussions of the first group worry at the problem by worrying at a conception of composition in which this fails to be the case. The discussions of the second group provide both models and examples of composition that respect and privilege this constraint.

Note, in this connection, that, although I shall be much concerned with the nature of a whole as an individual, the term 'individual' in my usage can as easily apply to a type as to a token. In this, I am guided by Plato's own discussions, in which the nature of composition is discussed both for tokens and for types and in a way which seems orthogonal to the type–token distinction. It is sometimes assumed that the relation between part and whole is an exclusively spatial relation. Plato makes no such assumption. Indeed, as we shall see, the majority of his examples of wholes are abstract types. But not all of his examples are types. Further, while one might have a different theory for the composition of types and for the composition of tokens, there is no evidence that Plato did so.

The relation between part and whole is a central topic in ontology. As such, the topic of this book is intimately related to the wider concerns of Plato's later metaphysics. However, I have

chosen to construe my brief quite strictly as focused on understanding Plato's views about composition, both because these
seem to me of independent interest and importance and for
reasons of practicability and space. While I would hope that this
book makes some contribution to our understanding of Plato's
late ontology, it is not itself a book about Plato's late ontology. In
particular, I shall not be concerned with the question of what
happens to forms. Thus, I do not propose to attempt to adjudicate which, if any, of the type objects which are offered as examples of wholes might properly be described as 'forms' and how, if
at all, such objects might be compared to the objects described as
forms in works such as the *Phaedo* or *Republic*, or indeed the
Timaeus. And I shall not be concerned with how the forms of the
Timaeus may relate to those of the *Phaedo* and *Republic*. My
focus is the nature of the theory of composition itself rather than
the nature of the objects to which the theory is applied.

Although this is a book about Plato's discussions of part and
whole, and not about part and whole in general, the book is
framed by consideration of what connections there are between
Plato's discussions and some of the dominant trends in modern
discussions of composition. This is not out of a belief that Plato's
views on some subject can only be of interest if they can be
brought into line with modern thought. Rather, it is because, as I
shall seek to show, there are fruitful points of contact between
Platonic and modern discussions of composition, reflection upon
which helps to shed light on both parties to the discussion and
provides a philosophical framework within which to evaluate the
Platonic discussions.

The problems to which Plato will be seen to be responding in
his discussion of the model of composition that he rejects are
problems central to any metaphysical investigation of composition. In particular, I argue, they are problems which may be seen
to lie behind certain tensions in one dominant line of thinking
about composition in modern times, particularly as espoused by
David Lewis. Further, the conception of composition that
emerges from the second group of Plato's discussions of composition is one which may fruitfully be compared and contrasted
with that of Lewis. In this way, I hope that this book enables

some sort of dialogue between Platonic and modern approaches to composition which may be of benefit to our understanding of both.

To this end, in Chapter 1, I spend considerable time examining some modern discussions of composition, especially those of Lewis, with the aim of framing a shared question about composition. Consideration of a passage from the *Theaetetus*, in §1.6, gives content to the points of contact established between Platonic and modern discussions of composition and provides the first example of Plato's concern with the model of composition that he rejects. Plato's examination of this rejected model, in the *Parmenides* especially, is then the focus of Chapter 2. Two out of the three contexts in which Plato explores this inadequate model suggest that he associates it with his predecessors, the Eleatics. The philosophical basis for this association is considered at the end of Chapter 2 (§2.5).

Chapters 1 and 2 have examined the philosophical framework within which Plato sets out to develop an alternative model of composition. Chapters 3 and 4 then focus on this alternative. In Chapter 3, I return to the *Parmenides*, from which the outline of an alternative theory emerges. In addition, I return to both the *Theaetetus* and the *Sophist* to recover some of the broader context of Plato's problem of composition. It is within this broader context that his solution to the problem takes shape. Central to this solution is the role given to structure in his account of the constitution of a whole. I thus begin Chapter 4 with some general considerations about structure and the role it might be thought to play in the constitution of a whole (§4.1). I then turn to Plato's own account of composition and of structure. Plato's own conception of wholes is identified through an examination of his discussions of combining and of mixing in the *Sophist*, *Philebus*, and *Timaeus*. In Chapter 5, I conclude by (briefly) considering the place of this conception of wholes in the broader context of his (late) philosophical work, and what, independently of this context, one might say about this conception, considered as such.

CHAPTER I

The Problem of Composition

COMPOSITE objects—wholes of parts—are ubiquitous. You and I are composites. So are some, perhaps all, of our parts: our bodily organs, their component cells, their component atoms (atoms in the physical sense, belying their name). My computer is a composite; so is this sentence; the (token) word 'sentence'; perhaps also, but more controversially, the word type 'sentence' of which there are three tokens in this paragraph. Most, if not all, of these are fairly ordinary examples. But even if it should turn out that what there *really* is is somewhat different from what we ordinarily think there is, almost any ontology will include composite objects. (Almost any: one might think that what there is has no parts; is a single incomposite object. Alternatively, one might think that none of the many things there are compose anything; that the world is made up of a number of distinct, and themselves incomposite, objects.) These exceptions aside, the part–whole relation—and an understanding of it—is central to ontology.

However, the part–whole relation is not well understood. Consider some examples: my hand is a part of me; the letter 'p' is part of the word 'part'; the Kyrie is part of the Requiem; being rational is part of being human; the philosophy department is part of the university. Are these examples of the same part–whole relation? That is, is there only one 'part of' relation, or are there several?[1] And are these all genuine examples of (some) part–whole relation? That is, do all these and other contexts in which it is acceptable in English to talk of one thing being part of another refer to one or more clearly definable part–whole relations, or are some mere modes of speaking? In particular, do abstract objects have parts, or should talk as if they do so be paraphrased away?

How should we even set about thinking about composition? Should we focus on the relation between any one part and the whole? Or should we focus on the relation between the many parts and the whole they compose? And how should we proceed? No doubt, there is more than one way to think about composition. But some are more fruitful than others. In this first part of the book I reflect on ways in which one might think about composition with the intention of framing a question about composition which is both philosophically fruitful and, since this is a book about Plato on composition, of particular relevance to Plato's treatment of composition.

1.1 IS A WHOLE (JUST) THE SUM OF ITS PARTS?

One way in which the problem of composition has sometimes been formulated is to debate whether or not a whole is (just) the sum of its parts. On one side are those who claim that a whole is indeed just the sum of its parts. Their opponents typically claim that a whole is more than, or greater than, the sum of its parts.[2] Prima facie, however, neither of these slogans is all that helpful in

---

[1] There is another possibility: that the terms 'part', 'whole', etc. are ambiguous, so that it might be ambiguously true that there is only one 'part of' relation.

[2] Alternatively, the contrast is between the claim that the whole is *equal to* the sum of its parts and that it is more than the sum. The history of these slogans has proved hard to trace. Already in Locke an early version of the first is described as a 'Maxim': that 'the whole is equal to all its parts' (*Essay concerning Human Understanding* IV. 7: Locke 1894: ii. 284). The claim that 'the whole is more than the sum of its parts' is offered as a translation of von Ehrenfels's first criterion for gestalt qualities in Rescher and Oppenheim (1955: 94). This slogan at least is now in popular use. Both slogans are the subject of critical scrutiny in Nagel (1952).

framing a question about composition. This is, in part, because it is not at all clear what either of them means.

Consider the claim that a whole is (just) the sum of its parts. The difficulty is this. What are we to understand by 'the sum'? Immediate associations come from arithmetic. Doing sums is adding things together. So, a sum is the result of adding things together. But if the claim is merely that a whole is what results from adding its parts together, it looks rather as if the claim that a whole is (just) the sum of its parts is simply another way of saying that a whole is a composite of its parts.[3] This, of course, is trivially true. Wholes are composites of parts. The relation between a whole and its parts is the relation of composition. All this may be agreed. But precisely what is up for discussion is how we are to understand the relation of composition.

Perhaps this is too hasty. Perhaps the identification of a whole with the sum of its parts is meant, in addition, to tell us something about the way in which a whole is composed of its parts. If so, it is not altogether transparent from the slogan what this might be. I shall consider below one somewhat technical suggestion which may be hidden in the term 'sum'. For now, let us stick with the immediate arithmetical associations of the term. Perhaps the thought is that composition is an operation on the parts or a relation between the parts which is either equivalent to or somehow like the arithmetical operation of addition.

Equivalence is, I suppose, a non-starter. An operation on the parts like addition might be putting the parts in contact or fastening them together. But this, at least apparently, will not do. The sad fact is that if you chop an elephant's trunk off and then place the trunk in contact with the remaining stump, you do not return the elephant to its former glory. More would have to be said here. (What about microsurgery?) Peter Van Inwagen has argued at length that no appeal to a single straightforward relation of bonding could explain the composition of a whole by its

---

[3] This is not quite true, since the use of the definite article in the phrase 'the sum' implies uniqueness in a way 'a composite' does not. However, to say this is already to move beyond the slogan to the kind of theory of composition such slogans may be intended to flag. Such theories are the subject of §1.2.

parts.[4] His arguments are not uncontroversial. What is clear, however, is that to discuss these matters properly would take us far from reflections on whether a whole is or is not the sum of its parts. And that is my point: that the choice between these two slogans does not provide a useful framework in which to think about composition.

For my money, the real problem with the term 'sum' is that it is singular.[5] Prima facie, the mystery about composition is how one thing—a whole—can be made up of many things—its parts. The identification of a whole with 'the sum of its parts' simply sidesteps this issue by coining another singular term with which to identify the whole. This one-many dimension will be of central importance in what follows. It is right at the heart of Plato's discussions of composition. But it is not always well understood. I shall return to it frequently.

As to the alternative slogan—the whole is more than the sum of its parts—this simply inherits all the difficulties associated with the term 'sum' and adds one of its own. Its own peculiar difficulty lies in the phrase 'more than'. To say that a whole is more than the sum of its parts, on any ordinary understanding of the phrase 'more than', is to say that a whole has something extra in addition to its parts (or indeed to the sum of its parts). Is this something extra a part? It had better not be, for the familiar reason that, if it is, then all that we have is another sum of parts (the original one plus the something extra). So, either we should concede that a whole is, after all, the sum of its parts—and if it is this one, why not the original one?—or regress threatens: the whole is more than this new sum also. (To my knowledge, the first person to formulate this argument explicitly was Aristotle. See *Metaphysics* VII. 17, 1041^{b}12–33.)

I have focused on the debate as to whether or not a whole is the sum of its parts, and concentrated on problems associated with the term 'sum'. Alternatively, one might find a whole identified with the fusion of its parts or the aggregate of its parts.[6] Such

---

[4] Van Inwagen (1990, esp. §§3, 6, and 7).

[5] Cf. here Van Inwagen (1990: 22).

[6] The term 'fusion' is that favoured by David Lewis in his discussions of composition, which are examined in §1.2, where the term is defined (p. 15).

alternatives suffer from the same or sufficiently comparable problems. An identity claim founded on any of these terms offers us a singular term with which to identify the whole, and a term which implies some way of putting the parts together: summing, fusing, or aggregating. And again, at least prima facie, it is not clear what more such a claim tells us than we already know: that a whole is one thing which is composed of its parts. But this, I take it, is not what people are denying when they deny that a whole is the sum, or fusion, or aggregate of its parts.

There still remains one substantive thesis which may lie behind claims that a whole is the sum, or fusion, or aggregate of its parts. Terms like 'sum', 'fusion', or 'aggregate' may, as it were, fall out of some particular formal or quasi-formal system describing the part–whole relation. Sums, or fusions, or aggregates would be values of variables of the formal system in question. The claim that a whole is identical to the sum, or fusion, or aggregate of its parts would be the claim that a certain formal system is an accurate representation of the metaphysical relation of composition; an accurate representation not just of *a* relation of composition (remembering that there might be more than one), but of *the* metaphysical relation of composition. This, I take it, would be the implication of the identity thesis: that all (and only) wholes of parts may be identified with the sums, or fusions, or aggregates which feature in the system.

This is indeed a substantive thesis and raises a host of different, and difficult, questions. Up for debate is whether or not it is true that the formal system in question accurately represents some or all instances of composition; whether it captures all those instances we think are instances of composition and only those; whether there is indeed only one relation of composition; and there will be other questions too. In modern metaphysical discussions, the problem of composition is now often debated in terms of the adequacy or otherwise of certain formal systems to capture relation(s) of composition.

1.2 MEREOLOGY OR MAGIC?

The term 'mereology' requires some explanation. Taken generally, and literally, it means simply any theory of parthood or composition. Taken this generally, Plato might be said to have a mereology, although he does not set about presenting it as such. In particular, he does not attempt to set out formal axioms governing the 'part of' relation. Nor shall I attempt to do so on his behalf, in part because I think the project would be ill-conceived. Plato is doing metaphysics, not logic.

Taken more narrowly, 'mereology' may refer to any formal system describing the behaviour of one or more 'part of' predicates. Taken more narrowly still, it refers to a particular family of such systems which share certain key formal features, namely, classical extensional mereology.[7] To prevent confusion I shall capitalize 'Mereology' when referring to a version of classical extensional mereology.[8]

David Lewis has claimed that Mereology is the only correct theory of composition; that all composition is Mereological. On the basis of this claim he has proposed a revision of the metaphysics of classes.[9] In addition, this claim about composition plays a central role in his debate with David Armstrong about the nature of universals and of states of affairs. Commitment to Mereology is the principal reason for Lewis's rejection of structural universals and of states of affairs, since both are composed in ways which violate a central tenet of Mereology.[10] Debates about universals and states of affairs and about the metaphysics of classes are not immediately relevant to the subject of this book. But the debate about composition which underlies them is.

[7] See the comprehensive study by Simons (1987). The family of systems referred to as classical extensional mereology descends from two principal ancestors: the Mereology of Leśniewski and the Calculus of Individuals of Leonard and Goodman. For details of the family and its ancestry, see Simons (1987, esp. ch. 2).

[8] Note, therefore, that my practice differs from that of Simons (1987), in which 'Mereology' refers exclusively to Leśniewski's ancestral version of classical extensional mereology.

[9] Lewis (1991).   [10] See e.g. Lewis (1986a, esp. 36–9; 1986b).

Mereology is a formal system, or a family of such systems, and, as such, it is in one sense unobjectionable. Historically, its evolution was associated with the desire to find alternatives to set theory for those with nominalist qualms about commitment to abstract objects like sets.[11] However, Lewis's claim is about the applicability of Mereology: that one can, as it were, read off the metaphysics of composition from the axioms of this formal system; and that anything we call 'composition' which fails to conform to these axioms is not composition at all: at best it is magic.[12] It is to this claim that objections may be (and have been) put. And it is Mereology's history that gives rise to the axioms that cause the trouble.

Lewis picks out three axioms central to Mereology as he conceives it:

> *Transitivity*: If x is part of some part of y, then x is part of y.

> *Unrestricted Composition*: Whenever there are some things, then there exists a fusion of those things.

> *Uniqueness of Composition*: It never happens that the same things have two different fusions.[13]

This list is not a presentation of the formal system Mereology. Nor is it intended to be. But these are axioms central to the family of systems known as classical extensional mereology. This is not to say that one cannot find more or less developed formal mereologies that do not share all these axioms.[14] Of the three, it is the Axioms of Uniqueness of Composition and/or Unrestricted Composition which prompt doubts about Lewis's claims for the applicability of Mereology.[15]

[11] On this, see Simons (1982, esp. 116).

[12] The reference to magic stems from Lewis (1986a).

[13] Lewis (1991: 74). His 'Uniqueness of Composition' axiom enshrines the Mereological principle of extensionality: objects with the same parts are identical.

[14] David Bostock (1979: 112–30) has developed a mereology with a considerably more restricted axiom governing the existence of sums or fusions. Peter Simons (1987) considers ways in which one might develop a mereology without either extensionality or unrestricted composition.

[15] Transitivity is widely, although not universally, accepted as characteristic of the part–whole relation. For doubts about transitivity, see e.g. Rescher (1955) and Lowe (1989: 94 n. 9). In what follows, I shall have very little to say regarding questions about transitivity.

The notion of a fusion falls out of Mereology and is a technical notion. Lewis defines it thus: 'Something is a *fusion* of some things iff it has all of them as parts and has no part that is distinct [i.e. disjoint] from each of them.'[16] Lewis's claim about the applicability of Mereology provokes two questions. Are wholes fusions? And are all fusions wholes? Consideration of these questions will move us closer to the goal of identifying a question about composition which it will be both profitable and relevant to pursue.

The first question—are wholes fusions?—gets a negative answer from those who think that wholes, unlike fusions, are not extensional; who think, that is, that it is possible for two distinct wholes to share all the same parts; or that it is possible for one and the same whole to have different parts at different times.[17] Such wholes would be composed in ways that violate the Axiom of Uniqueness of Composition.[18] The second question—are all fusions wholes?—gets a negative answer from those who think that Mereology generates more fusions than there are wholes. If all fusions are wholes, then Mereology's Axiom of Unrestricted Composition posits wholes whenever there are many things. Thus, consider some things: say, the *Mona Lisa*, my copy of Lewis's *Parts of Classes*, and your left leg. By Unrestricted

[16] Lewis (1991: 73). By 'distinct' Lewis understands 'disjoint'.

[17] Here and elsewhere, except where noted, I use the term 'part' to mean 'proper part'. Note that, in doing so, I differ from a practice common in Mereological discussions, in which 'part' is used for the technical notion of 'improper part'. Improper parthood, unlike proper parthood, is reflexive; thus a whole is an improper part of itself.

[18] This needs teasing out in the case of change of parts over time. Consider a car that breaks down on Monday and has a new fuel pump put in on Tuesday. The parts that compose the car on Monday differ from the parts that compose the car on Tuesday. Thus the car cannot be identical both with the fusion of its parts on Monday and with the fusion of its parts on Tuesday without being different from itself. But there is no principled reason for identifying the car with the fusion of its parts on one day as opposed to the other. Thus the car is not identical with the fusion of its parts on Monday nor with the fusion of its parts on Tuesday. Now consider the car and the fusion of its parts on Monday, supposing this fusion exists. (It is not open to the defender of Mereology to deny its existence.) The car and the fusion have the same parts, but are not identical, and thus violate Uniqueness. (This argument is by no means conclusive. Discussion of change of parts over time very quickly becomes complicated, not least because it raises the question of temporal parts. However, these complications need not detain us here.)

Composition there exists a fusion of these things. The second question gets a negative answer from those who think that the composition of wholes is more restricted than this would suggest.[19]

The Axiom of Uniqueness of Composition is the principal bone of contention between Lewis and Armstrong. Armstrong defends the existence of structural universals and of states of affairs; such entities have a central role in his ontology.[20] However, both structural universals and states of affairs provide counter-examples to Uniqueness. For example, the structural universals methane and butane are different wholes, but each has the same parts: carbon, hydrogen, and the dyadic relation bonded. Likewise, the state of affairs of Jack loving Jill is different from the state of affairs of Jill loving Jack, but each has the same parts: Jack, Jill, and the non-symmetrical relation loving. Nor are these the only kind of counter-examples to the Axiom of Uniqueness of Composition which could be suggested. Two different words—types or tokens—might be composed of the same letters, like 'dog' and 'god'. And many of the familiar composite objects around us, including ourselves, appear to have different parts at different times, through such ordinary processes as hair loss or the change of filters in one's car.

However, although there are relatively easy (and familiar) ways in which to generate apparent counter-examples to the Axiom of Uniqueness, it is rather harder to sustain such counter-examples in the face of determined opposition.[21] They become all too quickly mired in broader ontological disputes. Lewis, for example, has a ready response to each of the counter-examples mentioned.[22] Several are dismissed as resting on an account of

---

[19] Those who deny that the composition of wholes is either unique or unrestricted will, of course, answer 'no' to both questions. Thus no wholes will be fusions and no fusions will be wholes. This opens the question of whether one should accept the existence of fusions at all. This question is distinct from the question of whether Mereology provides a good account of the composition of wholes. This latter question is my principal concern.

[20] See e.g. Armstrong (1989, 1991).

[21] Debates about Uniqueness often go under the heading of debates about the thesis that constitution is identity. See e.g. Johnston (1992); Noonan (1993); and Baker (1997).

[22] See Lewis (1991: 78–9 with n. 8), together with Lewis (1986a).

the persistence conditions of objects which Lewis rejects, namely the view that objects are three-dimensional continuants which
endure, wholly present, through time. (There go examples of one
and the same object having different parts at different times, or
of different objects having the same parts at different times.) The
only counter-examples Lewis concedes as genuine are those
involving structural universals or states of affairs. But their vio-
lation of the Axiom of Uniqueness is precisely Lewis's ground
for rejecting the view that there are such things. Of course,
Lewis's responses are themselves not uncontroversial. But discussion of them would take us far from the central ground of
composition.

One might think that puzzles about Uniqueness of Composition would be central to Plato's discussions of composition. After
all, Plato is notoriously committed to the existence of types of a
sort, and, as we shall see, to complex types: just the kind of objects
which prompt counter-examples to Uniqueness.[23] However,
while it is true, as we shall see, that the majority of Plato's examples of wholes, in his discussions of composition, are complex
types, the question of whether or not two distinct objects could be
composed of the very same parts does not emerge as central.[24]
Perhaps surprisingly, it is in fact the second of the questions above
which has more of a connection with Plato's discussions: are all
fusions wholes?[25] To see this, however, one must start from a different question.

Suppose one asks: when is it the case that many things compose one thing, a whole? Assuming that 'fusion' and 'whole' are
coextensive, Lewis answers: whenever there are many things.
Plato, I shall argue, would disagree. And the question asked is
closely related to issues central to his discussions of composition.

[23] Complex types prompt counter-examples to Uniqueness because one may
readily envisage two different complex types composed of the same component
types.

[24] In *Symposium* 207d–208b Diotima asserts that human beings, being mortal,
persist through constant replenishment of their bodily constituents and psychologi-
cal states. However, the passage does not explicitly problematize the metaphysical
issues raised and is not framed in terms of discussion of part and whole.

[25] This need not mean that Plato's answer to this question will have no implications for the question about Uniqueness. My point is simply that Plato's discussions
of composition nowhere explicitly focus on questions about Uniqueness.

Nor is he alone in this. For a modern example of discussion of composition in these terms, consider the work of Van Inwagen. My question quite deliberately echoes what Van Inwagen calls 'the Special Composition Question', namely, 'When is it true that y the xs compose y?', or 'Less formally, in what circumstances do things add up to or compose something? When does unity arise out of plurality?'[26] This is the question about composition that Van Inwagen addresses (for the restricted field material objects, which is his focus). And he rejects an unrestricted answer of the sort Lewis gives.

Lewis himself is again unmoved by objections to Unrestricted Composition.[27] Of course, Lewis accepts that many fusions are not among those objects which we ordinarily talk of and which we might ordinarily think of as 'wholes'. For example, there is, by Unrestricted Composition, such a thing as the front half of a trout plus the back half of a turkey, a 'trout-turkey' as Lewis dubs it.[28] But it is not much talked of outside discussions of Lewis's book. This, Lewis suggests, is because we ordinarily, and quite properly, speak with restricted quantification about only some of the things there are. However, the fact that we are entitled, for everyday purposes, to ignore such things is not, he says, grounds for denying that they exist. In the case of the dispute about Unrestricted Composition, as opposed to that about Uniqueness, there is profit in pursuing the matter.

1.3 RESTRICTIONS UPON COMPOSITION?

Lewis has good reason not to worry about Unrestricted Composition and its proliferation of fusions. First, he has what he takes to be a good argument against the imposition of any restrictions upon composition. Second, he has a conception of fusions in light of which he views their proliferation as innocuous. The second is more important for the purposes of this book. I shall return to it below. First, however, a word about Lewis's

---

[26] Van Inwagen (1990: 30–1).

[27] Lewis (1991: 79–81; cf. Lewis 1986c: 212–13).

[28] Lewis (1991: 7 and elsewhere).

argument is in order. If Lewis were to have a knockdown argument against restrictions upon composition, pursuit of the dispute about Unrestricted Composition would be superfluous. My aim here is simply to say enough to show that one need not suppose that he does.

Lewis's argument against restrictions upon composition is (roughly) as follows.[29] Any attempt to restrict composition according to some specification of the conditions under which some group of things compose something must result in a vague restriction. But if a restriction on composition is vague, then composition itself must be vague. And if composition is vague, then existence is vague. But vagueness of existence is incoherent. Vagueness of existence is here understood as the claim that there is something such that it is a vague matter whether or not it exists. But, as Lewis says, 'once you've said "there is" your game is up'.[30] Lewis's argument takes the form of a *reductio*. From the attempt to impose restrictions upon composition, he purports to derive a contradiction: that if *there is* something which vaguely exists, there is nothing vague about its existence.

There are, I think, three possible strategies for responding to this argument. The first is simply to bite the bullet; to accept that any attempt to impose a restriction on composition must lead to vagueness of composition, and so of existence, but to deny that vagueness of existence is incoherent in the way Lewis suggests. This is the strategy adopted by Van Inwagen.[31]

The second possible strategy is to challenge the argument. The argument has two main steps: (i) from the inevitable vagueness of any attempt to impose a restriction on composition (that is, of any such restriction) to the vagueness of composition; and (ii) from the vagueness of composition to the vagueness of existence. However,

---

[29] The argument is to be found, briefly, in Lewis (1991: 80–1) and, at somewhat greater length, in Lewis (1986c: 211–13). It is a moot question whether and how the argument might be stated more precisely.

[30] Lewis (1991: 81).

[31] Van Inwagen (1990) defends a restricted conception of composition, according to which some things compose something if and only if the activity of those things constitutes a life (see esp. §9). Van Inwagen accepts that it is a consequence of this thesis that composition, existence, and identity are vague. He sets out to defend the coherence of this consequence in §§17–19.

nowhere that I can discover does Lewis state, with any precision, the details of the arguments required for these two steps, particularly the second. And the second, in particular, seems open to question. Suppose, for the sake of argument, that there are some things such that it is a vague matter whether there is something they compose. It is not clear it follows from this that there is something such that it is a vague matter whether it is composed by those things, let alone that there is something such that it is a vague matter whether it exists.[32]

Note that there are two ways in which vagueness of composition might be understood. Vagueness of composition might be understood as the claim that it is a vague matter whether something, *a*, is part of something, *b*. Here, quite clearly, there is no vague something. There is simply some (non-vague) thing, namely *b*, regarding which it is a vague matter whether or not *a* is part of it.[33] Alternatively, vagueness of composition might be understood as the claim that there are some things, the *a*s, such that it is a vague matter whether there is something the *a*s compose. This is how Lewis appears to understand vagueness of composition. Thus he supposes that an attempt to restrict composition according to some intuitive desiderata for composition must, perforce, have the result that it will be 'a vague matter whether a given class satisfies our intuitive *desiderata* for composition'.[34] (The term 'class' is here used loosely, simply as a way

---

[32] Van Inwagen questions the inference from 'it is indefinite whether anything is the sum of the *x*s' to 'something is such that it is indefinite whether it is the sum of the *x*s' and creates a semantics for inferences involving indefinite truth in which the inference fails (Van Inwagen 1990: 273–6). For a careful analysis of Lewis's argument, see also Walker (2000, ch. 5, §2.1). I am grateful to George Walker for discussion of these matters and for providing me with a copy of his thesis.

[33] Given Uniqueness of Composition, according to which the identity of a whole is determined according to the identity of its parts, then vagueness as to what are the parts of a thing leads to vagueness as to the identity of a thing, and it seems a short step from vagueness of identity to vagueness of existence. This may well be what makes the argument seem so straightforward to Lewis. However, an argument by this route is not topic-neutral, since it cannot be expected to persuade an opponent who rejects both the Axiom of Unrestricted Composition and that of Uniqueness. (Van Inwagen, we may note, who broadly accepts the consequences of the argument, if not its form, is himself committed to Uniqueness: 1990: 5.)

[34] Lewis (1986*c*: 212).

of referring to some things.) The third possible strategy for responding to Lewis is to challenge the legitimacy of this starting point; the assumption that there are some things which may readily be turned into parts.

For the present, the details of this response must remain a promissory note. The question of how precisely one should formulate a rejection of the Axiom of Unrestricted Composition requires careful consideration. In particular, the opponent may be ill advised to conceive such a rejection as a simple negation of the axiom as stated. Why this is so is a matter I shall take up only later, for it is only when one has an alternative to the Mereological model in view that one has a standpoint from which the assumption from which Lewis's argument takes off can be exposed to question.[35]

So much, for the present, then, for Lewis's argument against restrictions upon composition. I now turn to the reason for Lewis's lack of concern about the proliferation of fusions which Unrestricted Composition would entail.

1.4 ONTOLOGICAL INNOCENCE

According to Lewis, Mereology's principal virtue is its ontological innocence. And this is the reason for Lewis's lack of concern about Mereology's proliferation of fusions. So what, if Mereology posits fusions whenever there are many things no matter what those things may be? A commitment to fusions is as innocent as can be. Here's how Lewis puts it (at least at first):

given a prior commitment to cats, say, a commitment to cat-fusions is not a *further* commitment. The fusion is nothing over and above the cats that compose it. It just *is* them. They just *are* it. Take them together or take them separately, the cats are the same portion of Reality either way. Commit yourself to their existence all together or one at a time, it's the same commitment either way. If you draw up an inventory of Reality according to your scheme of things, it would be double counting to list the cats and then also list their fusion. In general, if you are already committed to some things, you incur no further commitment

---

[35] This promissory note will not be redeemed until Ch. 5.

when you affirm the existence of their fusion. The new commitment is redundant, given the old one.[36]

One may be sceptical about this claim to innocence.[37] (There's no such thing as an ontological free lunch.) By any Quinean standard, Mereological commitment to fusions *is* a commitment. Imagine a world in which there are two distinct (mereological) atoms.[38] By Mereology, the cardinality of the domain of quantification is three (in general, for n objects, $2^n - 1$). Of course, Lewis will say that in committing ourselves to fusions, we are not being committed to anything we were not committed to before ('given a commitment to cats, say . . .'). And that is true, *by* Mereology as Lewis conceives it. But that is unlikely to persuade anyone not already committed to Mereology.

The mainstay of Lewis's claim that Mereology is ontologically innocent is his identification of an analogy between the relation of composition and the relation of identity.

I say that composition—the relation of part to whole, or, better, the many-one relation of many parts to their fusion—is like identity. The 'are' of composition is, *so to speak*, the plural form of the 'is' of identity. Call this the Thesis of *Composition as Identity*.[39] It is in virtue of this thesis that mereology is ontologically innocent: it commits us only to things that are identical, *so to speak*, to what we were committed to before.[40]

I shall return to the important and mysterious waiver clause: things that are identical only 'so to speak'. Again, there are grounds for scepticism. Van Inwagen rightly points out that

---

[36] Lewis (1991: 81–2).

[37] Such scepticism is nicely expressed by Oliver (1994) and by Van Inwagen (1994).

[38] A mereological atom is an object which has no (proper) parts. Cf. Simons (1987: 16).

[39] Here and in what follows, this thesis should be distinguished from the similarly named thesis that constitution is identity, on which see above, n. 21. Proponents of the latter are concerned to deny that two distinct objects could share all the same parts; Lewis's thesis of composition as identity concerns the composition relation as such—the relation between the many parts and the whole they compose—and claims an analogy between this relation and the identity relation. The two theses are distinct, although they are not unrelated.

[40] Lewis (1991: 82); my emphasis on 'so to speak'.

there is already a perfectly good candidate for being the plural form of the 'is' of identity: the 'are' of identity, as in 'the Joneses are the people next door'.[41] Identity is indeed ontologically innocent in Lewis's sense. If you are committed to the existence of something, *a*, then you are already committed to the existence of anything identical with *a*. By analogy, Lewis suggests, if you are already committed to the existence of *a* and *b*, then you are already committed to the existence of the fusion of *a* and *b*. But this second is controversial in a way the first is not, because the fusion of *a* and *b* is not identical with *a* and/or *b*, not even 'so to speak'. And Lewis in fact admits as much (hence the waiver clause): 'What's true of the many [the parts] is not exactly what's true of the one [the fusion]. After all they are many while it is one.'[42]

Being a relation like identity is not being identity any more than being like butter is being butter. Two of the ways in which Lewis claims that Mereology is like identity are its ontological innocence and Unrestricted Composition.[43] But it is the thesis of composition as identity that is meant to support Mereology's claim to ontological innocence. And it is the ontological innocence of Mereology that is meant to demonstrate that Unrestricted Composition is unobjectionable. Again, there is little here to persuade the detractor.

Lewis's claim to an analogy between composition and identity is nonetheless important, not because it shows that composition is ontologically innocent—it does not—but because it shows how to make it so: take it to be like identity. Or, go yet further. Lewisian Mereology fails to be truly innocent because Lewis does not quite take composition to be (a kind of) identity, only 'so to speak'. Donald Baxter (to whom Lewis refers) goes the extra mile. Baxter does indeed take composition to be a kind of identity, what he calls 'many-one' or 'cross-count' identity.[44]

Baxter's position, in brief, appears to be this. Many parts are identical to the whole they compose. Prima facie, this is paradoxical. The paradox can be resolved, Baxter suggests, by appealing to the fact that there are two different senses of 'identity' (an idea

---

[41] Van Inwagen (1994: 211). [42] Lewis (1991: 87).
[43] Lewis (1991: 85). [44] Baxter (1988*a*, 1988*b*).

he traces back to Joseph Butler): a strict and philosophical sense and a loose sense. In addition, there are different 'counts' of what exist, some strict, some loose, and which may be better or worse, depending on context. Crucially, neither strict nor loose counting is any more real than the other, and both are exhaustive. The parts count as many, strictly and philosophically speaking; loosely, they count as one. In addition to there being two different senses of 'identity', there are two kinds of identity. (Beware: senses of 'identity' and kinds of identity do not straightforwardly line up.) There is the kind of identity that one thing has with itself (strictly counted). There is also a kind of identity which holds between many things (counted strictly) and one thing (counted loosely), hence 'cross-count' identity. What count as many on the strict count *are* what count as one on the loose count. The whole, as Baxter puts it, is 'the many parts counted as one'.[45]

On Baxter's view, composition does indeed appear to inherit the innocence of identity, for it is identity of a kind. But this innocence comes at a cost of a different sort. Recall why Lewis in the end withdrew from asserting a full-blooded thesis of composition as identity. Fusions, he said, are one; their parts are many. And many things cannot be identical to one thing, at least on any ordinary understanding of identity. Baxter proposes an extraordinary understanding of identity (although he might not see it this way) according to which many can indeed be identical with one. But, at least on my part, this has the consequence that I no longer understand what he means by such apparently ordinary terms as 'one', 'many', and 'identical'. And I am not alone in this.[46]

Alongside the question of how innocent composition could be is a second, just as important, question: how innocent *should* it be? 'Innocence', of course, is a favourable word. But we should not be carried away by its favourable connotations; they are no substitute for argument. Lewis hopes to persuade us of Mereology's virtue by proclaiming its innocence. However, as

[45] Baxter (1988a: 578).
[46] Cf. Van Inwagen's comment on Baxter's claim that the whole is 'the many parts counted as one': 'No one will be able to get anything out of Baxter unless he understands this sentence, and I . . . do not understand it' (1994: 214).

we have seen, innocence can be something of an illusion. In Lewis it is not clear that Mereology is all that innocent; nor that such innocence as it may lay claim to provides any independent motivation for accepting Mereology. In Baxter innocence turns out to have its own costs. And the desire for innocence is not, it seems, universally shared.

Consider Van Inwagen's discussion of the suggestion that to get some *x*s to compose something, one might simply fasten them together. Suppose, he suggests, that you and I shake hands and that, at the very instant of shaking hands, our hands become paralysed in such a way that we are fastened together. Do we now jointly compose something? Van Inwagen says not, observing that 'Our paralysis has not added to the furniture of [the] earth.'[47] Thus, for Van Inwagen, it counts against an answer to his Special Composition Question that a candidate for being a composite adds nothing to the furniture of the earth. Innocence is here a vice, not a virtue.

So, should composition be ontologically innocent? Lewis says 'yes'. Van Inwagen says 'no'. Plato, I shall argue, would agree with Van Inwagen. And it is no surprise, I think, that the central puzzle at the heart of his discussions of composition is regularly associated with his predecessors the Eleatics, notoriously among the most ontologically commitment-shy philosophers there have ever been. As we shall see, the Platonic discussions of composition on which I shall focus in the first half of this book set out to expose the problems that arise from adopting an innocent conception of composition. And the Eleatics will be seen to be associated with this conception in light of their desire for ontological innocence. The question of whether or not composition should be ontologically innocent is thus of central importance to Plato's discussions of composition. Indeed, we are now quite close to an understanding of the problem of composition which it will be both profitable and relevant to pursue.

---

[47] Van Inwagen (1990: 58).

1.5 COMPOSITION AND THE PROBLEM OF THE ONE AND THE MANY

Recall my claim that, at least prima facie, the mystery of composition is how one thing—a whole—can be made up of many things—the parts; and that this one–many dimension is of central importance to Plato's discussions of composition. Discussion of composition is one aspect of his discussion of the multifaceted problem of the one and the many. Consider, for example, a passage of the *Parmenides* (to which I shall return) in which Socrates purports to show how easily an individual human being such as himself might be shown to be many.

> . . . when someone wishes to show that I am many, he will say that the [parts] on the right of me are one thing, the [parts] on the left another, that my front [parts] are one thing, my back [parts] another, and likewise upper and lower—for, I suppose, I have a share of many. (129c5–8)[48]

Some one thing can be shown to be many (as well)—this being the general form of the problem of the one and the many—simply by pointing to its having many parts. So, in the *Philebus* (14c8–e4) Socrates lists precisely this puzzle under the heading of puzzles that show that one thing is many and many things one. (He does so, I shall argue, with the *Parmenides* very much to mind.)

This version of the ancient problem of the one and the many was, in essence, why Lewis withdrew from the claim that composition *is* identity, endorsing only an analogy between them. Baxter, by contrast, quite self-consciously takes the problem on and attempts to defuse the paradox in contending that one thing may, after all, be many. The problem is not absent from Van Inwagen's discussion either. Hence, one informal version of his Special Composition Question asks 'When does unity arise

---

[48] In my translation I supply the term 'parts' as a natural completion of the neuter plural articles in phrases such as 'the [things] on the right of me' (τὰ ἐπὶ δεξία μού, 129c6). I shall return to this point, when I discuss this passage more fully in §2.1 below. Note that '[things] on the right of me' should be understood as my 'rightward things', and not as things separate from me, on my right.

out of plurality?'[49] Here, the terms of the ancient and modern discussions coincide. The comparison is revealing in two ways especially.

First, the comparison reveals what might be called the 'logical core' of this version of the one–many problem: the treatment of composition as identity. (I shall have much more to say on this in what follows.) Second, the comparison reveals what is at stake: the choice, when theorizing about composition, between ontological innocence and commitment. What innocence threatens is the status of a whole as an individual; as one thing composed of many things and not just many things. And the question it raises is how an account of composition can respect the fact that a whole is an individual, rather than a collection. (The term 'collection', of course, is grammatically singular. However, here and in what follows, I use the term 'collection' as a convenient way in which to refer, in the plural, to many things. A collection is a plurality, or, better, many things, plurally quantified.)

The relation between composition and identity; and the ontological innocence or otherwise of composition: these are both matters right at the heart of Plato's discussions of composition. But the fact that they are so is easily obscured. Despite the connections between ancient and modern discussions which emerge, upon investigation, the terms of Plato's discussions of composition can seem alien to the modern context. This, I think, is for two connected reasons.

The first concerns 'number'. It has become a commonplace to point out that the Greek notion of *arithmos* (from which derives 'arithmetic' etc.) is far removed from our modern notion of number.[50] We think of the number three as one of the positive integers in the natural number series (whatever else we may think about the ontology of numbers). An *arithmos*, by contrast, is an enumerable collection—a collection of units, in Euclid; in the case of three, a trio. And one is not an *arithmos*, by definition;

[49] Van Inwagen (1990: 31).

[50] For a recent statement of the point, see Pritchard (1995). While this may not be the only conception of *arithmos* available in ancient philosophical discussions, where the nature of *arithmoi* comes in for considerable discussion, it is the conception of ordinary Greek mathematics, and it is this ordinary conception which will be at work in the Platonic passages I shall be discussing.

although it is, of course, in our sense, a number. Thus, the puzzle about whether a whole is one, or many, or both is not primarily, if at all, a puzzle about counting. Rather, it is precisely about whether a whole is an individual or an (enumerable) collection. Hence it is natural for Plato to make play, as we shall see that he does, with the possibility that a whole is in fact like an *arithmos* (is a collection) in a way that is likely to seem odd, if we think he is comparing a whole with a number, whatever our views on composition may be.

The figure perhaps most responsible for destroying this notion of 'number' as a collection of units was Frege.[51] And here we find the second and connected reason for the apparently alien quality of Plato's treatment of the problem of composition. In considering what I shall call the 'compositional version' of the problem of the one and the many, there is a temptation (as indeed in many other contexts) to wonder whether Frege did not sort all this out.[52] After all, there is that famous passage of the *Foundations of Arithmetic* in which Frege notes: 'While looking at one and the same external phenomenon, I can say with equal truth both "It is a copse" and "It is five trees", or both "Here are four companies" and "Here are 500 men" ' (§46). For Frege, the shift from one assertion to the other in each of these cases is a 'sign that one concept has been substituted for another'. And this in turn is part of his argument that 'a statement of number is an assertion about a concept'.

Frege's remarks, however, are focused on what we number, as part and parcel of his revolution of our understanding of number. His remarks, that is, are addressed to a curious feature of *counting*: that we can count 'the same thing' (or not, in fact, as Frege points out) in different ways. And the moral of his remarks is that, in counting, numbers are ascribed not to things, as such, but to the various concepts under which any given collection of things may fall. In contrast, Plato's problem is not about counting. It is,

---

[51] Above all in his *Foundations of Arithmetic*; I quote from Austin's translation, Frege (1953).

[52] This is not just idle speculation on my part; I have been asked as much in discussion. Cf. Baxter (1988a: 582), with whom I agree, at least on this, that the problem at issue is not the one that Frege is solving in *Foundations*.

rather, an ontological problem about the status of the things which Frege is out to deny are the bearers of numbers.

This problem of Plato's is not, in fact, entirely absent from the Fregean passage quoted. However, as Wiggins has noted, it is a problem about which Frege himself maintains a regrettable silence.[53] Consider Frege's own example: the copse and the trees. In what sense may 'one and the same external phenomenon' be both one copse and five trees?[54] A copse is something which is composed of some number of trees. Thus Frege should not be taken to be simply *identifying* the copse with the trees, unless we suppose that Frege is himself committed to the view that composition is identity. And, if he is so committed, this commitment can and should be detached from the otherwise successful moral of his remarks.[55]

Plato's compositional version of the problem of the one and the many itself depends, or so I shall argue, on assuming that composition is identity. It depends, that is, on the identification of a whole with its parts. Such an identification is problematic, it seems, because it identifies one thing (the whole) with many things (its parts). But what is problematic about this does need to be carefully stated in order to distinguish it from the legitimate moral of Frege's remarks.

One might put the point in terms of quantification. The problem is not that some thing or things turn out to be countably one or many according to the concept under which it or they are subsumed. The problem is rather that the identification of a whole with its parts means that something(s) is/are both one thing—singularly quantified—and many things—plurally quantified.[56] But there is a difference between singular quantification over individuals and plural quantification over many things. It is this

[53] Wiggins (1980: 43–4).

[54] The phrase 'one and the same' raises the spectre of alternative theories of identity. And Frege's point about numbers has sometimes been assimilated to Geach's theory of relative identity. Against such an assimilation, see Blanchette (1999).

[55] Wiggins in fact offers the Fregean passage quoted as an example of how even a philosopher of the calibre of Frege can sometimes give a bad argument for a correct view (Wiggins 1980: 44).

[56] The difficulty over singular and plural subjects and verbs is part of the point.

fundamental distinction between an individual and many things that is threatened by the identification of a whole with its parts.

Lewis recognizes the problem, which is why he withdraws from the claim that composition *is* identity, claiming only an analogy between them. 'What's true of the many [the parts] is not exactly what's true of the one [the fusion]. After all they are many while it is one.'[57] The problem, however, is not that there is no sense in which 'they' could be one, but that 'they' are not an 'it', nor 'it' a 'they'. The same goes for Plato's puzzle. According to the puzzle, a whole of parts is both one and many. But one might better understand this as the claim that a whole is both *a* one and *a* many; that is, is both an individual and a collection, where the term 'collection', recall, is merely a convenient way of referring to many.

Plato's problem is not the problem that Frege sets out to solve. But its clarification in contrast with that of Frege allows for a clearer perspective on the issue which I have identified as being at stake. What is at stake, I have argued, when theorizing about composition, is the question of whether a whole is a (complex) individual or a collection. Or, rather, since composition appears, pre-eminently, to be a many–*one* relation, the question is how best to respect the fact that a whole is an individual, rather than a collection. And the problem which, I shall argue, Plato sets out to solve is the problem of how to give an account of composition in such a way as to allow that a whole is an individual, rather than a collection.

This problem is in fact something which Plato shares with Lewis, despite what Lewis sometimes says. In saying this, I do not mean that Lewis explicitly sets out to show that a whole is an individual, rather than a collection; he does not.[58] However, especially in his *Parts of Classes*, Lewis displays a certain ambivalence about the innocence of composition and about the relation between composition and identity. He claims that Mereology is innocent, but that a fusion is one, not many. He claims that composition is not in fact identity, but that it is, in the

---

[57] Lewis (1991: 87).

[58] Indeed, the explicit goal, at least of Lewis (1991), is to give an account not of composition, but of the theory of classes.

relevant respects, like identity. Behind this ambivalence is the question of innocence.

Of course, one could, if one wished, have a genuinely innocent ontology. An ontology of collections, conceived in the way I have suggested, using plural quantification, might be used to avoid giving an account of composition; that is, to explain away alleged cases of composition by redescribing them in terms of plural quantification over simples.[59] An ontology of this sort is properly innocent. But it involves denying that there are any (genuine) cases of composition.[60]

In contrast, Lewis's ontology is not properly innocent. A Lewisian fusion is not a collection, in the sense stipulated above, since Lewis does suppose that a fusion is one thing composed of many, and not just many things. For this reason a Lewisian fusion is not as ontologically innocent as Lewis makes out. However, because of Lewis's desire for ontological innocence, a Lewisian fusion is, one might think, an entity which is so denuded of ontological commitment as not to offer an adequately robust account of a composite individual. Why might one think so? Because, given Unrestricted Composition, there are very many fusions. Given Unrestricted Composition, there are thus very many candidate individuals—too many, one might think. Lewisian innocence does not breed ontological economy. And it is this lack of economy that might be taken to suggest that the conception of an individual at work in Mereology is far too weak to do the job required.

It is Lewis's ambivalence about innocence which makes consideration of Lewisian Mereology and the issues it raises a useful starting point for my examination of Plato. Such consideration provides a way to set out the philosophical issues which I take to be at work in Plato's discussions of composition. Questions

[59] A project of this kind is undertaken in Hossack (2000).

[60] Since my principal concern is Plato's discussions of composition—and Plato nowhere doubts that composite objects exist—I do not propose to defend the assumption that composition sometimes occurs. However, one may note that the alternative—redescription of all apparent cases of composition in terms of plural quantification over simples—commits one to atomism. It might be preferable if one's ontology did not legislate for or against the existence of atoms; mereological atoms, that is.

about ontological innocence and about the relation between composition and identity form the backdrop against which Plato offers his own account of wholes as complex individuals, or so I shall argue. I shall further argue that this account is at least a viable alternative to that of Lewis.[61]

We now have a grip on (a) problem of composition conducive to discussion of Plato and a framework within which such discussion may take place. With this in hand, I now turn to a foundational text among Plato's discussions of composition, in which talk of one and many is not in fact to the fore. Nonetheless, it contains the philosophical core of the compositional version of the problem of the one and the many. It is with this problem, considered as a problem, that my examination of Plato's treatment of composition really begins.

1.6 *THEAETETUS* 203–206

First, some context. The *Theaetetus* considers and finally rejects three definitions of knowledge proposed by the young Theaetetus. The passage which concerns me[62] arises in the context of discussion of his third proposed definition—that knowledge is true judgement with an 'account' (λόγος).[63] Immediately following Theaetetus' dim recollection of once

---

[61] Talk of Plato having an alternative to Lewisian fusions is in fact somewhat over-simplified, because one might accept the alternative and still believe in fusions; that is, one might have fusions as well. One would then have (at least) two different kinds of composition, one Mereological, one not. I shall not be addressing this possibility, because I shall not be addressing the question of whether or not one should sign up to fusions at all, as well or instead. My aim is rather to set out the account of the relation between a whole and its parts which I find in Plato, and which offers an account of complex individuals which seems to me interestingly different from that of Lewisian Mereology.

[62] I am not the first to see connections between this passage of the *Theaetetus* and the modern debate about composition involving Lewis. Scaltsas (1990) draws connections between the arguments of this passage, passages of Aristotle, and the views of David Lewis and David Armstrong. However, I disagree with Scaltsas both about the interpretation of the *Theaetetus* passage and about the nature of its connections with the modern debate.

[63] For present purposes, it will not be necessary to worry about the translation of the multifaceted term λόγος.

having heard this definition proposed, Socrates offers an expansion of it in his report of a dream. Central to the dream is what I shall call 'the Asymmetry Thesis'—the thesis that there is an epistemological asymmetry between elements and complexes: elements are unknowable, complexes are knowable. We are given little information about the nature of these elements and complexes. Elements, we learn, are what 'we and everything else are made up of' (201e2). Letters and syllables serve as specific examples of elements and complexes in the discussion that follows.

Note that the paired terms 'letter' and 'syllable' and 'element' and 'complex' respectively translate the same Greek terms, στοιχεῖον and συλλαβή. Which use of the Greek term is intended is clearly marked in context by the use of examples. The arguments using letters and syllables as examples are generalized, in conclusion, so as to refer to the elements and complexes of the dream. These same arguments also include talk of 'part' (μέρος) and 'whole' (ὅλον). However, complexes and syllables should not immediately be identified as wholes with elements and letters as their respective parts. Rather, the relation between element or letter and complex or syllable serves as a place-holder onto which the part–whole relation will be mapped only under certain conditions. This feature of the discussion is crucial, and often ignored; I shall return to it.

Following the dream, and taking letters and syllables as examples of elements and complexes, Socrates presents two different refutations of the Asymmetry Thesis. The first—the passage which will concern us—takes the form of a dilemma in which Socrates argues that elements and complexes are either just as knowable as each other or just as unknowable as each other. That is, he argues for epistemological symmetry between elements and complexes.[64] In the second refutation—an argument from experience—Socrates argues that elements are in fact more

[64] For the claim to symmetry, see the stress on ὁμοίως ('likewise' or 'similarly') at 205b2–3, d8, and e2–3: this, notwithstanding the suggestion, at 203d7–9, that one must have prior knowledge (προγιγνώσκειν) of the elements if one is to know the entire complex. Whatever priority is implied here must be weak, given the argument's conclusion. I suggest it reflects the fact that one knows the complex only in and through knowing its elements, this because, in this argument, a complex just is its elements, on which more below. I am grateful to Lesley Brown for discussion of this point.

knowable than complexes. Here, then, he argues for epistemological asymmetry between elements and complexes, but an asymmetry of a different kind from that of the dream.

These two refutations of the Asymmetry Thesis have incompatible conclusions: the dilemma defends epistemological symmetry; the argument from experience defends an epistemological asymmetry alternative to that of the dream. Such incompatibility already calls into question (at least) one of these conclusions: that of the dilemma or that of the argument from experience. And if a conclusion is called into question, then the argument to that conclusion must be at fault. It is, I shall argue, the arguments of the dilemma, the first of the two refutations, that are at fault.

Of course, as a matter of logic alone, the argument from experience could equally be at fault (as well or instead). Later, I shall argue that the argument from experience is similarly culpable, in so far as it continues to assume, but here only implicitly, the faulty assumption which, I shall argue, the arguments of the dilemma are designed to expose.[65] There are, however, several reasons to identify the dilemma as the principal argument against which suspicions are to be raised. First, it is, I suggest, dramatically more effective to have a second, conflicting refutation call the status of the first into question retrospectively, than to add a second refutation one expects to be called into question in light of the first. Second, the dilemma—unlike the argument from experience—is sufficiently elaborate to give us some chance of identifying what may be at fault within it. The arguments of the dilemma are tricky; they are, I suggest, designed to provoke.

At their start Socrates and Theaetetus set out to investigate the following question: 'Look here, what do we mean by "the syllable"? The two letters (or if there are more, all the letters)? Or do we mean some single form ($\mu\acute{\iota}\alpha\nu$ $\tau\iota\nu\grave{\alpha}$ $\iota\delta\acute{\epsilon}\alpha\nu$) produced by their combination?' (203c4–6).[66] The investigation of this question gives rise to the dilemma, both horns of which challenge the dream's Asymmetry Thesis. The first horn proposes that

---

[65] The status of the respective epistemological conclusions of the two refutations will not, note, be my concern here.

[66] Translations from the *Theaetetus* are taken, with modifications where noted, from the Burnyeat–Levett translation found in Burnyeat (1990).

elements are just as knowable as complexes; the second horn proposes that complexes are just as unknowable as elements. On each horn Socrates makes judicious use of some aspect of the dream theorist's argument for asymmetry. On the first, he supposes, with the dream theorist, that complexes (here, syllables) are knowable. On the second, he supposes, again with the dream theorist, that simples (here, letters, indeed anything incomposite) are unknowable.

Judicious use of an opponent's assumptions is quite capable of producing a perfectly reasonable *ad hominem* refutation of the opponent's thesis. So, why have the second refutation, the argument from experience, whose conclusion contradicts that of the first? If one denies the conclusion of an argument, one should either show that argument to be invalid, or reject at least one of its premises. Socrates does neither explicitly in the argument from experience. But the incompatibility between the conclusions of his two refutations invites us to do so. I shall argue that a faulty premiss is in fact highlighted by the arguments of the dilemma themselves. It is the sole premiss on which both horns of the dilemma depend. That premiss is the identification of a whole with its parts.[67]

Whole–Parts Identity in the Dilemma

The dilemma arguments begin, then, from the question of whether a syllable is the same as its letters (or, simply, is its letters—Socrates uses these two phrases interchangeably) or is 'some single form' resulting from the combination of the letters.[68] The first horn of the dilemma is relatively swift. Assuming that a syllable is in fact the same as its letters, Socrates argues that if, as the dream theorist supposes, we know the syllable 'so', then, since the syllable 'so' is the same as the two letters

---

[67] Cf. Burnyeat (1990: 191–208), who also argues that the dilemma arguments depend on identifying a whole with its parts (his 'WP') and who takes this to be the false assumption the arguments challenge us to spot. My account of the arguments will thus retread and, in places, expand upon the ground of his illuminating discussion of the passage.

[68] I shall return to the significance of the phrase 'a single form' below.

's' and 'o', we know the two letters also. And thus, he infers, each letter is just as knowable as the syllable.

Already there is a certain uneasiness about this argument. To a modern eye, at least, it appears to involve two fallacies: first, a substitution of identicals into an opaque context—inferring knowledge of the letters from knowledge of the syllable on the grounds of their identity;[69] and second, a fallacy of division— inferring that 's' is knowable and 'o' is knowable from the fact that 's' and 'o' are (jointly) knowable. In general, one cannot infer from the fact that some pair of things has some property that any one member of that pair has the same property.

However, while formally fallacious, in context each inference seems defensible. The apparent fallacy of substitution is more like an inference from my knowing the name 'Marcus Tullius' to my knowing the names 'Marcus' and 'Tullius' than an inference from knowledge of Cicero to knowledge of Tully. Nor is the diagnosis of a fallacy of division for the predicate 'knowable' straightforward.[70] In fact, it seems plausible to infer that if 's' and 'o' are (jointly) knowable, 's' is knowable and 'o' is knowable, providing, that is, that the 'and' marks no more than the conjunction of the letters. This latter point is crucial. Both of the troubling inferences depend on the assumption that a syllable is the same as its letters. And this is also what rescues them, if the claim that a syllable is the same as its letters implies that a syllable is just a collection of letters,[71] if, that is, the composition of a syllable is assumed to be innocent. And so it is, although not without argument.

Since the central premiss of the first horn of the dilemma is the identification of a syllable with its letters, it might seem straightforward to say that the central premiss of the first horn of the dilemma is the identification of a whole with its parts. Simply take 'syllable' and 'letter' to be equivalent to 'whole' and 'part',

---

[69] The terminology is that of Quine (1953, essay VIII).

[70] Contrast the blatant fallacy of division, presented—and, we may note, identified—at *Hippias Major* 301d–302b, where the absurdity of supposing that, if Socrates and Hippias are two people, Socrates is two people, is brought to Hippias' attention. I owe the reference to Nicholas Denyer.

[71] Cf. Bostock (1988: 212).

and the question with which the dilemma began—about the relation between a syllable and its letters—is already a question about the relation between a whole and its parts. But to read the passage thus is to ignore the careful way in which Socrates manipulates the letter–syllable relation within the arguments of the dilemma.[72] It functions as a place-holder onto which the part–whole relation is mapped only under certain conditions. Socrates in fact begins by assuming a position on the relation between a whole and its parts, and uses this assumption to guide and constrain his conclusion about the relation between a syllable and its letters.

To see this, consider the second horn of the dilemma, where the strategy is clearest. I take up the discussion at the point at which the first horn of the dilemma, working on the assumption that a syllable is the same as its letters, has demolished the Asymmetry Thesis by concluding that syllables and letters— and so, complexes and elements—are just as knowable as each other. Socrates begins the second horn by questioning the working assumption of the first. What follows is the first stage of the ensuing discussion.

SOCRATES. . . . Perhaps we ought not to have supposed the syllable to be the letters; perhaps we ought to have made it some single form produced out of them, having its own single nature—something different from the letters.

THEAETETUS. Yes, certainly, that might be more like it.

SOC. We must look into the matter; we have no right to betray a great and imposing theory [the dream] in this faint-hearted manner.

THT. Certainly not.

SOC. Then let it be as we are now suggesting. Let the complex be a single form resulting from the combination of the several elements when they fit together, and let this hold both of language and of things in general.[73]

THT. Yes, certainly.

SOC. Then it [the complex, e.g. the syllable] must have no parts.

THT. Why is that now?

---

[72] As, for example, does Scaltsas (1990).

[73] The general form of Socrates' remarks supports Burnyeat–Levett's choice of 'element' and 'complex' here. Once again, letters and syllables will be the examples in what follows.

soc. Because when a thing has parts, the whole is necessarily all the parts. (203e2–204a8)

Here, in a nutshell, is the argument of the second horn of the dilemma. There is as much and more again of text remaining, because Socrates will argue for the identification of a whole and its parts against Theaetetus' resistance. But the conclusion (and the strategy) is encapsulated in this brief opening section. Socrates' argument is swift: if a syllable is different from its letters, it does not have parts, because, when a thing has parts, the whole is necessarily all the parts.

Notice that the leading premiss to this argument concerns the relation between a whole and its parts: that a whole is necessarily all its parts. Given this assumption, it is then precisely because the syllable is here taken to be different from its letters that Socrates argues that it cannot be a whole of which its letters are parts; indeed, it cannot be a whole of parts at all, since it is not identical with its letters, its candidate parts. The argument, as quoted, is not yet complete, but can be made so by the addition of some premisses which emerge in the rest of the discussion, in which Socrates develops this brief opening argument. (For the present, I omit premisses to the argument for the identification of a whole with its parts, which I shall discuss below.)

(1) If the syllable has parts, its letters are its parts (205b).
(2) Parts are parts of a whole (204e11).

Given these premisses, and the leading assumption that a whole is necessarily all its parts, Socrates argues validly to his conclusion: since, *ex hypothesi*, a syllable is not the same as its letters, it cannot be a whole and does not have parts.

The structure of Socrates' argument makes clear that the relation between a syllable and its letters does not inform our theorizing about the relation between a whole and its parts, but vice versa. The syllable is a whole of which its letters are parts, if, and *only* if, the relation between a syllable and its letters conforms to the independently established relation between whole and parts. It is in this way that the identification of a whole with its parts is the chief premiss of the second horn of the dilemma. It is also the central premiss of the first horn, as is confirmed by the first part of the final statement of the dilemmatic conclusion, in which a generalized conclusion about elements and complexes is extrapolated from the discussion of letters and syllables.

SOCRATES. Well now, if the complex is both many elements and a whole, with them as its parts, then complexes and elements are equally capable of being known and expressed, since all the parts turn out to be the same thing as the whole.

THEAETETUS. Yes, surely.

SOC. But if, on the other hand, the complex is single and without parts, then complexes and elements are equally unaccountable and unknowable—both of them for the same reason. (205d7-e4)

Both horns of the dilemma thus depend upon identifying a whole with its parts. How should we understand this identification? The attempt to salvage the arguments of the first horn from the charge of fallacy suggested that we should understand the composition of a whole—the syllable, *only if* identical to its letters—as having the ontological innocence to which Lewis aspired and which Baxter might claim to have achieved. As in Baxter, the identification of a whole with its parts, so understood, involves the (apparently) absurd identification of one thing with many things at which Lewis baulked.

What is Plato's attitude to this identification of a whole with its parts? To some extent, of course, the answer to such a question must be a matter for speculation. However, since the identification of a whole with its parts is the (sole) shared premiss on which both horns of the dilemma depend, if there is something at fault in the arguments of the dilemma, which Plato intends to highlight, this identification is the most likely candidate. The ensuing argument from experience, whose conclusion contradicts that of the dilemma, suggests that something may well be at fault in the arguments of the dilemma. Reasons to be suspicious of this identification are also provided by the lengths to which Socrates goes to defend it and the lengths to which Theaetetus goes to try to resist it. As we shall see, Theaetetus puts up a considerable fight against the identification of a whole with its parts. And his eventual capitulation is marked by less than enthusiastic assent.[74]

[74] On which, see n. 78 below.

In a highly compressed passage of text, the grounds for the identification of a whole with its parts are presented for our consideration at comparatively great length. In examining these grounds we shall see that the comparison with Baxter and Lewis is quite germane. What Socrates gives us is a prototype of an argument for the thesis that composition is identity.

Composition and Identity

Socrates' defence of the identification of a whole with its parts depends on two premisses, each of which is the result of tricky argument.

(1) All of it ($\tau\grave{o}$ $\pi\hat{a}\nu$)—where 'it' is something with parts—is the same as all of them ($\tau\grave{a}$ $\pi\acute{a}\nu\tau a$)—where 'they' are its parts.[75]

(2) The whole of something is the same as all of it.

Like the target identification of a whole with its parts, the identification of all of it with all of them (premiss 1) also involves an identification of one thing with many things, as indicated by the shift from singular to plural: identifying all of *it* with all of *them*. By far the greater part of Socrates' argument is taken up by his effort to get Theaetetus to agree to this latter identification.

I shall go through the argument slowly because of its importance. After his quick once-through of the argument, quoted in the previous section, to the effect that a syllable different from its letters does not have its letters as parts, Socrates offers and Theaetetus takes an escape route. The escape route is obvious: deny the chief premiss of that argument, the identification of a whole with its parts. Socrates suggests that, just as they had hypothesized that a syllable might be a single form arising from the combination of its letters, so one might take a whole to be 'a single form arising out of the parts, but different from all the parts' (204a8–9). Theaetetus adopts this hypothesis. Socrates then asks him whether or not he thinks that a whole is the same as

---

[75] In what follows, I adopt the translations 'all of it' and 'all of them'—suggested to me by Nicholas Denyer—as what seem to me the best way to capture what, in Greek, is marked by the singular and plural of the same noun-phrase: $\tau\grave{o}$ $\pi\hat{a}\nu$, $\tau\grave{a}$ $\pi\acute{a}\nu\tau a$. This has the advantage of avoiding the misleading implications of the Burnyeat–Levett translation 'sum' for the singular phrase.

all of it. Theaetetus decides that a whole is different from all of it. Whence the argument begins.

First, and most importantly, Socrates argues that all of it—where it has parts—is all of them—where they are its parts (premiss 1).

SOCRATES. Well now, is there any difference between all of them and all of it? For instance, when we say 'one, two, three, four, five, six'; or, 'twice three', or 'three times two', 'four and two', 'three and two and one'; are we speaking of the same thing in all these cases or different things?

THEAETETUS. The same thing.

SOC. That is, six?

THT. Precisely.

SOC. Then with each expression have we not spoken of all the six?

THT. Yes.

SOC. And when we speak of all of them, aren't we speaking of all of it?

THT. We must be.

SOC. That is, six?

THT. Precisely.

SOC. *Then in all things made up of number* (ἐξ ἀριθμοῦ), *at any rate, by 'all of it' and 'all of them' we mean the same thing?*

THT. So it seems.

SOC. Now let us talk about them in this way. The number of an acre is the same thing as an acre, isn't it?

THT. Yes.

SOC. Similarly with a mile.

THT. Yes.

SOC. And the number of an army is the same as the army? And so always with things of this sort; their total number is all of what each of them is.

THT. Yes.

SOC. But is the number of each anything other than its parts?

THT. No.

SOC. *Now things which have parts consist of parts* (ἐκ μερῶν)?

THT. That seems true.

SOC. And it is agreed that all the parts are all of it, seeing that the total number is all of it.

THT. That is so.

SOC. Then the whole does not consist of parts. For if it did, it would be all the parts and so would be all of it.

THT. It looks as if it doesn't. (204b10-e10; I emphasize the crucial claims, on which see below.)

There is much that is difficult in this argument, which, arguably, leads into difficult issues in Greek philosophy of mathematics.[76] I shall return to some of the difficulties later. For now, my concern is to show that Socrates' argument is an argument to the effect that composition is identity.

Socrates' aim in the passage quoted is to identify all of it with all of them; that is, to establish premiss 1 (above). His first example involves number (better, *arithmos*). 'Four and two', 'three and two and one', 'twice three' are all ways of talking about six. Further, to speak of all of them—say 'one, two, three, four, five, six'—is to speak of all of it, six.[77] Socrates now generalizes from this, in the first passage italicized above: for all things made up of (ἐκ) number, all of it is the same as all of them. Let me restate this: anything which is made up of—that is, is composed of—number is identical to all the things that compose it. In other words, composition—for the case of composition by number—is identity.

Socrates proceeds to develop the argument to include, first, things measured by number—an acre, a mile—and, second, numbers of things—an army, here identified (perhaps question-beggingly) as some number of soldiers. In the case of things of this sort, he claims, their number is their parts. In the second passage italicized above, he again emphasizes composition: things which have parts *are composed of* (ἐκ) parts. Socrates now sees the way clear to his conclusion without the restriction to composition by number. Since it has been agreed—for composition by number—that all of it is all of them;[78] and since composition by parts has been assimilated to composition by number, then, for anything which has parts, all of it is the same as all of them. That is, things composed of parts are identical to the parts

[76] See Burnyeat (1990: 205–9) for both the argument and the issues.

[77] Remember that an *arithmos* ('number') should here be thought of as a collection of units. That is why, as Burnyeat notes (1990: 205–9), Theaetetus—the promising young mathematician—is happy to accept such claims. Here is one instance of the (to us, rather alien) comparison between numbers and wholes I mentioned before. I shall consider how loaded the comparison may be hereafter.

[78] Notice, however, that the three points at which Theaetetus' responses might be taken to indicate uncertainty or reluctance—when he agrees only that the conclusion appears to follow (204d3, e4, e10)—are exactly those points at which Socrates takes composition to involve identity. Theaetetus' responses are worth watching.

that compose them. What Socrates defends is indeed the thesis that composition is identity, the thesis underlying both Lewis's and Baxter's (more or less successful) claims to the innocence of composition.

Socrates' overall argument is not yet complete. Recall that his defence of the identification of a whole with its parts depends on two premisses:

(1) All of it—where 'it' is something with parts—is the same as all of them—where 'they' are its parts.

(2) The whole of something is the same as all of it.

Thus far, he has gained premiss 1, but has yet to gain premiss 2. What he has ensured is that anything which has parts is the same as all its parts. Thus, as he concludes in the passage quoted, a whole cannot be composed of parts, for if it were, it would be the same as all its parts, and so, by the transitivity of identity, the same as all of it. If a whole has parts, then, premiss 2 follows from premiss 1. Theaetetus is prepared, for a short time, to defend the view that a whole does not have parts in order to avoid the consequent identification of a whole with all of it. (And if this is not a heavy authorial hint to look carefully at this identification, I don't know what is.) But Socrates quickly persuades him to accept the identification on the grounds that both a whole and all of it may be characterized as 'that from which nothing is absent' (205a4–7). Thus Theaetetus eventually grants Socrates both premiss 1 and premiss 2. The identification of a whole with its parts is thereby secured.

Socrates' characterization of a whole, at 205a4–7, as 'that from which nothing is absent' is interestingly different from the characterization of a whole, at *Parmenides* 137c7–8, as 'that from which no *part* is lacking', subsequently repeated by Aristotle (*Metaphysics* v. 1023^{b}26). The two characterizations are equivalent, of course, if a whole is to be identified with its parts, since there is nothing other than a part to be lacking. Aristotle in fact denies that this is all there is to be lacking, in an argument in *Metaphysics* VII. 17, on the grounds that the parts appear to be able to survive the dissolution of the whole. I suggest that one of the troubling features of Socrates' argument in the *Theaetetus* is the way in which he carefully chooses his examples to diminish the appeal of Aristotle's worry about the differential survival of parts and whole.

The Ontology of the Dilemma and Aristotle's Worry

The number six (the *arithmos*, that is), an acre, a mile, and an army: this rather odd assortment is what Socrates gives us by way of concrete examples of composition. There is a certain natural progression in his list, as I suggested: from the initial numerical examples to things measured by number or *arithmos* (the acre, the mile) to numbers of things (the army). The lead example, through its association between composition and *arithmos*, governs the entire list. Thus, Socrates first establishes his conclusion for the case of 'composition by number' and then assimilates composition by parts to this.

The association between composition and *arithmos* has two aspects. First, and most obviously, an *arithmos*—six, the sextet— is an example of something composite. This, while alien to our modern conception of number in the ways I have discussed, is in line with the Greek notion of *arithmos* as a collection of units.[79] Second, Socrates claims that, for each of his examples, 'their number (or *arithmos*)' is their parts. How should this claim be understood? Again, reflection on the Greek conception of *arithmos* is helpful. Small collections of units may go to make up larger collections; if, for example, a trio and a duet combine, a quintet is formed.[80]

---

[79] So, for example, Euclid talks of numbers or *arithmoi* as having parts, which parts are other, lesser numbers. See e.g. *Elements* VII, definitions 3 and 4, text and translation of which may be found in Heath (1956, vol. ii).

[80] This account of legitimate combinations of parts of an *arithmos* would need refinement. Since there is more than one way to divide an *arithmos* into its parts, one would need to preclude combining overlapping parts, such as a quartet (the quintet minus one member) and a duet (the quintet minus three members), taken from different legitimate, but incompatible, divisions of the *arithmos*. Otherwise, one would end up with the absurdity of parts of the quintet combining to make a sextet. The notion required is that of a 'partition', on which see Simons (1987: 219): adapting from Simons, a partition of an *arithmos* might be defined as a class of parts of the *arithmos* whose members are disjoint (have no part in common) and jointly compose the *arithmos*.

Is this association between composition and *arithmos* loaded? I think so. *Arithmoi* are enumerable collections. A unit of measurement—an acre or mile—is fairly readily assimilated to this conception, being a spatial extent containing smaller such extents: an acre comprises 4,840 square yards; a mile comprises 1,760 yards. What of an army? Is an army just an enumerable collection of soldiers? What about lines of command? battalions and brigades? (An army should be distinct from a rabble. And do we suppose that the identity of the army fluctuates dramatically on a day when casualties are especially high?) At least, however, an army is clearly (some kind of) collective entity. Socrates' conclusion, however, is utterly general; it applies to anything with parts. Recall his rather hasty generalization after the example of the army: 'And the number of an army is the same as the army? And so always with things of this sort; their total number is all of what each of them is' (204d9–11). What are 'things of this sort'? The question is hidden in the generalization. Socrates generalizes the numerical conception of composition to include all cases of composition. And this is why the association between *arithmos* and composition is loaded.

By the argument of the dilemma, any whole of parts is an enumerable collection. And such a view sits well with what I dubbed the 'compositional version' of the problem of the one and the many, for such a whole is many, as many as its parts. (Its parts, recall, are its number.) Enumerable collections are not the only things in Socrates' ontology here. They are, however, the only composite things. Consider the two conceptions of a syllable on offer in the dilemma. The letter–syllable relation has functioned as a place-holder onto which the part–whole relation may be mapped only under certain conditions. On the first horn of the dilemma, the syllable turns out to be a collection—some letters. Being the same as its letters, it may be taken to be a whole of which its letters are parts, and all wholes of parts are enumerable collections. If, however, as the second horn of the dilemma supposes, the syllable is not the same as its letters, it is, for this reason, not a whole and has no parts. Just this, recall, is what Socrates' argument that composition is identity is designed to show. Considered thus, the syllable is a mereological atom; an object which has no (proper) parts. And this exhausts the ontology of the dilemma: enumerable collections and mereological atoms.

What Socrates' examples omit, we may feel, particularly if we are moved by Aristotle's worry, is any reference to structure. Atoms—mereological atoms, that is—have no internal structure. But (at least some) wholes of parts are notable for the complex structural arrangement of their parts. (Consider the list of examples I gave at the beginning: wholes such as human beings, computers, and sentences.) What should we say about such structure in relation to composition? Should we take the structural arrangement of parts to have ontological significance? Should we use it to restrict our notion of composition: to distinguish one kind of composition from another, say, or to distinguish genuine composition from what is not composition at all? So Aristotle supposes. That is why he supposes that parts can survive the dissolution—the loss of structure—of the whole they compose, where the whole cannot. I shall argue that Plato's own position is broadly similar, as we shall see, much later, when we turn to those passages in which he discusses composition in a more positive vein.[81]

Alternatively, we might stick out for ontological innocence. We might see the relation between structure and composition as a matter not for ontology, but for ideology, to be dealt with by an apparatus of predicates.[82] So (I suppose) Lewis might argue. Recall his claim that, given Unrestricted Composition, we ordinarily (and, in his view, quite legitimately) speak with restricted quantification about only some of the things there are: about trouts and turkeys, but not, at least not ordinarily, about trout-turkeys (the Mereological fusion, you may recall, of the front half of a trout and the back half of a turkey). But the difference between them is not one of ontological significance.

---

[81] The question of the survival of parts is complicated, however, both for Plato and for Aristotle, despite what he says in *Metaphysics* VII. 17. I shall return to these complications in Chs. 4 and 5.

[82] The terminology is that of Quine (1953, essay VII). In Quine's terms, the 'ontology' of a theory is the entities to whose existence the theory is committed; its 'ideology' is its capacity to mark out some group of objects among these entities without further adding to its ontology.

Once again, what reflection on the relation between composition and identity brings into focus is the question of the ontological innocence or otherwise of composition. In the course of this book, I shall argue that structure plays a central role in Plato's account of the kind of complex individual a whole should be taken to be. But it is no easy task to show how this is so, not least because the notion of structure itself requires clarification, and is one which has, in general, been relatively underexplored. Investigation of the way in which considerations of structure might feature in an account of composition will provide one way in which to frame the difference between Plato's account of composition and that of Lewis.

Our *Theaetetus* passage does not mention structure.[83] Indeed, it is, I would say, conspicuous in its failure to mention it.[84] Its failure to do so is part of the strategy of Socrates' argument for the view of composition as identity. But this view of composition is here to be problematized, not endorsed. As such, the *Theaetetus* passage provides the first instance of a pattern we shall find repeated and expanded in the texts which I shall consider in Chapter 2.

---

[83] The phrase 'μία τὶς ἰδέα' (Burnyeat–Levett: one single form) is tantalizing, however. This is the phrase that Socrates chooses to describe the syllable considered as different from its letters, which turns out to be a mereological atom. It turns up again in the *Parmenides*, as we shall see, used to describe a whole of parts and meant, I shall argue, to flag the significance of structure to the constitution of a whole.

[84] By this, I do not mean that there is some Greek word which Plato could have used in this passage, but conspicuously does not. Rather, I mean that a significant feature of Socrates' strategy in this passage, manifest particularly in his choice of examples, is that he talks about composition in a way which distracts one's attention from any significance one might attach to the structural arrangement of the parts of a whole, and this despite the fact that the passage purports to be a discussion of letters and syllables, a context in which the order of the letters makes a significant difference to which, if any, syllable they compose.

CHAPTER 2

Composition as Identity in the *Parmenides* and *Sophist*

THE *Parmenides* may be considered the *locus classicus* of Plato's treatment of part and whole. Arguments involving parts and wholes recur frequently throughout the dialogue. They feature in the initial conversation between Socrates and Zeno; in Parmenides' and Socrates' subsequent discussion of forms; and in Parmenides' deductions about the One, which make up the latter and largest part of the dialogue.[1] Further, these arguments involving parts and wholes are of a particular kind. Like the passage of the *Theaetetus* discussed above, and an equally brief passage of the *Sophist* to be discussed below, they treat the part–whole relation at a level of considerable abstraction. Indeed, the arguments of the *Parmenides* are by far the richest source for Plato's treatment of the part–whole relation as such.

The *Parmenides* is a notoriously puzzling dialogue. My discussion is not aimed at providing a comprehensive interpretation of the dialogue as a whole. Rather, I concentrate on one of its dominant themes—the relation between part and whole; a theme which is closely related to what has some claim to be *the* dominant theme—the relation between one and many. My approach to the *Parmenides* stands squarely in the tradition of Owen's work

---

[1] I adopt the translation 'the One' for τὸ ἕν , the subject of the deductions.

on the dialogue, which itself had antecedents in that of Ryle.[2] Owen took the nerve of Plato's argument, at least in the deductions about the One, to be the strategic opposition of premisses central to more than one argument; and he took the *Parmenides* to set the stage for problems on which Plato would focus in other late works.[3] At least in the case of arguments about composition, however, I take such opposition of premisses to run throughout the dialogue, indicating a greater unity of focus than is sometimes accorded to the dialogue's different parts. Further, whereas Owen's 'map' of the dialogue is static, I shall argue that, at least in the arguments about composition, there is a definite progression over the course of the dialogue.

Aside from their similarity of topic, the *Parmenides* gives no explicit indication of a relation between its various discussions of part and whole. However, when examined together, I shall argue, they can be seen to mount a sustained exploration of the relation between part and whole, forming what I shall call a 'mereological undercurrent' to the dialogue as a whole.[4] Further, if one reads through the dialogue focusing on these various discussions of part and whole, and on the relation between them, one gets an inexorable sense of a progression of argument. The mereological undercurrent to the dialogue comes in two phases: one negative

[2] See Owen (1970*a*; repr. in Owen 1986; references to the latter) and Ryle (1939).

[3] As evidence for this approach, Owen had already shown how, in the *Physics*, Aristotle may be seen to be treating the *Parmenides* as a source for problems to be solved (Owen 1961). Regarding Plato, the question of the relation between part and whole is one of Owen's own examples of the kind of problem which would be pursued in other Platonic works (Owen 1986: 93, 99–100). This book as a whole might be taken as an affirmation—and elaboration—of this view.

[4] Franz von Kutschera has advanced an interpretation of the *Parmenides* in which he argues that, in the deductions about the One, Parmenides may be seen, albeit only implicitly, to be using the resources of a formal mereology as a way of explicating the communion of forms (Kutschera 1995). I am certainly sympathetic to the idea that, in the *Parmenides*, there is significant theorizing of the part–whole relation. However, in my view, von Kutschera's enthusiasm for the attempt to formalize the principles that lie behind such theorizing leads him too quickly to assume a uniform theory of part and whole across the dialogue's various discussions of their relation; and to assimilate that theory to classical extensional mereology (see esp. §§5.1–3). Nonetheless, as the only other sustained treatment of the *Parmenides*' discussions of part and whole of which I am aware, von Kutschera's work may be usefully compared—and contrasted—with my own.

movement and one positive movement.[5] In the first and negative movement, an escalating series of puzzles is driven by the assumption that a whole is identical to its parts. This assumption, in turn, is shown to create difficulties for a composite's claim to unity. Against this, the arguments of the positive movement stand in relief. They offer a direct challenge to the assumption of whole–parts identity, which is the basis of the puzzles, and a consequent reappraisal of the unity of a whole.

In this chapter I shall concentrate on the negative movement of the mereological undercurrent to the *Parmenides* and its series of puzzles.[6] There are four puzzles in the series.[7] Each is an instance of the same general pattern of puzzle. I shall seek to identify and explore the treatment of part and whole on which this pattern of puzzle is based. The puzzle series will be seen to develop, on a larger scale, the understanding of composition identified and problematized in the *Theaetetus* dilemma. As in the *Theaetetus*, I argue, this understanding of composition is here to be problematized, not endorsed. Both here and elsewhere I take this understanding of composition to be one which Plato views as false, but whose problems he is concerned to expose and explore. In closing, I shall consider the Eleatic antecedents of this understanding of composition through discussion of a related passage of the *Sophist*. Taken together, Plato's investigations of this—as he takes it to be—inadequate conception of composition form the backdrop against which he will be seen to offer his own account of composition as an alternative.[8]

2.1 SOCRATES' PUZZLE: THE CONVERSATION WITH ZENO

The reported dialogue of the *Parmenides*, beginning at 127d6, consists of three conversations. It begins with a conversation

---

[5] 'Negative' and 'positive' here flag what I take to be Plato's attitude to the conceptions of composition involved in each movement.

[6] I shall discuss the positive movement in Ch. 3.

[7] These are puzzles that I shall identify among the arguments of the dialogue. Especially in the early stages of the series, they are not explicitly set out as such.

[8] This account will be the subject of my discussion in Chs. 3 and 4.

between Socrates and Zeno in which Socrates introduces a nascent theory of forms in response to some arguments put forward by Zeno.[9] It continues with a conversation between Parmenides and Socrates in which Parmenides raises a number of questions about this nascent theory.[10] It concludes with a lengthy series of deductions presented by Parmenides for which a young man called Aristotle, who would later become one of the thirty tyrants (127d2–3), serves as respondent.[11] These deductions are offered as an example of the kind of training that Parmenides prescribes for the young and somewhat precocious Socrates. Two opposing hypotheses are examined in turn: first, that One is, and, second, that One is not. For each hypothesis, separate consequences are deduced for the One and for the Others.[12] Further, in each case, two separate and apparently conflicting sets of consequences are drawn for the One and for the Others. There are thus eight deductions in total.[13]

Establishing the relation between these three conversations of the reported dialogue is one of the central interpretative problems of the *Parmenides*. Demonstrating that there is an intelligible

[9] This nascent theory clearly corresponds in significant respects to the characterization of forms in works such as the *Phaedo* (72–8 and, perhaps especially, 96–106) and the *Republic* (esp. books v–vii). What more than this might be said about the relation between the *Parmenides'* theory and the *Phaedo's* and *Republic's* discussions of forms will not concern me here; nor will the theory itself as such.

[10] After questioning Socrates as to what forms there are, Parmenides' questions centre on two main issues: the relation (or lack of relation) between forms and their participants and Socrates' claim that each form is one.

[11] It stretches the point somewhat to describe this latter as a 'conversation', since Aristotle's contribution is limited to the most minimal replies. However, the deductions are, at least, interactive in spirit. In the preliminary discussion of procedure, there is discussion as to who should act as respondent, but not of whether there should be a respondent. See 137b6–8 and contrast *Sophist* 217c2–d3, where the Eleatic Stranger does consider whether to adopt the mode of question and answer or to give a long speech.

[12] Parmenides nowhere expands on the identity of the things other than the One, consequences for which are deduced in the third, fourth, seventh, and eighth deductions. I capitalize 'Others' to indicate that this is a collective name for whatever is other than the One and to avoid confusion with the term 'other'.

[13] Like most readers of the *Parmenides* in recent times, I take the discussion of the 'instant' (155e4–157b5) to be, not a separate deduction, but an appendix to the first and second deductions. Cf. Owen (1986: 95); Meinwald (1991: 117–24); and M. L. Gill (1996: 55). Sayre (1996: 240–1) takes this passage to be an appendix to the second deduction only.

relation between them is crucial to establishing some unity of purpose for the dialogue as a whole. And the *Parmenides* is a dialogue whose overall unity has been questioned, either by taking the deductions in the latter (and largest) part of the dialogue to be a laborious joke or by taking the deductions to be a later appendix.[14] Much interpretative effort has duly been expended on exploring the relation between the deductions and the conversation between Parmenides and Socrates, in which is found Parmenides' infamous apparent criticism of forms. In particular, interpreters have sought to identify in the deductions some response to the criticism levelled at Socrates' conception of forms, whether by way of defusing the criticism or by way of revising or jettisoning the theory of forms.[15]

All too often this interest in examining the relation between the deductions and Parmenides' criticisms of forms has been at the expense of consideration of the initial conversation between Socrates and Zeno.[16] No doubt this is because the relation between this initial conversation and the remainder of the dialogue appears comparably clear. The initial conversation provides the setting for Socrates' introduction of forms, the introduction of which is the basis for Parmenides' subsequent searching examination of them. However, there is more to be gleaned from this initial conversation than an excuse for the introduction of forms. In particular, for present purposes, this initial conversation between Socrates and Zeno provides the first puzzle in the escalating series of puzzles with which I shall be concerned.

I begin, not with the puzzle, but with a passage which occurs towards the end of Socrates' conversation with Zeno, in which he issues the following challenge:

---

[14] See, respectively, Taylor (1934) and the Afterword to Ryle (1939), published on its reprinting in Allen (1965: 145–7). For a survey of approaches to the interpretation of the *Parmenides*, see Sayre (1996: pp. xi–xx). However, Sayre's restriction to book-length treatments devoted to the *Parmenides* omits many valuable contributions to the literature on the dialogue which have come in the form of articles or books with a wider brief.

[15] The defusion strategy has been exemplified most recently by Meinwald (1991), the revisionist approach by Sayre (1996). For an approach to the interpretation of the dialogue which places the 'whither forms?' question away from centre stage, see McCabe (1994, esp. ch. 3, §§4–7, and ch. 4).

[16] Exceptions include Allen (1983) and McCabe (1996).

If someone should undertake to show that the same thing is one and many, regarding sticks and stones and the like, we shall say that he has shown that same thing to be one and many, but not that the one is many nor the many one; he has not said anything remarkable, but things on which we all might agree. If, however, someone were first to distinguish the forms I just mentioned, just by themselves, such as likeness and unlikeness, multitude and the one, rest and change, and all such things, and were then to show that these things in themselves can be combined and separated, then, Zeno, I would really be amazed. I think that you have dealt very bravely with the former. However, as I say, I would admire it much more if someone could show that this same puzzle is thoroughly interwoven among the forms themselves; that, among the things we grasp by reason, it turns out to be just as you have shown it to be among the things we see.[17] (129d2–130a2)

When, much later, in the second of his deductions about the One, Parmenides argues that the One itself is both one and many (142b5–145a3), his argument is a direct response to Socrates' challenge. As per Socrates' challenge, he reproduces the Zenonian style puzzle among the 'things we grasp by reason'; this much at least is clear about the entities involved in the deductions.[18] In doing so, he uses the very same terms with which Socrates had introduced his challenge: that is, one and many. These are also the very terms which Socrates himself had used, immediately prior to his challenge, in saying that it would be no concern to him if someone were to show that he himself were one and many (129c4–d2). Socrates and Parmenides each presents a one–many puzzle: some object (Socrates, the One) is shown to be both one and many.

The correspondence does not end here. Both Socrates' and Parmenides' puzzles are part–whole puzzles. Each exploits the same assumption about the relation between part and whole. Each exploits the assumption that parts pluralize. Call this the 'Pluralizing Parts Principle'. If some single object has parts, then, according to the Pluralizing Parts Principle, that single object is many—just as many as its parts. In the context of the *Parmenides*, I shall argue, applications of the Pluralizing Parts

[17] Translations of the *Parmenides* are my own, but I have consulted, and often broadly followed, the translations of others, in particular that of Allen (1983), and of Mary Louise Gill and Paul Ryan in M. L. Gill (1996).

[18] See 135d8–e4, which explicitly recalls the terms of Socrates' challenge.

Principle depend on the assumption that a whole is identical to its parts. They depend, that is, on assuming that composition is identity. This assumption underlies each of the four puzzles on which I shall focus. Socrates' puzzle is the first in the series; Parmenides' puzzle is the culmination both of the series and of the negative movement of the mereological undercurrent to the *Parmenides*.

This mereological undercurrent is neither explicit nor developed in the early stages of the dialogue. Nonetheless, it is worth following the order of the puzzles as they occur in the dialogue, so as to bring out the progression of argument as the dialogue proceeds. The recurrence of the same pattern of puzzle provides one thematic connection between all three of the conversations of the reported dialogue. As is appropriate for a puzzle which is introduced in a conversation with Zeno, the puzzle has recognizably Eleatic, and indeed Zenonian, origins. The Zenonian credentials of the assumption that parts pluralize are recorded in a report of Eudemus, preserved in Simplicius:

Eudemus says in the *Physics* '. . . they say that Zeno said that if anyone would demonstrate to him what the one is, he would be able to speak of the things that are. He was puzzled, it seems, because each perceptible thing may be called many both predicatively (κατηγορικῶς) and in virtue of having parts (μερισμῷ), whereas the point (στιγμή) may be supposed to be nothing . . .' (Simplicius, *in Ph.* 138. 30–139. 1 = Eudemus fr. 37a)[19]

According to Eudemus, then, Zeno thought that sensible objects were many both because they have many properties and because

[19] There is a question as to the boundaries of Simplicius' quotation from Eudemus here. Diels (1882, ad loc.) takes the quotation to run from 138. 31–139. 3. However, as Han Baltussen points out to me, one might instead have only a short direct quote in 138. 31 (not given) and take φασιν (they say), in 138. 32, from which my translation begins, to be Simplicius himself attributing the view of Zeno which follows to both Eudemus and Alexander. In either case, however, Eudemus will be (one of) the sources for the view ascribed to Zeno. On Simplicius' quotation habits in general and his use of Eudemus in particular, see Baltussen (2002, forthcoming). Since Eudemus' status as a source for Zeno's thought is unclear, we should be appropriately cautious about the evidential value of this report. Among surviving Eleatic texts, the most direct application of the Pluralizing Parts Principle I have found is ascribed to Melissus (B9 = Simplicius, *in Ph.* 87. 6–7, 110. 1–2). Interestingly, however, Kirk, Raven, and Schofield (1983: 401 n. 1) question Simplicius' ascription of the remark to Melissus and suggest it may rather be a fragment of Zeno.

they have many parts. In the *Parmenides*, as we shall see, these two grounds for pluralization will be brought together by taking an object's properties to be parts of that object.[20] First, however, I consider how the assumption that parts pluralize is introduced for the case of spatial parts in the first of our puzzles, Socrates' puzzle.

Pluralizing Parts

Socrates' puzzle occurs during the course of his response to Zeno. Zeno is armed with a battery of arguments that purport to show that plurality is impossible. He has been reading through them from his book before the reported dialogue begins. The reported dialogue opens with Socrates' repetition of, and then commentary upon, the first of Zeno's arguments. 'If things are many, then the very same things must be both like and unlike. But this is impossible, for unlike things cannot be like, nor like things unlike' (127e1–4).

Zeno's argument is enigmatically brief, but its point is clear: it is designed as a reductio of the supposition of plurality (cf. 127e6–8). The argument takes the form of a modus tollens, as follows: (1) if things are many, the very same things are both like and unlike; but (2) it is impossible that the very same things are both like and unlike; thus (3) it is impossible that things are many. Socrates' subsequent remarks make clear that this argument is representative of the pattern of Zeno's arguments in general, and that these arguments are all designed to demonstrate the impossibility of plurality. Thus, the general form of Zeno's arguments is this: if things are many, the very same things are both F and not-F for some list of properties. But this is impossible, or so Zeno says.

In the course of his response to Zeno, Socrates offers his own Zenonian style puzzle.[21] His Zenonian puzzle involves an

---

[20] Cf. Owen (1986: 90).

[21] Socrates does not present this puzzle as puzzling, because he takes himself to have a solution to it. However, I call it a puzzle, because Socrates takes it to require a solution (on which more below), and in order to highlight its connection with the puzzles of the same pattern which occur later in the series of which this is the first member. Just as the assumptions on which the puzzles depend are less explicit in the early occurrences of the pattern than in its later occurrences, so too their character as puzzles is less explicit earlier than later. The sense in which Socrates' puzzle (and the puzzles in general) are Zenonian in character will be made clearer below.

account of how someone might show that he, Socrates, is both one and many, as follows:

> when someone wishes to show that I am many, he will say that the [parts] on the right of me are one thing, the [parts] on the left another, that my front [parts] are one thing, my back [parts] another, and likewise upper and lower—for, I suppose, I have a share of many; when he wants to show that I am one, he will say that I am one person of the seven of us present, having a share of the one also. (129c5–d2)

Socrates does not talk directly of parts here. In my translation I have supplied the term 'parts' as a natural completion of the neuter plural articles in phrases such as 'the [things] on the right of me' (τὰ ἐπὶ δεξία μού, 129c6). But even if such a completion were disputed, it is clear that what makes Socrates many is having many parts: his left side, his right side, etc. Socrates is one in so far as he is one of the seven people present; he is many in so far as he has many different spatial parts. This is the first occurrence of the assumption that parts pluralize. By examining the relation between this puzzle and Zeno's argument, the implications of this assumption may be unpacked.

Socrates' puzzle—that he himself is both one and many—is explicitly presented as offering an illustration of his general response to Zeno. The strategy of his response is to challenge premiss (2) of Zeno's argument, as outlined above: the claim that it is impossible that the very same things are both like and unlike (or F and not-F in general). Socrates proposes that, for some things, under certain conditions, premiss (2) is false (and thus is false *simpliciter*). His puzzle is offered as a way of providing an example of the falsity of premiss (2). Given this strategy of response, Socrates' puzzle must provide us with a situation precisely analogous to that of Zeno's premiss (2). It is in this sense that Socrates' puzzle may be described as Zenonian in character.

One might dispute this claim to analogy. One might notice that, in Socrates' puzzle, Socrates spells out the relevant respects in which he is both one and many. He is one in respect of being one person and many in respect of having many different parts. Zeno, by contrast, at least according to Socrates' report of his argument, had not spelled out the relevant respects in which a plurality of things must be both like and unlike.[22] And one might think that, once Socrates spells out the relevant respects, he has already blown Zeno's cover; that there is nothing at all puzzling about things being one and many—or like and unlike—in different respects. It is then tempting simply to dismiss Zeno's argument as a sophism, in which Zeno deliberately fails to state the relevant respects in which a plurality of things must be both like and unlike.[23] After all, the only sense in which it is impossible for the same things to be like and unlike is if they are like and unlike the same things, in the same respects, and at the same times. But no pluralist need concede that things being like and unlike in this sense is a necessary feature of plurality.

However, tempting as such a diagnosis may seem, it is out of step with Socrates' own response to Zeno.[24] Socrates responds to Zeno's argument by bringing in a metaphysical hypothesis about forms: that they exist and that they stand in certain relations to the things around us. Despite the fact that his own Zenonian puzzle is stated with the relevant respects included, Socrates finds the (apparent) contradiction of his being one (in one respect) and many (in a different respect) sufficiently philosophically worrying to require the involvement of forms. This need come as no surprise, since such (apparent) contradictions— things being F (in one respect) and not-F (in a different respect)—illustrate the 'compresence of opposites' often associated with Socrates' introduction of forms.[25] Socrates' Zenonian puzzle is an example of the compresence of opposites. For it to be

---

[22] However, we may not have a complete account of Zeno's argument. Socrates is described as asking to hear the first 'hypothesis' of the first argument again (127d7). It is unclear whether this is all that he then reports or whether he reports the entire first argument. If, as seems more plausible, the former is the case, it seems likely that, in the remainder of the first argument, Zeno gave the grounds and thus the respects in which he contends that a plurality of things must be both like and unlike.

[23] See e.g. Brumbaugh (1961: 30–2).

[24] Cf. Allen (1983: 67), who observes that 'no man trundles in artillery to shoot fleas'.

[25] See e.g. *Phaedo* 74b7–c3 (at least on one, dominant interpretation of these lines); *Republic* v. 479a5–b8; and, for an example involving one and many—and, by implication, part and whole—*Republic* vii. 525a–e. For 'compresence of opposites', see pp. 175 and 177 of Owen (1957; repr. in Owen 1986; references to the latter); and Irwin (1977: 9).

so, however, requires an additional assumption, peculiar to this example. It is this additional assumption—and not the compresence of opposites as such—that will be the focus of my concern.

Socrates' solution to his Zenonian puzzle, and his response to Zeno's arguments generally, is to say that such (apparent) contradictions can be resolved, (1) if there are forms, and (2) if particular objects, like himself, stand in certain relations to forms. In Socrates' example, Socrates is one because he has a share of the form One, and is many because he has a share of the form Many. It is then important, in Socrates' response, that forms are not in turn vulnerable to such (apparent) contradictions; that the form One, for example, is not both one and many. This is the basis of the challenge he makes at the end of his conversation with Zeno. This basis will later be threatened, when Parmenides argues that the One is indeed both one and many.

Why Socrates should take it to be important that forms are not themselves vulnerable to such (apparent) contradictions is a good, but complex, question. Speaking generally, it is, no doubt, a function of the kind of epistemological and ontological concerns that one might identify as the general motivation for the introduction of forms. I do not propose to tackle these broader issues here. For the specific case in question, concerning one and many, it is a sign that Socrates himself assumes that there is something problematic about the unity of something that is both one and many, such that he seeks, as it were, to underwrite its unity by appeal to some unity that is not similarly affected. The effect which this has on his conception of the form One is something I shall discuss further below. In general, however, what matters most for my purposes is less why than *that* this is important to Socrates, since this brings out the structure of his response to Zeno. Attention to this structure will reveal the additional assumption underlying Socrates' chosen example of the Zenonian puzzle.

The structure of Socrates' response to Zeno—and the role of his own Zenonian puzzle within it—shows that Socrates himself sees no significant difference between his own puzzle, which is stated with suitable qualifications, and the puzzling situation envisaged in premiss (2) of Zeno's argument, which was not stated with such qualifications. He takes his own puzzle to be precisely analogous to that of Zeno's premiss (2), requiring the same solution. In light of this, we may now examine more closely the way in which Socrates' Zenonian puzzle must work.

Recall the general form of Zeno's arguments. From the hypothesis that things are many, he draws an (allegedly) impossible consequence: that the very same things are both *F* and not-*F*. For Socrates' puzzle to provide an instance of this (allegedly) impossible consequence, it must conclude that the very same thing is both one and many (or one and not one).[26] The thing in question, in Socrates' puzzle, is a whole of parts, Socrates himself.[27] Socrates is one in so far as he is one person and many in so far as he has many parts. We should distinguish the respect in which Socrates is one—being one person—from *what* is one. The whole—the person Socrates—is one; Socrates' parts are many. Does it then follow that the very same thing—Socrates— is both one and many? It can be made to follow, but only if Socrates further assumes that a whole is identical to its parts.

Let me spell out how this goes. The whole—Socrates—is one; his parts are many. Add the assumption that a whole is identical to its parts, and substitute identicals. The whole, being identical to its parts, is also many. The parts, being identical to the whole, are also one. Thus, the whole—or, for that matter, the parts—is or are both one and many. Socrates' own statement of the puzzle emphasizes the conclusion that the whole, Socrates, is both one and many. He could equally well have argued that his parts are both many and one. Since the puzzle trades on an identity between whole and parts, it could always be set up either way.[28]

---

[26] This equivalence is important; I shall return to it.

[27] Socrates no more explicitly talks of wholes here than he does of parts. However, just as it is clear that Socrates is here identified as having many parts, so it is clear that, if he has parts, he is a whole of those parts. ('Part' and 'whole' are correlative terms, as the *Parmenides* itself will later make clear.) As I have said, in the early puzzles in the series—especially this and the next—the assumptions on which the puzzles depend are nowhere explicit. However, the fact that Socrates' puzzle is a part–whole puzzle is confirmed, at least retrospectively, both by comparison with later puzzles in the *Parmenides*' series and by the explicit back reference to this very puzzle at *Philebus* 14c8–e4, which I shall discuss in §4.3 below.

[28] Here, too, compare *Philebus* 14c8–e4, where differentiating a person's limbs and parts leads us to be forced to admit both that one thing is many *and* that many are one.

Only on the assumption that a whole is identical to its parts does Socrates have a puzzle of the form required for his response to Zeno. In context, therefore, Socrates' assumption that parts pluralize—and pluralize the very thing whose parts they are—must depend on the identification of a whole with its parts.

This may seem a surprising result. The surprise comes, I think, from a tendency to take a benign interpretation of the Pluralizing Parts Principle. According to the benign interpretation, something with parts is many only in the sense of 'consists of many', what Wiggins has called 'the "is" of constitution'.[29] However, this benign interpretation of the Pluralizing Parts Principle will not yield the required puzzle. For Socrates' puzzle to have the same form as that of Zeno's premiss (2), he must show that he both is one and is many. No comparable puzzle arises from the claim that he is one and consists of many.

The benign interpretation seems tempting, because it is so reasonable to say that Socrates *consists of* many parts, or that he *has* many parts. However, Socrates' puzzle requires that he may be said to *be* many parts. And he can only be said to *be* many parts if he *is* what he consists of. This is no benign principle. To assume that he is what he consists of is to assume that composition is identity, the view of composition identified and problematized in the *Theaetetus* dilemma. This view of composition is precisely what Socrates must implicitly assume when he argues that he both is one and is many, being a whole of many parts.

Pluralizing Parts and Conceptions of Unity

If parts pluralize, the unity of a whole is problematic.[30] This much is clear from Socrates' puzzle. It is because Socrates has parts, and parts pluralize, that the whole—Socrates—is many, in

---

[29] Wiggins (1980: 30–1 with n. 19).

[30] Note that, here and elsewhere, the term 'whole' applies only to things which have (proper) parts. There are contexts in which the term 'whole' might also be applied to a mereological atom. Talk involving improper parthood (on which see Ch. 1 n. 17) is one such context. Everything is an (improper) part of itself. Thus, a mereological atom is a part, and thus also a whole, of itself. This use of the expression 'whole' seems to me the exception, not the norm. In any case, it is not the way in which Plato uses the expression.

addition to being one. Socrates' use of the Pluralizing Parts Principle, I have argued, is, albeit implicitly, premissed on the assumption that a whole is identical to its parts. The consequences of this implicit assumption for his conception of unity may likewise be extrapolated from what he says.

The only unproblematic examples of unity consistent with the assumptions which underlie Socrates' puzzle are mereological atoms. This is by default: having no parts, they are simply unaffected by the assumptions underlying the puzzle. Socrates' tolerance of this pattern of puzzle, in its first appearance, relies on the assumption of one such mereological atom. Socrates takes his own claim to be one to be dependent on his having a share of the form One, and on this form, One, not in turn being both one and many. This is the substance of his response to Zeno and the basis of his concluding challenge. Given the Pluralizing Parts Principle, the form One must be a mereological atom. As such, it is unaffected by the thesis that a whole is identical to its parts, except in so far as it is governed by the following counterfactual: if it were to have parts, it would be many. Parmenides will trade on this counterfactual later in the series of puzzles.

There is a story to be told about plurality also, although the *Parmenides* is, I think, rather less concerned to tell it.[31] If parts and whole are identical, then the parts, like the whole, are one, in addition to being many. Once again, Socrates' tolerance of the puzzle relies on his assumption of a form Many, which cannot be one. It is, we may suppose, a bare plurality, whatever that may be. (This, of course, plays hell with Socrates' repeated insistence that each form is one.[32])

---

[31] Discussion of plurality is not, however, entirely absent. Conceptions of plurality come to the fore in the latter phases of the deductions. I shall discuss these below. In general, however, both in the *Parmenides* and, in consequence, in my discussion, it is conceptions of unity or of being one that are in focus. This asymmetry as regards the consequences of the puzzle is curious, given the symmetry of the identity claim on which the puzzle depends. Perhaps, however, the thought is that a plurality is a plurality of units, and thus that an understanding of plurality will itself depend on resolving the problem about being one.

[32] Socrates' insistence that each form is one is a central focus for Parmenides' subsequent questions about forms; see e.g. 131c9–10, 132a1, and cf. *Republic* v. 475e9–476a7.

At the start of the *Parmenides*, then, Socrates' one–many puzzle presents us with three kinds of one and/or many: (1) a whole, which is, paradoxically, both one and many, the paradox of which is resolved by making its unity and plurality dependent on its relation to (2) a mereological atom—a one that is not many; and (3) a bare plurality—a many that is not one. Of the three options on offer—paradoxical many–ones, atomic ones, and bare pluralities—the last two may be compared with the two alternative conceptions of a syllable in the *Theaetetus* dilemma, discussed in Chapter 1. There, a syllable was either a mereological atom—it was not a whole of which its letters were parts—or a collection—some letters. These are the only options that avoid the puzzle, but are consistent with its assumptions.

The Thematic Significance of One and Many

Socrates' puzzle is a one–many puzzle. So, indeed, is each of the puzzles on which I shall focus. The one in question is, in each case, a whole of parts; in Socrates' puzzle, Socrates himself. The one–many motif is the surface presentation of the puzzle. Its logical basis is the thesis that composition is identity. It is this thesis that claims an identity between a whole and its parts. It is this identity between whole and parts that drives the assumption that parts pluralize, and makes a whole a many as much as a one.

The mereological assumptions on which Socrates' one–many puzzle depends are not explicit in the opening pages of the dialogue. Nor is the relation between these assumptions and his conception of what is involved in being one or many. But the theme of one and many does get considerable emphasis in the immediate context. I take this to be an invitation to think more closely about Socrates' puzzle and its successors in the remainder of the dialogue.

Before Socrates produces his response to Zeno, he spends some time teasing the two Eleatics present. He puns heavily on the terms 'one' and 'many' in his characterization of Parmenides and Zeno. Zeno, he suggests, thinks that there are as many proofs that there are not many (things) as the arguments he has written (127d11–128a1). And, despite their efforts to disguise the fact, Zeno and Parmenides have simply said the same thing: Parmenides saying 'one', Zeno saying 'not many', and these being the same thing, Socrates says (128a4-b6). Irony is at work here. Just as it is unfortunate for Zeno to have denied plurality by a plurality of denials, so it would, no doubt, be deeply unfortunate for two monists to have two distinct theses. (Indeed, it would be better if they themselves were not distinct.) Behind the irony, there is an important point.

Socrates' description of the combined Eleatic thesis—one, i.e. not many—picks out precisely the way in which he himself characterizes the form One: as a one that is not (and cannot be) many. This similarity between his characterization of the form One and of the Eleatics' thesis illustrates an important feature of Socrates' response to Zeno. Socrates does not tackle the assumptions on which Zeno's puzzles are based. He accepts Zeno's characterization as applied to particulars. Specifically, therefore, he accepts that the unity of a composite particular is paradoxical: having parts, it is many, in addition to being one. He accepts this characterization, I have argued, because he implicitly accepts that a whole is identical to its parts.

Socrates seeks to defuse the paradox which particulars engender by shifting the goalposts. The level at which the combined Eleatic thesis applies is the level of forms. Provided no analogous puzzle applies to forms, and provided particulars stand in appropriate relations to forms, Zeno's characterization of the phenomenal world need not worry us. Specifically, therefore, a whole gets some derivative unity from its relation to the form One, and the paradox—its being both one and many—is defused by its relations to the forms One and Many. However, just as Socrates' example of the Zenonian puzzle, expressed in terms of one and many, depends upon an additional assumption about parts and whole, so this additional assumption has a knock-on effect on the terms of his solution; in particular, on his conception of the form One. And—whatever else one may make of it—his solution is correspondingly fragile in just this respect. This pattern of puzzle becomes urgent, therefore, when it reappears at the level of forms. It is here too, as I shall show, that the mereological assumptions on which this pattern of puzzle is based come to the fore.

2.2 TWO KINDS OF 'PART' IN THE DILEMMA OF PARTICIPATION: *PARMENIDES* 131A–C

It is crucial to Socrates' response to his own Zenonian puzzle that *a* form—the form One—cannot have parts. In the Dilemma of Participation[33] Parmenides will argue Socrates into supposing that *any* form has parts, just in virtue of many particulars participating in it. This forestalls one swift defence of the claim that the form One cannot have parts. Socrates' Zenonian puzzle had used the core spatial notion of parthood. Socrates was many, because Socrates had many different spatial parts: his left side, his right side, etc. And spatial parthood—if not the only kind of parthood—is clearly the central case. But a form, one might then suppose, simply cannot have parts, since a form is not the kind of spatio-temporal individual that might have spatial parts.[34]

The Dilemma of Participation threatens the atomicity of forms. In doing so, it prompts the question of what kind of parts a form might have, and of the varieties of parthood in general. The Dilemma also provides the second in the series of one–many puzzles with which I am concerned. As with Socrates' puzzle, however, the mereological assumptions on which this pattern of puzzle is based, and the questions it raises, are not yet explicit at this stage in the series.

The Dilemma

Parmenides begins the Dilemma by presenting Socrates with a choice of ways in which to describe participation in forms:

---

[33] I take this label from Allen (1983). In the context of Parmenides' questioning of Socrates' nascent theory of forms, the Dilemma of Participation constitutes Parmenides' first attempt to get Socrates to clarify the relation between a form and its participants.

[34] For an example of scepticism about claims that abstract objects have parts, see e.g. Oliver (1994: 217). Oliver's paper is a criticism of Lewis, who himself defends abstract parthood; Lewis (1991: 75–6).

Does each thing which has a share of a form have either the whole form or part of the form as its share? Or is there some other way of having a share distinct from these?—How could there be? he said. (131a4–7)

On the first horn of the Dilemma, he supposes that each participant has the whole form as its share; and reasons as follows:

Do you think, then, that the whole form, being one, is in each of the many?—What prevents it, Parmenides? said Socrates.—Then, being one and the same, the whole will be present in many separate things at the same time, and would thus be separate from itself. (131a8–b2)

In an attempt to avoid this consequence, Socrates proposes that each form might be like a day, which 'being one and the same is in many places at once and is not thus separate from itself' (131b3–5). Parmenides responds to this analogy with an analogy of his own: that a form will thus be like a single sail spread over many people. Here, however, it is not the whole, but only part of the sail that is over each person. This feature of Parmenides' analogy leads Socrates on to the second horn of the Dilemma. On this second horn, each participant has not the whole, but only part of the form as its share. Parmenides then argues as follows:

Then, Socrates, forms themselves are divisible into parts, and things that have a share of them would have a part as their share, and in each [participant] would no longer be the whole, but part of each [form].—It certainly appears so.—But, Socrates, are you willing to say that one form is really divided into parts ($\mu\epsilon\rho i\zeta\epsilon\sigma\theta\alpha\iota$) and is yet one?—Not at all, he said. (131c5–11)

It is here, in the discussion of the second horn of the Dilemma, that we find the second in the series of puzzles with which I am concerned, although it is here presented only indirectly.

In the Dilemma as a whole, Parmenides presents Socrates with what purport to be exhaustive options for participation in forms: that the participant's share is the whole form or that the participant's share is a part of the form. On either option, he further assumes that a participant's share is, in some sense, present in the participant itself.[35] Parmenides then argues, first, that the

---

[35] The wider issues concerning this assumption have been cogently discussed in G. Fine (1986).

suggestion that a participant's share is the whole form leads to absurdity—a form separate from itself, being, as a whole, in many separate participants—and, second, that the remaining alternative that a participant's share is part of the form undermines Socrates' claim that each form is one.

Dialectically, this Dilemma is effective against Socrates. Socrates explicitly agrees to the assumption that the alternatives (whole or part) are exhaustive options for participation. And he nowhere challenges the assumption that a participant's share is present in that participant. This latter assumption is the lever by which Parmenides derives absurdity on the first horn of the Dilemma—that the form, being wholly present in many separate things, is separate from itself. It is given emphasis on the second horn of the Dilemma also, thus: 'and in each [participant] would no longer be the whole, but part of each [form]' (131c6–7). We need not be surprised that Socrates nowhere questions this assumption that a participant's share is present in that participant. He articulated it himself in the *Phaedo*: 'whenever you say that Simmias is larger than Socrates and smaller than Phaedo, you mean that both things are in Simmias, largeness and smallness?' (102b4–6).

Parmenides' Dilemma is asymmetric in structure.[36] The first horn purports to derive actual impossibility from the assumption that each participant's share is the whole form. The second horn is *ad hominem*. It turns on Socrates' assumption that each form is one, together with his agreement that, if a form were to have parts, it would thereby be many, not one. Once again, parts pluralize. Here, we may note, Parmenides portrays the form not just as having parts, but as being actually divided into these parts.[37] But the

---

[36] Cf. Allen (1983: 114, 118).

[37] At least, this appears to be the effect of his proposal that each form is 'really divided into parts' (τῇ ἀληθείᾳ μερίζεσθαι, 131c10). Appeal to the analogy of the sail, we may note, would not suffice to support this proposal, so understood, since, in the analogy, the sail is not actually divided. Thus, if Parmenides does assume an actual division of forms—as he appears to—his support for doing so must be found elsewhere. Perhaps, as in the argument of the first horn of the Dilemma, we are meant to recall that each of the participants to which—here, a part of—the form is present is (spatially) separated from all of the others. However, the point need not detain us, since the parallel I propose with the other puzzles in the series would, if anything, only be stronger, if Parmenides does not here mean to propose an actual division of forms.

significance of this discrepancy should not be overstated. Socrates' own earlier puzzle portrayed a whole as many, which was divisible, but not divided (thankfully not, from Socrates' perspective, he being the whole in question). Simply having parts suffices to pluralize a whole. In the Dilemma Socrates' instant acceptance that a form divided into parts cannot be one shows that he continues to assume that a composite object cannot (unproblematically) be one. As I argued above, such is the consequence of his continued implicit assumption of whole–parts identity. Here, however underdeveloped, is the second puzzle in our series, now applied to forms.

Parmenides proposes—and Socrates accepts—that a form, divided into parts, would be many, not one. Why many, not one, rather than many and one? In his own earlier puzzle Socrates had portrayed a whole as both many and one. He had, however, continued to assume that one and many are exclusive: that if something is many, it is not one; and that if something is one, it is not many. We saw this in his inclination to identify the two theses associated with the two Eleatics present: Zeno's assertion of 'not many' makes the very same claim as Parmenides' assertion of 'one'.

The identification of 'one' and 'not many' was also implicit in Socrates' use of the claim that he himself is both one and many as an example of the kind of puzzling situation envisaged in Zeno's arguments. Zeno's arguments turned on the (alleged) impossibility of the very same thing(s) being both F and not-F. Socrates' claim that he himself is both one and many is offered as an example of this (alleged) impossibility. However, being one and many may be represented as being F and not-F only if to be many is to be not one. Fully stated, therefore, Socrates' puzzle in fact involves the claim that he, being composite, is both one (and so not many) and many (and so not one). In the second horn of the Dilemma, Parmenides exploits only the second half of this fuller version of the puzzle form, underdeveloped as it is in its second appearance.

The underdeveloped character of the second occurrence of this pattern of puzzle may be due to the lack of resources which Socrates has at his disposal once this pattern of puzzle is applied to forms. Recall that, in his response to Zeno, Socrates took the unity of a composite particular to be derivative, dependent upon its relation to the form One. Arguably, this means of allowing some derivative unity to a composite is not available to Socrates when it comes to participated forms. This is so for two reasons. First, the unity of a participated form would thus be paradoxical, since, like the composite particular before it, it would be both many and one. But Socrates is committed to the claim that such paradoxes do not arise at the level of forms; on this his response to Zeno depends. Second, he is further committed to the claim that forms do not 'combine' (συγκεράννυμι, 129e2); this claim was part of the challenge with which he ended his response to Zeno. What, more precisely, he means by this is unclear. At the least, he again means to deny that forms can be the bearer of contrary properties. But he may also mean to rule out any interrelations between forms. If so, this would provide a second reason why he is unable to allow a participated form even a derivative unity.

In the Dilemma the divided form in question is not the form One, but any participated form. (Of course, this carries implications for the form One also, since it has participants, not least Socrates himself, as we have seen. But the 'full-blooded' version of this pattern of puzzle, applied to One itself, is not yet explicit.) The participated form does, however, suffer the fate of the form One, as the mereological assumptions which drive the puzzle go to work on the consequent conceptions of unity. Recall the position of the form One in the opening passage. Since parts pluralize, and the form One cannot be many, the form One must be a mereological atom. As such, it could remain unaffected by the assumption that a whole is identical to its parts, except in so far as it was governed by the following counterfactual: if it were to have parts, it would be many. Parmenides' argument on the second horn of the Dilemma is an elliptical application of this same counterfactual: if a form had many parts (its parts being present in many participants), it would be (many and) not one.

Again, none of this is explicit; Socrates simply accepts on the second horn of the Dilemma that a divided form cannot be one. Within the broader context of the dialogue's discussions of composition, however, his instant acceptance can, I argue, be seen as a result of implicit acceptance that a whole is identical to its parts. Once again, the assumption that a whole is identical to its parts allows no (unproblematic) conception of a composite unity.

Property-Parts and Instance-Parts

Where Socrates' Zenonian puzzle involved spatial parthood, the Dilemma concerns predication, more specifically, the share of a form that is present in a particular when a form may be predicated of it. How should we think of this share of a form—to use the *Phaedo* example, the largeness in Simmias, or George, or John? How does it relate to the form? And how does it relate to the particular whose share it is? The Dilemma turns on two alternative answers to the first question. On the first horn, a participant's share is the whole form. On the second and, for my purposes, the more significant horn, a participant's share is a part of the form. As to the relation of a participant's share to the participant itself, the Dilemma is less than clear. A participant's share is *present* in it. But what does that mean?

One possibility is that a participant's share is a part of that participant, where this need not imply that it is a spatial part of it.[38] The Dilemma neither confirms nor denies this possibility. Later in the *Parmenides*, as we shall see in due course, Parmenides will treat the properties present in a subject as if they were parts of a sort. In interpreting the Dilemma, however, we may simply suppose, for the sake of argument at this stage, that, on both horns of the Dilemma, a participant's share might be understood to be part of that participant and, on the second horn of the Dilemma, as part of the relevant form.[39]

---

[38] This view has its defenders as an interpretation of the *Phaedo*. For example, Jordan (1983: 43) refers to the largeness in Simmias as a 'logical part'; and the view that the *Phaedo* canvasses something very like an 'ingredient model' of predication has been proposed by Denyer (1983). The interpretation of the *Phaedo* is complicated, however, by controversy surrounding the status of entities such as the largeness in Simmias, and is not my concern here.

[39] Whatever may be true, in the *Phaedo*, of the relation between Simmias and the largeness present within him, there is no suggestion that this share of largeness is part of the relevant form. Indeed, at least earlier in the *Phaedo*, forms were explicitly presented as being incomposite (78c7–9). In the *Parmenides*, too, Socrates is striving to keep them that way.

This gives us two different kinds of parthood, relating to two different aspects of predication.[40]

If an object *a* has some property, *F*-ness, then *F*-ness is present in *a*. The *F*-ness in *a* is, first, a part of *a*. Call a part of this kind a 'property-part'.[41] The *F*-ness in *a* is, second, a part of the form *F*-ness. Call a part of this kind an 'instance-part'. What is predicated of an object, on this account, is not only a property-part of it, but also an instance-part of the property in question. For example, if Anne is smaller than Harry, smallness is present in Anne. The smallness in Anne is both a property-part of Anne and an instance-part of the form smallness.

Neither instance-parts nor property-parts are obvious examples of spatial parthood. In particular, if, as one might assume, forms are not spatio-temporal individuals, but abstract objects, the instance-parts of a form cannot be spatial parts. In context, however, there is a question as to how safe this assumption about forms might be. After all, the second horn of the Dilemma of Participation is followed by three brief arguments involving predications of size: large, equal, and small (131c12–e2). Each of these arguments is designed as a reductio of the supposition that each participant's share might be part of the relevant form. Cornford complained that these arguments take ' "part" and "whole" in the most gross and material sense'.[42] And, of course, if one has a gross and material treatment of the parts and wholes of forms, one has a gross and material treatment of forms.

Cornford is right about the treatment, although he may be wrong to lay the complaint at Parmenides' door. In the Dilemma of Participation, in response to the argument of the first horn of the

---

[40] That participation is understood as a mereological relation is the starting point of von Kutschera's interpretation of the *Parmenides*; for which, see esp. Kutschera (1995, §3.1.3). However, von Kutschera does not attend to the difference between the two kinds of parthood that are here seen to be involved in participation and that are put to work again in the second deduction (for which, see my discussion in §2.3 below and contrast Kutschera 1995, §§3.3.1–2).

[41] Property-parthood has affinities to what McCabe calls 'natural inherence' (McCabe 1994: 29–37 and elsewhere), according to which the properties of particulars are real components of those particulars and hence make particulars complex. One might think of this as a 'Pluralizing Properties Principle'. My own interest in pluralizing properties is as a special case of pluralizing *parts*.

[42] Cornford (1939: 85).

Dilemma (for which, see above), Socrates offers his own, indeterminate analogy for forms: that each form might be like a day (131b3). In doing so, Socrates himself compares forms to an individual of sorts. If he means to compare a form to a (token) daytime, like Wednesday, he is comparing a form to an abstract individual. But if he means to compare a form to daylight, he is comparing a form to material stuff, to a spatially extended and homogeneous concrete individual.[43] Parmenides plumps for the latter in trading Socrates' analogy for a comparison with a sail; the form is like a sail spread over many individuals (131b7–9). Again, and more clearly, a form is here compared to a concrete spatio-temporal individual.

In the case of instance-parts, our instinct—supported by the immaterial characterization of forms common elsewhere[44]—may be to assume that we have here an example of non-spatial parthood referring to the parts of an abstract object. But the imagery of the Dilemma and of the three subsequent arguments involving predications of size leaves it unclear whether, in fact, forms are being treated as concrete individuals and instance-parthood assimilated to the spatial case. Likewise, in the case of property-parts, the arguments involving predications of size talk of the property-parts of objects in suggestively concrete terms. For example, the third such argument, concerning predications of smallness, turns, in part, on the absurdity of thinking that it should be by *adding* a part of smallness to an object *a* that it comes to be smaller, rather than larger, than before (131d9–e1). Prima facie, the addition of something (and here is where one thinks in concrete terms), no matter how small, should make something larger not smaller than before.[45]

The second in our series of puzzles, found in the second horn of the Dilemma of Participation, canvasses two kinds of parthood—property-parthood and instance-parthood—each apparently different from the core notion of spatial parthood employed in the

---

[43] For these two possible understandings of Socrates' analogy, cf. Proclus, *in Prm.* IV. 862, trans. in Morrow and Dillon (1987).

[44] As seen, for example, in the characterization of forms as intelligible, rather than sensible: e.g. *Parmenides* 129d6–130a2; *Phaedo* 78c10–79a5.

[45] This, I think, is the correct interpretation of this argument, taking it to turn on the operation of addition, and taking into account the emphasis on a temporal process ('smaller, not larger, *than before*', e1). Cf. Cornford (1939: 86 with n. 1).

first. However, while the Dilemma has given us different *examples* of parts, the context of the passage fails entirely to divorce the corresponding kinds of parthood from the original spatial case. Further, if these are different kinds of part, giving us three in all, the logical behaviour of all three is at bottom the same. In the second puzzle, as in the first, the puzzle turns on the assumption that a whole is identical to its parts, that is, that composition is identity.

The Transitional Nature of the Dilemma

In the series of four puzzles with which I am concerned, the Dilemma's puzzle is transitional. It is the least developed of them all. Although it does deal explicitly with parts and whole, the puzzle in question is flagged only by Parmenides' question, and Socrates' negative response, as to whether a form, divided into parts, could still be one.

In the first incarnation of this pattern of puzzle, applied to a concrete particular, Socrates had tried to defuse the consequent puzzlement about the unity of a whole through its participation in the form One, taken to exclude plurality. The Dilemma turns Socrates' solution against him. If a participant's share is part of the form, participation itself will in turn pluralize both the participant—because of its property-parts—and, more significantly, the form—because of its instance-parts. The Dilemma does not mention the form One directly—that version of the puzzle is yet to come—but it threatens the atomicity of forms in general.

If forms are abstract objects, they should at least be free of spatial parts.[46] The Dilemma, at least on one possible interpretation, introduces two different kinds of parts, based on two different aspects of predication: property-parts and instance-parts. The latter are the (putative) parts of participated forms. But if this marks a step in the direction of abstract parts, the Dilemma continues to treat forms—and hence the parts of forms—on spatial lines. These two kinds of parthood will be put to work again, in the second deduction about the One.

The mereological assumptions on which this pattern of puzzle is based are, if anything, less explicit in its second version than in

---

[46] At least on one understanding of the slippery term 'abstract'.

its first. It is only in the first and second deductions that these assumptions come to the surface. And it is here that the negative movement of the mereological undercurrent to the dialogue reaches it culmination.

2.3 ATOMIC ONES AND INFINITE COLLECTIONS: THE FIRST AND SECOND DEDUCTIONS

The surface manifestation of each of the two puzzles considered thus far is a one–many puzzle: a whole of parts is a many as much as, or instead of, a one; and only a mereological atom is just one. The same holds of the remaining two occurrences of this pattern of puzzle, in the first and second deductions. In the first deduction Parmenides begins by arguing that the One cannot be many. Like the form One, at the start of the dialogue, the One excludes plurality and is thus atomic, here explicitly so. In the second deduction, by contrast, Parmenides begins by twice arguing that the One is infinitely many, in addition to being one. Here, the One has the paradoxical unity of the composite Socrates at the start of the dialogue, being both one and (infinitely) many, having an unlimited number of parts.

These arguments of the first and second deductions provide the third and fourth of our puzzles respectively. It is with the fourth and last puzzle that Parmenides finally meets Socrates' opening challenge, showing the One to suffer from precisely the same (apparent) contradiction from which Socrates had sought to insulate it. Given the doubtful status of forms in the wake of Parmenides' questioning of them, the subject of the deductions— the One—cannot simply be identified with the form One.[47] It is, however, explicitly described as the kind of thing 'one might think to be a form' (135e3–5), being intelligible, rather than sensible, as per Socrates' own distinction. As such, it may be taken to fall within the remit of Socrates' challenge.

---

[47] This is not meant to prejudge the question of whether or not forms survive this questioning. My point is simply that Parmenides cannot, given the context, blithely continue talking of forms, as his own remarks make clear.

The arguments of the first and second deductions on which I shall focus have contradictory conclusions, but share a common premiss. That premiss is that a whole is identical to its parts, that is, that composition is identity. It first appears in the guise of the Pluralizing Parts Principle, and underlies the arguments of both deductions. The deductions differ only in how they use this premiss and in their prevailing attitudes to the One. In the first deduction the One is divorced from all relations whatsoever, with the unwelcome result that it can neither be named nor spoken of; indeed, it cannot even be. In the second deduction the One is steeped in relations, with the equally unwelcome result that it may be qualified by each of a set of opposing pairs of opposing properties. These different attitudes to the One influence the direction in which the shared premiss is used. The result is different conclusions—(the One is not many) versus (the One is (infinitely) many), (the One has no parts) versus (the One has an infinite number of parts)—from the shared premiss: if x has parts, x is as many as its parts.

As the puzzle series reaches its conclusion, the mereological assumptions on which it is based come to the fore. I shall discuss these assumptions hereafter. I begin by showing how the Pluralizing Parts Principle figures in the relevant passages of the first and second deductions; and how, in context, it may be seen to depend on the assumption that a whole is identical to its parts.

An Atomic One

Parmenides begins the first deduction by arguing that the One is not many. However, the interpretation of his opening argument is vexed in ways that cut across, although they do not substantially affect, my discussion. The Greek in which Parmenides expresses the hypothesis which governs the first deduction is ambiguous. The hypothesis could be: 'if One is'. It could also be: 'if it [the One] is one'.[48] There are arguments pro and con.

---

[48] The Greek is this: εἰ ἕν ἔστιν, 137c4. According to the first interpretation ἕν is the subject. According to the second, it is predicative, and the subject is taken from the main clause (τὸ ἕν, 137c4).

The second deduction is clearly governed by the hypothesis 'if One is'. But this, in itself, does not decide the interpretation of the first. At the start of the second deduction, considerable emphasis is placed on establishing the identity of the hypothesis under consideration (142c2–4). For this and other reasons, Gill, for one, has judged the two deductions to have different initial hypotheses.[49] But appeal to the second deduction cuts both ways, for the second deduction opens with the express intention of taking up the hypothesis again, from the beginning, to see if 'something else will emerge' (142b2). It would, at the least, be disingenuous to wonder if we might arrive at a different result, if we are about to take off from a different hypothesis.

There is a third possibility, which I offer for consideration. This is that, for Plato, at least in context, there is less of a difference than one might think between supposing that One is and supposing that One is one. Regarding the Greek verb 'to be' ($\epsilon\hat{\iota}\nu\alpha\iota$), Brown has persuasively shown, in arguments pertaining to the *Sophist*, that, for Plato, there need be no semantic shift involved in the move from something being to its being somehow qualified.[50] The lack of a completion in the hypothesis 'One is' need not, then, sharply distinguish it from the hypothesis 'One is one'. For the move from being to being *one*, the *Parmenides* itself, in the second deduction, will exploit the close connection between being and being one. And the same close connection can be seen at work in another Eleatic context, the puzzles about not being in the *Sophist* (237b6–239b5).[51]

[49] M. L. Gill (1996: 65–8). Gill takes the preamble to the second deduction explicitly to distinguish the hypothesis 'One is' from 'One is one', and takes the latter to have been at work in the first deduction. However, this part of her argument depends on a disputable translation of 142c3's εἰ ἓν ἕν, according to which the copula must be supplied, to give the hypothesis 'One is one'. In contrast, I am more inclined to follow Schofield (1973a: 31) in taking this discussion of the hypothesis to turn on linguistic substitution: if 'one' had (contrary to fact) the same semantic content as 'is', then one could substitute it into the hypothesis 'if One is'—giving 'if One one'—and get the same result. Appeal to the second deduction's discussion is, however, only part of Gill's case.

[50] Brown (1986).

[51] These puzzles turn, in part, on exploiting a close connection between being, being one, and being something (τι). See McCabe (1994, esp. ch. 7, §1) for an interpretation of these puzzles based on the centrality and importance of this close connection.

The Eleatic context is important, since, in the deductions of the *Parmenides*, we are, in some sense, exploring Parmenides' own hypothesis (see 137b3), and Parmenides, at least as he is presented in the *Parmenides*, is someone who began from a proposal about being and ended up with the One.[52] This Parmenidean One is not the form One, but it is the kind of thing 'one might think to be a form' (135e3–4). And Plato, notoriously, has his own reasons for being at home with the assumption that One is one.[53] Whatever one decides about the identity of the hypothesis in the first deduction, however, *both* the first and second deductions will exploit the assumption that the One is one.[54]

Regarding the opening argument of the first deduction, what matters most, for my purposes, is not the assumption, whether implicit or explicit, that the One is one, but rather the conclusion that Parmenides draws from his explicit denial that the One is many. He argues as follows:

If One is [alternatively: is one], isn't it the case that the One would not be many?—Of course.—Then it mustn't have any part, nor be a whole.—Why so?—Part, of course, is part of a whole.—Yes.—And what of the whole? Won't it be that from which no part is absent?— Indeed.—Then, on both grounds, the One would be composed of parts, both being a whole and having parts?—Necessarily.—Then on both grounds the One would thus be many and not one.—True.—But it must be not many, but one.—It must.—Then if the One will be one, it will neither be a whole nor have parts.—It won't. (137c4–d3)

Once again, we find the assumption that parts pluralize. If the One had parts, or were a whole, Parmenides argues, it would be

---

[52] See the characterizations of Parmenides' thesis at 128a8–b1 and 137b3, and compare *Sophist* 244b6–245e2.

[53] Exactly what this assumption may amount to has been the subject of much discussion. Owen and Moravcsik both take it to be an ordinary predication. See Owen (1970a) and Moravcsik (1982). Owen takes it to be the result of a confusion between identifying and predicative uses of the verb 'to be'. Moravcsik rather takes it to be a necessary feature of the form One that it be (predicatively) one, on the grounds that it is by participation in this form that other things are one. In contrast to both Owen and Moravcsik, Meinwald takes 'One is one' to be a special kind of predication, revealing the unitary nature of the One; see Meinwald (1991: 41–5 and 80–2).

[54] The first makes this assumption explicit at 137e11, if not already at the start. The second deduction makes this assumption at 143a8–9, if not before.

many, not one. Since, therefore, *ex hypothesi*, the One is (one and) not many, it neither has parts, nor is a whole.

Here Parmenides' use of the Pluralizing Parts Principle is counterfactual, as in the Dilemma of Participation. As in the Dilemma, the putative parts of the One would make the One many and not one, not many and one. Parmenides also argues that being a whole would make the One many, not one. This is a new, if obviously related, tactic. And it is this tactic, even more than the first, that reveals the way in which Parmenides' use of the Pluralizing Parts Principle here depends on the assumption that a whole is identical to its parts.

Prima facie, there is an asymmetry between the two claims of Parmenides' argument. So, for example, Schofield says that 'nobody would be inclined to deny that something correctly described as having parts is in some sense many; but a whole, it might be thought, need not be'.[55] Consider, first, therefore, the sense in which nobody would be inclined to deny that something with parts is many. All that follows non-controversially from an object's having parts is that it consists of many; it is many only in the sense of consisting of many. But it should then also be non-controversial to say that nothing in an object's consisting of many detracts from its being a single unitary object. Hence the apparent asymmetry between Parmenides' two claims, on which Schofield remarks.

Now consider Parmenides' argument once more. His first claim is that, both on the grounds of having parts and on the grounds of being a whole, the One would consist of parts. His justification for this is his interdefining of 'part' and 'whole': a whole is 'that from which no part is absent'. Thus any whole is a whole of parts, and whatever follows from an object's having parts also follows from its being a whole. So far, so good. Since it follows from an object's having parts that it consists of many, then, both on the grounds of having parts and on the grounds of being a whole, Parmenides can infer that the One consists of many. This inference, and the use it makes of the Pluralizing Parts Principle, would be benign and its conclusion correspondingly weak. If the

---

[55] Schofield (1973*b*: 6).

One were a whole or had parts, it would be many, but only in the sense of consisting of many, the sense compatible with its being a unitary object, or so one might reasonably suppose.[56]

Consider, however, Parmenides' second claim. Parmenides further claims that both on the grounds of having parts *and* on the grounds of being a whole, the One would be many *and not one*. By this claim, a whole is not only many; it fails to be one. Parmenides must suppose that if something consists of many, it is not one. This supposition is not benign. On this supposition, a whole not only consists of, but is identical to, a many, its many parts. Once again, the Pluralizing Parts Principle depends on an assumption of whole–parts identity: that a whole is composed of—and thus identical to—its many parts.

The Pluralizing Parts Principle has, on the face of it, a benign interpretation. However, its use in the *Parmenides* is never benign: it depends on the controversial thesis that composition is identity. As we have seen, this thesis provides no unproblematic understanding of the unity of a whole. The only example of a one compatible with this thesis is a mereological atom, and this is by default. Hence, in this first deduction Parmenides concludes that the One must be a mereological atom; it can neither be a whole, nor have parts. This conclusion is a direct consequence of his (as yet implicit) acceptance of the identity of whole and parts.

The One as Infinite Collection

Parmenides begins the second deduction by arguing twice, in direct opposition to the opening argument of the first deduction, that the One is not just many, but unlimited in number. Both arguments are long, and raise interpretative difficulties. In brief, however, Parmenides twice argues that the One is a whole, having an unlimited number of parts. On each occasion he concludes that the One is therefore unlimited in number. The arguments are followed by a companion piece to show that the One is also one, which I shall consider below.

---

[56] This appears to be Schofield's reading of how the argument works (1973*b*: 6), although a detailed examination of the argument is not his concern in this paper.

Each of Parmenides' two arguments is a direct application of the Pluralizing Parts Principle, which makes its first explicit appearance in the second argument: 'what is divisible [or: divided] into parts (μεριστόν) must be just as many as its parts' (144d4–5). The Greek term μεριστόν could mean divisible into parts or actually divided. In the context of the second deduction Parmenides may well mean to suggest an actual division of the One, for his argument explicitly recalls that of the Dilemma of Participation, dividing the One into parts in order to distribute it to all of the unlimited number of parts of being, to each of which it is present (see 144c6–d3). Within the puzzle series as a whole, however, pluralization follows simply from having parts, not just from being actually divided into parts. This is clear from Socrates' initial puzzle. The argument of the first deduction confirms the point. There the simple threat of having parts was enough to jeopardize the unity of the One.

The passage at 144d4–5 may be compared with an earlier passage from the first deduction. There Parmenides had argued that, if the One were of more or fewer measures—that is, were greater or lesser than something else—it would be of as many parts as measures, and thus as many as its measures (140c8–d2). There plurality is explicitly associated with number of measures, not parts. But number of measures is explicitly correlated with number of parts. And it is having measures—and thus parts— that pluralizes, not an actual division into these measures or parts. In the context of the first deduction, of course, this argument provided grounds for *denying* that the One has greater or fewer measures, just as it was denied that it has parts.

When, in the second deduction, Parmenides twice argues that the One is infinitely many on the grounds of its having an unlimited number of parts, the subject of his argument is identified somewhat differently in each case. The subject of the first of his arguments is 'the One which is' (141d1, 2, and 144e5). The subject of the second is 'the One itself' (143a6, 144e6). However, despite this difference in the way their subject is described, the subject of the two arguments is the same. Both proceed from the hypothesis that One is. The first is addressed to this One which is. The second considers that One 'which we say has a share of being' (143c6–7), but considers it just in itself, abstracted in thought. In each argument, we are concerned with the selfsame One, but adopt a different mode of consideration of it.

In his first argument Parmenides argues in two stages that the One which is must have an unlimited number of parts. First, he argues that the One which is must itself be a whole of which one and being are parts. Second, he argues that these parts of the One which is—namely, one and being—must themselves each have two parts—one and being—which in turn each have two parts, and so on. The interpretative crux regarding this argument turns on the move from the first to the second stage.[57] At least in the second stage, if not already in the first, the parts in question—one and being—are clearly properties. Since any part of the One both is and is one, any part will in turn have two parts, being and one, and so on.

In his second argument Parmenides begins by distinguishing the One from its property being. From the fact of their difference, he infers the existence of a third entity, namely, difference. Parmenides then turns to the numerical properties jointly and severally exemplified by these three items: that any pair of them is two, of which each is one; and that all together they are three. From these numerical properties—and in an argumentative tour de force which I shall not attempt to summarize here— Parmenides derives the existence of all numbers, or *arithmoi*. From the existence of all numbers, Parmenides goes on to derive the existence, first, of an unlimited number of beings, and, thence, of an unlimited number of parts of the One, considered in itself. The parts in question are instances of the One; that is, they are things that have the property of being one. Since all the beings that have been derived are, or have being, and, since everything that is is one, this unlimited collection of beings are parts, first, of being, and, more importantly, of the One itself.[58]

---

[57] See e.g. the contrasting views of Curd (1990) and Schofield (1973*a*).

[58] This is a very compressed account of a lengthy argument. I shall discuss some of its details further below. For consideration of the argument as a whole, see Schofield (1972); Allen (1974); and Curd (1990). For a recent account of both arguments, motivated by concerns very different from my own, see Palmer (1999, ch. 10).

Parmenides' two arguments involve different kinds of part, kinds we have met before in discussing the Dilemma of Participation (§2.2). In the first argument Parmenides shows the One to have an unlimited number of property-parts. Whatever the precise details of the structure of the argument here, it is clear that, at least by the second stage of the argument, the parts derived are properties. In the first stage of the argument the One which is is shown to be a whole of which one and being are parts. Each of these parts of the One which is both is and is one. That is, each has the properties one and being. And it is these properties that, in the second stage of the argument, are construed as the parts of one and being. But each of these parts in turn is and is one, and thus has parts, one and being, and so on. Thus the One which is is here shown to have an unlimited number of property-parts.

In the second argument Parmenides shows the One to have an unlimited number of instance-parts. His argument explicitly recalls that of the Dilemma of Participation, where instance-parthood was first exemplified. In the course of his argument Parmenides derives the existence of an unlimited number of beings. Each of this unlimited number is and is one. Thus, Parmenides concludes, neither One nor being is lacking to each of this unlimited number. One and being are properties of each and must be distributed to them all. The allusion to the Dilemma of Participation comes when Parmenides argues that the One, being one, cannot be in many places as a whole (144c8–d2). Instead, the One is present to each of the unlimited number of beings through having parts. Each of this unlimited number has a part of being and a part of the One. These parts of the One are thus its instance-parts.

Why have two different arguments to the same conclusion— that the One is (infinitely) many?[59] It is not because the arguments have two different subjects: they do not. Nor do I think it is because they involve different kinds of parthood—although they do. Rather, it is because the second of Parmenides' arguments,

---

[59] For the question and possible answers, compare Allen (1974), Curd (1990), and Kutschera (1995: 87).

even more than the first, directly responds to the challenge
with which Socrates had ended his conversation with Zeno.
Parmenides meets Socrates' challenge by taking Socrates' own
puzzle—that something (Socrates himself) be seen to be both one
and many by being a whole of many parts—and applying it to the
One. He twice argues that the One is (infinitely) many; he follows
these arguments with an argument to show that it is also one. In
the first of his arguments to show that the One is (infinitely) many,
Parmenides shows that the One, considered as being, is unlimited
in number. At this point, however, Socrates might yet object, he
has not yet shown that the One, just in itself, is (infinitely) many,
in addition to being one.[60] This, however, is precisely what
Parmenides goes on to do in his second argument. The second
argument is thus more vicious than the first; it is a more
inescapable meeting of Socrates' challenge than the first. These
two arguments—together with the companion argument to show
that the One is one, which I shall discuss below—are the culmination of our escalating series of puzzles.

Like the first in the series, Socrates' puzzle, Parmenides' arguments exploit the Pluralizing Parts Principle; in each argument
the One is shown to be infinitely many because it has an infinite
number of parts. As in Socrates' puzzle, the resulting paradox—
Socrates or the One being both one and many—depends upon an
identification of one thing with many things, a whole with its
parts. (I shall say more of how this works in Parmenides' version
hereafter.) Whereas Socrates had sought to defuse the paradox
by putting himself in relation to a one that is not many—the form
One—no such route is available in the second deduction. Here,
then, the unity of this composite—the One—is irredeemably
paradoxical.

The arguments of the second deduction provide a mirror
image of that of the first. In the first deduction the One excluded
plurality; it was not a whole and had no parts. In the second
deduction the One embraces plurality; it is both the whole and an
infinite collection of parts. Parmenides describes the One as
being '*both* the whole *and* the parts' (145a2–3). I shall return to

---

[60] Compare the use of καθ αὑτά formulations at 129d7–8 and at 143a7.

the context in which he does so below. For now, note that this description directly involves the identification of whole and parts on which all four of the puzzles have been based. Once the One itself falls victim to this identification, Parmenides' response to Socrates' challenge is complete.[61]

Pluralizing Parts and Parts that Measure

The first threat to the atomicity of intelligible objects arose in the Dilemma of Participation, which flagged the two kinds of parthood subsequently exploited in the arguments of the second deduction. In the Dilemma property-parts and instance-parts appeared not to be spatial parts, but were treated in quasi-spatial terms. What of the arguments of the deductions?

The deductions deal explicitly with things we grasp by reason, as opposed to things we can see (135d8–e4); with abstract, rather than concrete, entities. Socrates, of course, had made the same claim about his forms. Indeed, it is Socrates' own visible–intelligible distinction that Parmenides here applies, in taking the entities of the deductions to be the kind of things 'one might think to be forms' (135e3–4). Some features of the second of the two arguments of the second deduction suggest that the parts of the One may also be being treated in quasi-spatial terms.

The first argument of the second deduction—concerning the property-parts of the One—gives little further information as to the nature of the parts in question. The second argument—concerning the instance-parts of the One—contains unmistakable echoes of the Dilemma of Participation. Here the parts of the

---

[61] His response is complete, that is, at least as regards the terms with which Socrates had introduced his challenge: one and many. In so far as Socrates' challenge ranged more broadly—over one and many, but also over likeness and unlikeness, rest and motion, and all such things (129d8–e1)—Parmenides' response might not be said to be complete until the end of the eighth and final deduction. However, consideration of completeness in this regard raises a question as to whether and how there is any progression of argument over the course of the deductions, and of what form such progression might take. With regard to the arguments involving part and whole, I argue, there is a progression: one recurring and problematic pattern of argument culminates here in the second deduction; this pattern is challenged in the third deduction and there is no return to it thereafter. Whether arguments involving other key terms have a comparable shape is a question outside the scope of my investigation.

One are present to all those things that have a share of it. The One, like being, is 'chopped up into pieces' (κατακερματισμένον, 144e4; cf. 144b4–5), and distributed to each of the unlimited number of things that have been proven to be.

The verb 'chopping into pieces' (κατακερματίζειν) has a material ring. For example, its root verb (κερματίζω) is used by Plato for the division of body by heat (*Timaeus* 62a3). If this is the kind of image that comes to mind, then, like the images of the Dilemma of Participation, the image involves spatially extended magnitudes. But the verb is also used by Plato for the division of virtue (*Meno* 79a10); and can, in general, refer to the changing of money into smaller coin.[62] Perhaps the verb is a metaphor, although we may be hard-pressed to say what it is a metaphor for. The same condition of being chopped up (and the same verb) is applied to the kind Other, one of the kinds there identified as greatest, at *Sophist* 257c7. There too it is tempting to construe the verb metaphorically, and, again, it is hard to say what it is a metaphor for.[63] If Plato is grappling with the description of abstract parthood, he may not have a more obvious vocabulary ready to hand.

The guiding feature of the treatment of parts and wholes in the arguments of both the first and second deductions is the association between parts and measures. The association first occurs in a passage of the first deduction (140c8–d2), discussed above. Parmenides there argues that were the One to be greater, lesser, or equal to itself or another—none of which it will turn out to be, in this deduction—it would be of respectively greater, fewer, or an equal number of measures to itself or another. And it would be of as many parts as measures (140b6–c9). There is a quasi-spatial aspect to this treatment of parts and the One, inasmuch as it makes one think of discrete spatially extended magnitudes measured against each other and against some common unit of measure. This quasi-spatial aspect goes along with the more obvious mathematical, or geometrical, tone of the passage.[64]

---

[62] See Liddell, Scott, and Jones, *A Greek–English Lexicon* (Oxford: Clarendon Press, 1996; hereafter, LSJ), s.v. κατακερματίζω, κερματίζω and κέρμα.

[63] For one view, see Anscombe (1966).

[64] Thus Curd (1990: 31) talks of the 'geometrical sense' in which Plato takes 'part' and 'whole' here and elsewhere in the *Parmenides*.

What is striking about this association between parts and measures is the way in which it diminishes the significance of overall structure. This may sound odd. The notion of measure may be thought to carry connotations of structure—and elsewhere in Plato it does, or so I shall argue. Here, however, measure comes only with the parts; it is, as it were, 'part-led', imposed from without. It is not a guiding and constitutive feature of the whole in question.

To see this, consider two ways in which one might enumerate the parts of Socrates, the first example of our puzzle series. One might focus on the kind of thing Socrates is, a human being, and enumerate his parts accordingly: a head, a torso, two arms, two legs. An anatomy textbook might offer (no doubt, a more sophisticated version of) such an enumeration. Contrast this with the way in which Socrates in fact enumerated his parts: his right side, his left side, his front, his back, and so on (129c5–8). This reads more like an enumeration of the parts of any spatially extended magnitude. The enumeration of parts finds its own structure, in this case oriented around spatial axes. An enumeration of parts of this sort will divide any spatial extension; it is not specific to Socrates or to the kind of thing he is. The identification of parts and measures, especially in the geometrical setting in which it is first introduced, suggests an enumeration of parts of the second sort rather than the first. Take two spatially extended (commensurable) magnitudes, the second larger than the first. Pick an arbitrary common measure. The second will have a greater number of such measures than the first. No reference to the structure of the magnitudes in question is made or required.

This diminishing of the importance of structure is comparable to that of the *Theaetetus* dilemma (cf. §1.6). There Socrates' first example of composition was the composition of number, or *arithmos*, where this means an enumerable collection of units. He went on to consider things measured by number (an acre, a mile) and enumerable collections of things (an army) and to assimilate the number of something to its parts. The *Parmenides* too associates parts and *arithmoi*, but in a somewhat more complicated way.

In his second argument in the second deduction Parmenides deduces the existence of an infinite number of instance-parts of the One. More than half of his argument is devoted to a deduction of number (143c1–144a5).[65] It concludes with a curious passage, which appears to involve a division of number, or *arithmos*. Having deduced that, if there is *arithmos*, there will be many, indeed an unlimited number of things that are, Parmenides goes on to state that if 'all number' (πᾶς ἀριθμὸς) has a share of being, each part or portion (μόριον) of number does so also (144a5–9). Like others, I take each part of number to be individual numbers, or *arithmoi*.[66] In context, this need not be as odd as it may seem to us. If an *arithmos* is a collection of units, then 'all *arithmos*' is the total collection; indeed 'total collection' seems an alternative possible translation of πᾶς ἀριθμὸς. Each part or portion of this total collection, save for the unit, will be a (smaller) collection or *arithmos*. It is this enumerable collection of component *arithmoi* which are subsequently identified as the instance-parts of both being and the One.

One final passage, later in the second deduction, ties the notions of part, measure, and *arithmos* together (151b7–e2). This passage is the mirror image of the passage of the first deduction discussed above. It draws out the implications of the claim that the One is indeed equal to, greater, and lesser than itself and the Others. As in the first deduction, to be equal to, greater, or lesser than, is construed in terms of numbers of measures: having the same, a greater, or lesser number of measures than itself or another. Measures, once again, are linked to parts: if the One has the same, a greater, or smaller number of measures, it has the same, a greater, or smaller number of parts (151c1). And, if it has the same, a greater, or smaller number of measures and parts than itself or another, it is, correspondingly, the same, greater, or fewer in number than itself or another (151c2–e2). This, in effect, is a third and final statement of the Pluralizing Parts Principle, uniting the terms involved in the first and second. If

---

[65] Like others, I take Parmenides' argument to be, not a generation of number, but a proof of the existence of number; if not of every number—since it is not clear that Parmenides can accommodate the primes—at least of an infinite number of numbers, and this will do for Parmenides' purposes. Compare Allen (1970) and Schofield (1972).

[66] See e.g. Allen (1974: 715) and Curd (1990: 27). Contrast, however, Schofield (1972: 104–9).

something has measures, and hence parts, it is as many in number as its measures or parts.

The Pluralizing Parts Principle makes a whole as many as its parts. The treatment of parts which goes with this principle is the treatment of parts as enumerable measures. The relevant sense of 'measure' is that in which a measure provides a unit for counting. Such treatment of parts makes no appeal to structure in relation to the whole. It is directly comparable to two related ways in which Aristotle says that 'part' is said, in *Metaphysics* v. 25. 'Part', he says, is said in one sense of anything into which a quantity may be divided, that is, of any (smaller) quantity that may be subtracted from the original quantity. In a second, related sense, the term 'part' is restricted to factors of the quantity in question, that is, to anything that divides a quantity into multiples of itself (the divisor) without remainder. Aristotle's examples are *arithmoi*. In the first sense, two is part of three. In the second sense, two is not part of three, since it is not a factor of three; but two is in this sense part of four. Aristotle calls this second sense precisely 'parts which measure' (1023b15). The treatment of parts as enumerable measures is the conception of parts—be they spatial parts, property-parts, or instance-parts—that underlies the *Parmenides*' puzzles.[67]

The Puzzle Series in Review

With Parmenides' argument that the One, even considered just in itself, is unlimited in number, in addition to being one, his response to Socrates, and the puzzle series, is complete. Each of the four puzzles that make up the series has exploited the assumption that parts pluralize. In context, I have argued, their use of this assumption depends on an identification of parts and whole. This much and the treatment of parts that underlies this identification are common to the four.

[67] Compare, here, Curd (1990: 35 n. 27), who rightly identifies the connection to Aristotle's first definition of 'part'; and see, once again, Euclid, *Elements* vii, definition 3: 'a number is part of a number, the lesser of the greater, when it *measures* the greater' (my emphasis). In Euclid the term 'part' (μέρος) is restricted to factors; the term 'parts' (μέρη) to component numbers that are not factors (that do not measure). See Heath (1956, vol. ii, ad loc. *Elements* vii, definitions 3 and 4).

With regard to presentation, there are differences among the four. The first and fourth make positive use of the Pluralizing Parts Principle, and hence conclude with a paradox: a whole that is both many and one. The second and third puzzles are counterfactual. If a participated form or the One were to have parts, each would be many, not one. The claim that each would be many, not one—rather than many and one—gives only half of the puzzle form, which, at its fullest, I have argued, involves the claim that a whole is both one (and so not many) and many (and so not one). In the Dilemma of Participation, I suggested, this truncation of the puzzle form may be a consequence of the lack of resources at Socrates' disposal, once this pattern of puzzle comes to be applied to forms. It has some relation to the progression of the puzzles over the course of the series also.

Recall that the first of our puzzles—Socrates' puzzle—prompted his challenge. His tolerance of this puzzle depended on his having, through participation in forms, a relation to a one that is not many and a many that is not one. The form One, I argued, must therefore be a mereological atom. The second puzzle—in the Dilemma—threatened to turn Socrates' solution against him, for it threatened the atomicity of forms in general. However, the application of this to the form One was not there explicit, and the threat was in any case defused by Socrates' refusal of this model of participation. The threat to a One—not the form One, but something one might think to be the form One—is directly on offer in the third puzzle, in the first deduction. Again, however, the threat is defused; here the One remains resolutely atomic. It is only in the fourth and final puzzle that Socrates' challenge is finally met head on. Here, once again, the puzzle is stated in all its glory; the One, even considered just in itself, is both unlimited in number and one, being a whole of an unlimited number of parts.

Viewed as the stimulus for and as a progressive response to Socrates' challenge, the puzzles may be seen to escalate over the course of the series. In particular, the puzzles go up the scale of significant entities in the terms that Socrates first set out. The puzzles form an escalating series in a second way also. The Pluralizing Parts Principle, on which each depends, claims that parts pluralize the object whose parts they are, no matter how these parts are conceived. A first view of the puzzles, however, might suggest somewhat different grounds for pluralization. In the first puzzle what Socrates emphasizes is not that his left side and right side are *parts*, but that they are *different*. In the second puzzle the putative parts of a participated form are not different in character, but the form, unlike Socrates, appears to be actually divided. Thus, one might think that, in the first case, it is difference that gives rise to pluralization, and, in the second case, actual division. When we come to the deductions, however, it is parts, simply in virtue of being parts, that pluralize. Thus, as the puzzles escalate, they not only go up the scale of significant entities, they also become increasingly 'pure' cases of the pattern of puzzle at work.

2.4 COMPOSITION: IDENTITY OR DISTINCTNESS?

Two passages immediately following Parmenides' conclusion that the One itself is infinitely many complete the negative movement of the mereological undercurrent to the *Parmenides*. The second (145b7–145c7) finally makes explicit the identification of a whole and its parts on which each of the puzzles has depended. The first (144e3–145a3) has been taken by Owen to offer an alternative account of composition, according to which a whole is not identical to its collective parts.[68] I shall argue that Owen is right to see this first passage as presenting an alternative to the thesis that composition is identity. However, the way in which this alternative is framed is itself problematic, and the alternative is not a stable view within the passage in question. Reflection on the two passages, and on the somewhat complex relations between them, throws into relief the assumptions about composition on which the puzzles have turned. Neither passage appears to offer a satisfactory account of composition.

[68] Owen (1986: 92–3).

Composition and Containment: Parmenides *144e–145c*

The context of the passages in question is this. Having twice argued that the One is unlimited, because unlimited in number, as discussed above, Parmenides goes on to argue, first, that the One is also limited and, thence, from the combination of these arguments, that the One is both one and many, whole and parts, limited and unlimited. From this conjunctive conclusion, he then argues, first, that the One must have some shape or other, and second, that the One is both in itself and in another.

It is in the argument to show that the One is limited that Owen finds the view that a whole is not identical to its parts. This characterization of the relation between a whole and its parts is then upset by the argument to show that the One is in itself, since this latter argument entails that a whole is indeed identical to its parts. The relevant passages are these:

(A) Then the One itself, being chopped up by being, is both many and unlimited in multitude.—It appears so.—Then not only is the One which is many, but also the One itself must be many, having been distributed by being.—Certainly.—Further, because parts are parts of a whole, the One would be limited in respect of the whole. Or are not parts contained by the whole?—Necessarily.—Next, what contains would be a limit.—Of course.—Then the One, since it is, is surely both one and many, both whole and parts, and both limited and unlimited in multitude.—It appears so. (144e3–145a3)

(B) Each of the parts is surely in the whole and none is outside the whole.—That's so.—And are all the parts contained by the whole?—Yes.—Further, the One is all the parts of itself, and neither more nor less than all.—That's so.—And isn't the One also the whole?—Of course.—If, then, all the parts are in fact in the whole, and the One is both all of them and the whole itself, and all of them are contained by the whole, then the One would be contained by the One; and thus the One itself would indeed be in itself.—It appears so. (145b7–145c7)

According to Owen, passage A supports the view that a whole is not identical to its parts; passage B the view that a whole is identical to its parts.

First, then, consider the two passages in isolation. Considered thus, it is relatively easy to identify in each the view of composition that Owen suggests. In passage A Parmenides argues that, in so far as the One is a whole of parts, it is limited. His argument has three premisses:

(1) The One is a whole of parts.
(2) A whole is so related to its parts that it contains its parts.
(3) A container limits that which it contains.

The first premiss was established in the two arguments about the One considered above. The second and third premisses are agreed upon by Parmenides and Aristotle in the course of passage A. These three premisses are jointly sufficient to express the non-identity of whole and parts in the way in which Owen suggested, provided one takes a reasonably natural reading of premisses 2 and 3, such that a container is distinct from that which it contains. What more precisely it means for a container to be distinct from that which it contains and whether or not this is a good model for the relation between a whole and its parts are moot questions. I shall discuss them below.

In contrast to passage A, passage B has two premisses which jointly entail that a whole is identical to all its parts.

(4) The One is all its parts.
(5) The One is also the whole of those parts.

By substitution, premisses 4 and 5 jointly entail that a whole is (i.e. is identical to) all its parts. Passages A and B thus present precisely the opposing views of composition that Owen suggested they do.

The story becomes both more complicated and more interesting, however, if we reflect not only on the relation between these two passages, but also on their respective relations to related passages of the first deduction. Take passage A. If passage A is to imply that parts and whole are not identical, as Owen suggested, one must read the premisses involving the containment relation as taking a container to be distinct from that which it contains. And, as Owen suggested, such a reading is naturally taken to imply that a limit (the container) is external to, and not part of, what it limits.[69] However, as Owen himself saw, this consequence conflicts with an earlier argument from the first deduction, in which Parmenides implied that the limits of an object were in fact parts of that object. This earlier argument followed Parmenides' and Aristotle's agreement that the One is not a whole and has no parts (137c4–d3), the opening of the first deduction, which I discussed above. Parmenides subsequently argued, first, that the One thus has neither beginning, middle, nor end, since these would be parts of it; and second, that the One is thus unlimited, since the beginning and the end are the limits of each thing. The conjunction of these latter claims entails that the limit of an object is part of what it limits.

The reading of passage A that supports Owen's view thus conflicts with this passage of the first deduction. However, it is consistent with a later passage of the first deduction. At 138b2–3, as part of an argument to show that the One is not in itself, Parmenides had argued that what contains is one thing; what is contained another. Here, quite clearly, container and contained are not identical. Parmenides here treats a container as that which its contents are in (see 138b1).[70] This 'locative reading', as I shall call it, does indeed suggest that a container is external to, and not part of, what it contains, since that which something is in is not naturally construed as a part of what is within it. This later passage of the first deduction thus gives the conception of the containment relation that must be operative in premises 2 and 3 of passage A to give Owen's view. According to this conception, passage A presents the following view of the relation between a whole and its parts: a whole, *qua* container of its parts, is external to the parts it contains; it is thus not identical to those parts.

However, this view of the relation between a whole and its parts is not a stable view even within the argument of passage A. Note that premises 1–3 of passage A entail only that the One is a

---

[69] Owen (1986: 92).

[70] Compare also 138a3–4, where Parmenides argues that if the One were in another, it would be contained by that other.

limit. The conclusion of the argument is that the One is limited. This further conclusion follows only if the One not only is the container of its parts, but is also the parts contained. This fourth premiss is used in passage B, but it is already explicit at the end of passage A, at 145a3: 'the One is both one and many, both whole and parts'. The premiss that the One is its parts establishes that the One is limited, but upsets both the view that a container is external to what it contains and the consequent thesis that a whole is not identical to its parts.

Reflect, once again, on the relation between the argument of passage A and those of the first deduction. The assumption that a container is distinct from what it contains—necessary to passage A—is consistent with one of the arguments of the first deduction, according to which what contains is one thing, what is contained another. It is in conflict with another of the arguments of the first deduction, according to which the containing limits of an object are parts of that object. Were one to pursue this latter thought, one would take a containing whole to be itself some part(s) which it contains. Such a view has two consequences: first, that a whole is identical to its parts; and second, that a whole is in itself. Both these consequences are exploited in the second deduction, in passage B. But they are prompted by part of the conclusion to passage A: that the One is limited.

Passage B, as we have seen, has two premises which jointly entail that a whole is identical to its parts. These two premises, together with the continued assumption that a whole contains its parts, lead Parmenides to conclude that the One is contained by the One and thus is in itself. Passage B thus undermines the argument of passage A, which suggested that a container is external to, and not part of, what it contains. Each passage depends on a reading of the containment relation to present the alternative views on the relation between a whole and its parts that Owen suggested. Each passage's reading has precedents in the arguments of the first deduction.

The complex nature of the discussion of part and whole in these two passages of the second deduction should not surprise us. I have already suggested that the opening argument of the first deduction—to the effect that the One is not a whole and has

no parts—is a mirror image of the opening argument of the second deduction—that the One is a whole of an unlimited number
of parts. The two opening arguments derive conflicting conclusions from a shared premiss, the Pluralizing Parts Principle. The
conflicting characterizations of the relation between a whole and
its parts in passages A and B also share a premiss: that a whole
contains its parts. However, their respective understandings of
this containment relation differ. Each passage takes the relation
in a way that conflicts with one passage of the first deduction, but
is consistent with another.

Such is the nature of the arguments of the deductions of the
Parmenides. So much is grist for Owen's mill, for the arguments
within and between the deductions continually rebound off each
other in much the way he proposed. Considered on its own, the
conflict within the second deduction is generated by the fact that
the One is considered at different times as one or both of a whole
and parts. Thus Parmenides says that: 'In so far as the One is a
whole, it is in another. But in so far as it is all the parts, it is in
itself. And thus the One is both in itself and in another'
(145e3–5). Indeed, consideration of the One as one or both of the
whole and its parts governs all the conclusions in this passage. In
so far as the One is a whole, it is one, limited, and in another. In
so far as the One is all the parts, it is many, unlimited, and in itself.
Thus, in so far as the One is both the whole and the parts, it is
both one and many, both limited and unlimited, both in another
and in itself.

The final twist to these conclusions—the conjunctive conclusions—takes up the viewpoint of passage B. The One is both the
whole and the parts only if a whole is identical to its parts. The
final twist, therefore, depends on the identification of a whole
and its parts, on the view that composition is identity, the premiss
which has underlain all the puzzles about composition and about
the unity of a composite in the dialogue thus far.

Assessing the Alternatives

Of the two conceptions of the containment relation on offer, that
of passage A is by far the more natural. According to this con-

ception, a container is distinct from that which it contains. But what exactly does this mean? And does it provide a suitable model for the relation between a whole and its parts?

If a container is distinct from that which it contains, the least that this means is that a container is not identical to what it contains. And this seems to be Owen's understanding of the containment relation as conceived in passage A. Viewed as a model for the relation between a whole and its parts, this understanding has clear advantages with regard to the series of puzzles that I have considered. Take the first and last in this series—the one–many puzzle with which Socrates began and its complement, Parmenides' argument that the One itself is both one and many. Both of these puzzles turned on the identification of one thing with many things, a whole with its parts. The proposal that a whole is a container of parts, understood on the model of passage A, destroys this identification and thus averts the consequent puzzlement: that a whole of parts is both one and many.

Matters cannot rest here, however, for passage A's conception of the distinction between container and contained seems sharper than this suggests. Recall that passage A's conception of the containment relation is based on the locative reading of that relation to be found in an argument of the first deduction. This locative reading suggests that a container is distinct from its contents in such a way that a container is external to, and not part of, those contents. So far, so good, perhaps, since a whole is not itself among its parts.[71] However, the locative reading further suggests that the contents of a container are not part of that container.

In fact, this seems a natural way in which to understand the relation between a container and its contents. Consider a can of beans. The beans are in the can and are contained by it. But the beans are no more part of the can than the can of the beans.[72]

---

[71] It is not among its proper parts, at least, although in Mereological systems it is an (improper) part of itself.

[72] As Chris Hughes points out to me, '*x* is a container of *y*' and '*x* contains *y*' may function differently in this regard. If *a* is a container of *b*, then it seems straightforward to infer that *b* is not part of *a*. This inference is less straightforward if *a* contains *b*, at least in English. Suppose I fear that this book contains many mistakes. If I am right, I cannot, unfortunately, infer that the mistakes are not part of the book. However, the Greek word περισχεῖν, here translated 'contain', has core meanings: to

That this is a consequence of the locative reading of the containment relation may be confirmed by looking back to the first deduction once again. There Parmenides argued that what contains is one thing; what is contained another. And he supported this by arguing that the same thing cannot, as a whole, both contain and be contained (138b3–4). This allows that container and contents might both be (discrete) parts of the same thing; thus the can and the beans might each be part of something, the *can of beans*, say. But it precludes one being part of the other.

If this is the understanding of the containment relation involved in passage A, then a container is distinct from its contents in the sense of being disjoint from them. So understood, the distinction between container and contained cannot provide a suitable model for the relation between a whole and its parts. A whole cannot be distinct from its parts in the sense of being disjoint from them on pain of absurdity. Two things are disjoint if they do not have any part in common. Thus, if a whole were, *per absurdum*, to be disjoint from its parts, then none of the parts of the whole would be parts of the whole.

Does this mean that we must fall back on the second alternative, that of passage B, according to which a container—and so a whole—is identical to the parts it contains? It does not. The alternation between the two conceptions of the containment relation on offer is damaging, just in so far as it presents us with false alternatives for the relation between a whole and its parts. If a whole is not distinct from its parts in the sense of being disjoint from them, it is not for that reason identical to its parts. Rather, it may simply be non-identical to them.

---

encompass, embrace, or surround (see LSJ, s.v. περιέχω I. 1. a). This notion of what contains as something 'around the outside of' what it contains (evident in the prefix περι-) again suggests that what is contained is not part of what contains it. The term περισχεῖν has later, technical uses in which one might take what is contained to be part of what contains it (LSJ, s.v. περιέχω I. 4. b and I. 5). These, I take it, are not to the point here, since the *Parmenides* is, at most, preparing the ground for such later uses. LSJ also gives the meaning 'comprise', used of the relation between whole and parts, citing *Parmenides* 145c itself (ibid. I. 4. a). This, I think, is a mistake, since the *Parmenides* is a context in which the nature of the whole–parts relation, and its relation to containment, is precisely what is up for discussion.

Being clear about this distinction between non-identity and disjointness is important. Consider the following argument, put forward by Baxter, and designed to undermine the view that parts and whole are non-identical.

> Suppose a man owned some land which he divides into six parcels. Overcome with enthusiasm for the Non-Identity view [of the relation between parts and whole] he might try to perpetrate the following scam. He sells off the six parcels while retaining ownership of the whole. That way he gets some cash while hanging on to his land. Suppose the six buyers of the parcels argue that they jointly own the whole and the original owner now owns nothing. Their argument seems right. But it suggests that the whole was not a seventh thing.[73]

The argument has affinities with Lewis's accusation of double counting.[74] According to Lewis, we may recall, the whole or fusion of some parts—some cats, say—is nothing over and above the cats that compose it. Thus: 'If you draw up an inventory of Reality according to your scheme of things, it would be double counting to list the cats and then also list their fusion'.[75] It is with just such double counting that the perpetrator of Baxter's land scam appears to be charged.

However, the accusation of double counting is misplaced. Double counting is counting the same thing(s) twice.[76] Of course, if a whole *were* identical to its parts, then adding a whole to a list that already includes the parts of that whole would be double counting, since adding the whole would just be adding the parts all over again. But the accusation of double counting is here levelled at those who deny that a whole is identical to its parts. And for those who deny this, no double counting occurs. If a whole is not identical to its parts, then adding a whole to a list that already includes its parts is simply adding to the list something to which no item already included on the list is identical. This follows straightforwardly from the uncontroversial fact that no (proper) part is identical to the whole of which it is a part. Nothing is counted twice: not one part, nor all the parts. This is

[73] Baxter (1988a: 579).
[74] Lewis himself quotes Baxter's argument with approval (Lewis 1991: 83).
[75] Lewis (1991: 81); cf. discussion in §1.4 above.
[76] Cf. Van Inwagen (1994: 213).

why, as we may note, the addition of the whole to our list adds one to the total, and not the number of the parts.[77] Of course, what Lewis means to suggest is that, once my list includes *all* the parts of the whole, it is somehow redundant to add the whole as well. Again, however, while this might be true, if composition were identity, it is not a consequence for those who deny this.

What, then, is the answer to Baxter's argument? If a whole is not identical to its parts, why can I not sell the parts and yet keep the whole? I cannot do so for the simple reason that the whole is related to its parts, and it is so related to its parts that I cannot sell all of them without selling it, nor sell it without selling them.[78] No doubt this has as much to do with facts about buying and selling as with facts about the relation between parts and whole. But it is, I suggest, just this relation between parts and whole which an argument such as Baxter's might induce one to ignore. To ignore this relation would indeed be to treat a whole as though it were disjoint from, rather than merely non-identical to, its parts.[79] But this, as we have seen, is a false alternative to the view that a whole is identical to its parts.

The *Parmenides'* discussions of composition have thus far been dominated by the view that a whole is identical to its parts. Passage A offers an alternative view, according to which a whole is distinct from its parts. To this extent, I agree with Owen. But the alternative that passage A offers is a false one. A whole cannot be distinct from its parts in such a way as to have no connection

[77] Compare here the point about cardinality, which I have made before (§1.4). Even in the Mereological systems that Lewis favours, in a world in which there are two distinct (mereological) atoms, the cardinality of the domain of quantification is three, not two, and certainly not four. Cf. Van Inwagen (1994: 213–14).

[78] Of course, this is not an argument against the view that composition is identity. But it shows that one who denies this view can accommodate the intuition to which Baxter appeals. And this is all that is needed in the context.

[79] I do not here mean to suggest that either Baxter or Lewis ignores the fact that whole and parts are related, nor that they conflate being non-identical with being disjoint. It is their opponent who must guard against such a conflation. For defenders of composition as identity such as Baxter and (here, at least) Lewis, the accusation of double counting seems persuasive, since it would be a consequence of their view. To the extent that the argument might seem at all persuasive to an opponent of composition as identity, such an opponent would, I think, have been encouraged to elide the distinction between non-identity and disjointness by assuming that an item on a list of things is only an additional item, if it is disjoint from the other items listed.

with those parts; it is after all composed of them. The putative alternative account of composition of passage A fails precisely because it fails to give any content to this relation of composition between parts and whole.

An analogous criticism can be directed at passage B's identification of a whole and its parts. If a whole simply is its parts—if composition is identity—a whole is a many. Here too there is no room for composition. Composition makes one thing out of many things. If a whole is a many, it is not one thing composed of many. Parmenides, of course, also says that a whole is one. But he does not here say that a whole is one thing composed of many, but rather that it is *both* one *and* many (145a2). He gives no content to the claim that a whole is one; nor indeed to its parts being many.

According to the view of passage A, things which should be related by composition—the whole and its parts—cannot be so related because they are utterly distinct. According to the view of passage B, the whole and the parts are not sufficiently distinct for one to be composed of the other; the whole is simply identified with, not composed of, its parts. Thus Parmenides concludes not that the One is a whole *of parts*, one thing *composed of many*, but that the One is *both* the whole *and* the parts, *both* one *and* many.

The alternative to the identification of a whole and its parts that Owen found is ephemeral. First, it is not a stable view of the relation between a whole and its parts even within the argument of passage A; it is immediately countered and subsumed by the view of passage B, which latter provides the dialogue's most explicit statement of the identification of whole and parts. Second, the alternative account of composition is not a viable alternative to the view that composition is identity. Like the simple identification of a whole and its parts, it too fails to give content to the composition of a whole by its parts.

At this stage in the *Parmenides* all these issues stand in need of resolution. It is not until later in the second deduction that Parmenides makes a proposal crucial to the achievement of a viable alternative account of composition, and not until the third deduction that the thesis that composition is identity is finally challenged. I shall discuss this positive phase of the mereological undercurrent to the dialogue in Chapter 3. For now, it remains to complete the discussion of the negative movement through consideration of its Eleatic antecedents.

2.5 ELEATICISM AND ONTOLOGICAL INNOCENCE

It is perhaps no surprise to find the Eleatics complicit, at least by association, in Plato's discussions of the compositional version of the problem of the one and the many. Parmenides and, after him, Zeno are surely chief among the ancestors of the ancient problem of the one and the many.[80] At the start of the *Parmenides* we found Socrates presenting their combined thesis as the claim that there is one, not many. And we have seen evidence from Eudemus, reported in Simplicius, that Zeno took parts, like properties, to pluralize. Further, in two of the three late dialogues in which we find Plato discussing the part–whole relation at a level of considerable abstraction—the *Parmenides* itself and a short passage of the *Sophist*—the Eleatics are in the frame. Consideration of the *Sophist* passage reveals the philosophical issue at work in Plato's apparent concern with the genealogy of the puzzle.

The Discussion of the Monists in Sophist 244b6–245e2

In *Sophist* 244b6–245e2, as part of a broader investigation into theorists of being, the Eleatic Stranger (the *Sophist*'s main speaker) addresses a monist theory of being.[81] The Stranger's strategy is to involve the monists in a series of difficulties, which show ultimately that the monists can neither name nor describe monist being without falling into pluralism. Central to his discussion of the monists is movement from a linguistic problem

---

[80] So, Barnes (1988: 229 n. 15).

[81] The investigation into being follows the Stranger's and Theaetetus' investigation into not being, which itself was prompted by their search for the sophist, the dialogue's overall quest. The examination of the monists is preceded by an examination of certain dualist theorists of being as part of the examination of those who have views about how many beings there are, as well as, or instead of, having views about what the beings there are are like; for this grouping of the theorists examined, see 242c4–6.

that the monists are seen to have in attempting to characterize being to an associated problem about the characteristics that being thereby appears to have. There are thus two separate, but related, strands to the argument with the monists: (1) a puzzle about names (ὀνόματα) (244b6–d13) and (2) a puzzle about attributes (πάθη) (244d14–245e2).[82]

The general strategies of the two strands of argument are broadly parallel. Under (1) the Stranger argues that, if names are other than that which they name, and if the monists are committed to a plurality of names, the monists wind up with pluralism: a plurality of names and a plurality of named. If, on the other hand, names are the same as that which they (purport to) name, names are either empty or name themselves. Under (2) the Stranger argues that, if attributes are other than that of which they are attributes, a plurality of attributes implies a plurality of things. Earlier in the dialogue the thesis that attributes are in fact the same as that of which they are attributes had led dualist theorists of being into difficulties (243d6–244b5). The burden of the second strand of argument against the monists is to show that such an identification of the attributes of monist being—being both whole and one—cannot jointly be sustained.

I shall focus on this second strand of argument and shall not attempt an analysis of the first.[83] For my purposes, what matters is simply the moral of this first strand of argument: that, if the monists are to avoid pluralism, they must identify both all names and all named.[84] (Whether this response is tenable is, of course, a different matter.)

In what follows—the second strand of the argument—the Stranger argues that such an identification of the named—being, one, and whole—is impossible to maintain. His argument takes the form of a dilemma, constructed around a choice: the agreement or denial that monist being is a whole of parts.

[82] See the explicit references to names (ὀνόματα) at 244c8, d1, d3, d8; and to attributes (πάθη) at 245a1, a5, b4, c2.

[83] For a persuasive reading, see now McCabe (2000: 66–73).

[84] The first identification does not figure explicitly as an option in the text, but is surely necessary if the monists are to head off both of the problems that names generate: that, being themselves plural, they pluralize, as well as implying a plurality of things, both names and named.

The Monists' Dilemma

On the first horn of the dilemma (A), the Stranger supposes that monist being is indeed a whole of parts. This agrees with his characterization of the implications of Parmenides' position, established by reference to Parmenides' poem at the beginning of our passage.[85]

ELEATIC STRANGER. Next, will they say that the whole is other than the one which is or the same as it?

THEAETETUS. Of course they will and do say [that it is the same].[86]

ES. If, then, it is a whole,[87] just as indeed Parmenides says, 'resembling the mass of a sphere well-rounded on all sides, equally balanced from the middle in all directions; for there must not be something either more or less here than there',[88] then being, being such, has a middle and extremes, and, having these, absolutely must have parts, must it not?

THT. That's so. (244d14–e7)

As the Stranger and Theaetetus present the monists' position, not only do they take being to be a whole of parts, they also identify the whole with their one being ('the one which is'). Such an identification is necessary if the monists are to avoid pluralism; if, that is, they are to avoid there being (at least) two things: the whole and the one which is. It is this identification that the argument of the first horn of the dilemma (A) will challenge.

---

[85] Here and elsewhere my concern is with Plato's presentation of Eleaticism, and not with its historical validity. Palmer (1999, introd. and *passim*) has rightly stressed the importance of distinguishing the project of exploring Plato's engagement with Parmenides and his understanding of Parmenides' thought from that of interpreting Parmenides himself. Palmer himself offers an interpretation of this *Sophist* passage and of its relation to arguments of the deductions of the *Parmenides* that is substantially different from my own; see Palmer (1999, esp. 173–81).

[86] That this is how Theaetetus replies on the monists' behalf is indicated by the way in which, in his reply, he echoes φήσουσι (e1, echoing d15), which, in the question, was positioned in the second disjunct. Theaetetus' answer proves that he has learned (at least some of) the lessons of the first strand of the argument.

[87] With Cornford (1935) and Bluck (1975) I take being to be the subject of the antecedent, taken from the consequent (e6); it is assumed to be a whole on the basis of Theaetetus' identification of the one and the whole on the monists' behalf. Contrast the translations of Fowler (1921) and White, in Cooper (1997).

[88] The Stranger here quotes directly from Parmenides' poem, B8. 43–5.

On the second horn of the dilemma (B), the Stranger rather supposes that monist being is not a whole of parts.[89] Under (B) the monists have already broken faith with their own position, at least as extrapolated by the Stranger on the basis of Parmenides' poem.[90] Here, then, it looks as if the monists take up a last resort in defence of their position. The argument of the second horn is itself divided into consideration of two options. First (B1), we suppose that there is such a thing as wholeness, but that being lacks it.[91] Second (B2), we suppose that there is no such thing and, *a fortiori*, that being lacks it.

If the monists are to avoid pluralism, they must identify both of the attributes they ascribe to monist being—namely, being whole and being one—with being itself. The dilemma on which the monists are caught precludes just this identification. What the Stranger will show is that if any two of the three—being, one, and whole—are identified, the monists cannot complete the identification with the remaining term. Under (A) the pair, being and whole, are identified, but cannot further be identified with the one. Under (B), while nothing prevents the identification of being and one, this is only because the further identification with the whole has already been given up.[92]

---

[89] For the choice—being is a whole or being is not a whole—see 245b4–5; for the second option, see 245c1.

[90] The Stranger has extrapolated. His claim that monist being has parts is the result of an argument, based upon his interpretation of the consequences of the spatial imagery used in Parmenides B8. 43–5. He does not claim that B8. 43–5 itself directly asserts that being has parts. Well might he not, given that Parmenides himself had described being as indivisible, or at least as not divided: οὐδὲ διαιρετόν, B8. 22.

[91] In 245c2 I take αὐτὸ τὸ ὅλον as subject, rather than complement of ᾖ; translating the passage in which it occurs as follows: (245c1–3) 'Further, if being is not a whole through having been affected by the attribute provided by that [the one], but the whole itself is, it follows that being lacks something of itself.' How does it follow that being lacks something of itself? Either because of a (dubious) slide from not being (a) whole to being lacking to lacking something of oneself; or because there is something—the whole—which is, but which monist being is not, so that being lacks something of itself (being). Since the argument appears to be carried over to (B2) also, where the whole is not, the first seems more likely. Contrast White's translation in Cooper (1997). Contrast also Palmer (1999: 177–8), who, although appearing to take αὐτὸ τὸ ὅλον as subject, nonetheless interprets this passage as continuing to assume that being is a whole.

[92] In outline, at least, my reading of the dilemma is thus closest to that of Moravcsik (1962). Moravcsik, however, takes the goal of the argument to be to establish the

The arguments of the dilemma are extremely dense; I shall go through them slowly below. In outline, however, I take them to proceed as follows:

(A)   Suppose being is a whole of parts. Then, although it can be one whole of parts, it cannot be identified with the one itself,[93] because the one does not have parts. So, if being is a whole of parts, at least two things exist: being (the whole) and the one. (245a1–b9)

(B1)   Suppose being is not a whole of parts, but the whole exists. Then, first, since being lacks something of being, it turns out to be not being;[94] and, second, once again, at least two things exist: being (the one) and the whole. (245c1–10)

(B2)   Suppose being is not a whole of parts and the whole does not exist. Then, since being is not a whole, it can neither be, nor have come to be, nor be of any quantity. (245c11–d11)

Under (A) and (B1) the Stranger argues the monists into commitment to pluralism. Under (B2) the Stranger argues that the monists avoid pluralism only at the cost of losing being altogether. Thus, as a result of this dilemma, the monists are faced with what, from their perspective, is an impossible choice: pluralism or nothing. And so the discussion of the monists concludes.

Considered overall, I shall argue, what the dilemma urges is that, if the monists admit wholeness into their ontology— whether by characterizing being as a whole or simply by admitting that such a thing as wholeness exists—they wind up with pluralism. So, an admission of composition will add to the monists' ontology. Contrast this with the conception of composition that has dominated the arguments of the *Parmenides* as thus far considered. At the heart of the *Parmenides*' puzzles

---

non-identity of, first, being ('Existence' as he terms it) and the one and, second, of being and the whole. In contrast, I take the argument to deny the possibility of identifying all three—being, one, and whole—even granting the possibility of identifying the pairs (being, whole) or (being, one).

[93] See αὐτό τὸ ἕν at 245a5–6. I take this to be the attribute (πάθος)—being one— referred to at 245a1, by which the whole—monist being—has been affected (πεπονθὸς, 245a5).

[94] By an argument that is, undoubtedly, obscure. See above, n. 91.

about composition is the thesis that composition is identity. Considered thus, a whole adds nothing to an ontology that already includes its parts.

The *Sophist*'s dilemma arguments challenge this conception of composition. In doing so, they also reveal, by contrast, the reason why the Eleatics are a natural target for association with the view to be challenged. It is the Eleatics' desire to avoid ontological commitment that makes them natural progenitors of the innocent conception of composition here being challenged. This can be shown by considering more closely the several steps of the argument of the dilemma, paying particular attention to those explicitly concerned with composition, especially the argument of the first horn of the dilemma.

Composition and Innocence

Consider, first, the Stranger's opening gambit (244e2–7). It has been agreed that monist being is a whole. Indeed, the monist supposes that monist being may be identified with the whole that it is. The Stranger's first move is to show that, given Parmenides' characterization of this whole, it must have parts.

ELEATIC STRANGER. If, then, it is a whole, just as indeed Parmenides says, 'resembling the mass of a sphere well-rounded on all sides, equally balanced from the middle in all directions; for there must not be something either more or less here than there', then being, being such, has a middle and extremes, and, having these, absolutely must have parts, must it not?
THEAETETUS. That's so. (244e2–7)

Clearly the premiss to this argument is that anything which has a middle and extremes has parts. We have seen this premiss at work before, in the opening arguments of the first deduction of the *Parmenides*. There Parmenides argued that, since they have agreed that the One does not have parts, it follows that it cannot have a beginning, middle, and end, since these would be parts (137d4–5). In the *Sophist* this argument works in reverse. Since Parmenides' own imagery suggests that the whole—monist being—does indeed have a middle and extremes, it must have parts.

The Stranger's premiss appears innocuous enough, crucial though it is for getting the argument going. For my purposes, the significance of this opening gambit lies not so much in what the Stranger here says, as in what he does not do next. Consider what, in the end, he wants to end up showing: that the monists are committed to there being more than one thing. Familiarity with the *Parmenides'* puzzle suggests one quick and obvious route to this conclusion. The Stranger has shown that monist being has parts. The puzzle would say that monist being is therefore many, just as many as its parts. But this is not how the Stranger proceeds. Instead—and perversely, or so one might think—he goes on to stress that there is nothing to prevent this whole from being characterized as one. This is the first indication of a departure from the conception of composition underlying the *Parmenides'* puzzle and it appears to work in the monists' favour. Appearances can be misleading, however, as we shall see.

The second step of the Stranger's argument under (A), the first horn of the dilemma, may be thought of as the softener before the blow. What he says is this: 'Of course, nothing prevents what has parts (τό μεμερισμένον) from having the attribute of unity/being one over all its parts, and being in this way one, since it is both all and whole' (245a1–3).[95] The softening comes with the suggestion that monist being—considered as a whole of parts—is nonetheless one, at least in the sense of being a unified whole. The blow, for the monists, comes next. First, however, this passage warrants discussion.

Recall that the moral of the argument immediately preceding the dilemma was that the monists cannot afford to admit distinct names, referring to distinct entities: one, being, and whole. It was because Theaetetus had learned this moral well that he realized, at the start of the dilemma, that the monists must identify the whole with being. The Stranger's current claim that there is nothing to prevent the whole of parts that is monist being from being one appears a step in the right direction towards complet-

---

[95] I take πᾶν τε ὂν καὶ ὅλον to be a participial clause and one in which καὶ is not epexegetic. ἐν εἶναι is then coordinate with πάθος . . . τοῦ ἑνὸς ἔχειν. Compare Fowler (1921), and contrast the translations of Cornford (1935); Bluck (1975); and White, in Cooper (1997).

ing the necessary identification of being, whole, and one. Being—which, according to the monists, is the only thing there is—is at least one thing, a unified whole. This is why the Stranger's failure to apply the *Parmenides'* puzzle appears to work in the monists' favour. At this stage the monists look set to meet their requirement that there be only one thing.

The monists' requirement, however, is twofold. First, what is must be one—must have the attribute of unity or of being one. Second, it must be unique—there must be only one of it. This I take to be the implication of the monists' initial claim that 'the all' is one (244b6) and the claim that is in trouble when the Stranger twice claims that 'all thing*s*' (now in the plural) have turned out to be more than one (245b8–9 and 245c8).[96] The blow dealt by the Stranger's argument on the first horn of the dilemma will put pressure on the monists' ability jointly to maintain both of their requirements. If being is a unified whole of parts, he will argue, it cannot be all there is. It is this pressure that will force the monists to abandon the suggestion that being is a whole of parts and lead them on to the second horn of the dilemma (B).

Recall the quick and easy route it seemed the Stranger might have taken to his conclusion. Simply apply the *Parmenides'* puzzle: being—in so far as it is a whole of parts—is many, as many as its parts. Pluralism follows, or so it appears. There is, however, a flip side to the *Parmenides'* puzzle, albeit the *Parmenides* does not give the alternative version much attention. Since the puzzle turns on taking composition to be identity—the one whole to be identical with the many parts that compose it—it is, of course, reversible: the many are one. It is in this direction, one imagines, that the Eleatics themselves might exploit it and the Stranger be well advised to avoid it. And so he does, challenging, instead, the conception of composition on which the puzzle trades.

If monist being is a whole of parts, it can indeed, the Stranger suggests, be one. In fact, it must be one, or so the direction of the argument entails. What the argument of the first horn of the dilemma is designed to prove is that at least two things—being

[96] These references to all things, in the plural, so subversive from the monist perspective, act as punctuation for the arguments of the dilemma, indicating points where conclusions are drawn from different options (A and B1 respectively).

and the one—exist. That being and the one are distinct is a consequence of the next step in the Stranger's argument. This is the blow. The unified whole of parts that monist being is now considered to be cannot, the Stranger claims, be identical with the one, for what is truly one cannot have parts (245a5–10). I shall consider what we should make of this claim below. For now, consider the Stranger's account of a whole as something one.

Monist being has been agreed to be a whole of parts. As such, it can be one. But it cannot be the one. This, it might seem, is all that is needed for the Stranger's conclusion that two things exist: being and the one. Not so. The argument must indeed show that being and the one are not identical; and this much is explicit. But the monists might choose to deny the existence of the one and stick with the unified whole; to stick, that is, with the suggestion that this unified whole is indeed all there is. To get his conclusion, the Stranger must further assume that, if being is a unified whole of the sort he describes, the one must exist as a property of being in so far as it is whole. This whole not only may, but must, be one. Thus, the Stranger's argument has two components: (1) if being is a whole, then, since it is a whole, it must be one; it must, that is, have the property of being one, whose role is to give the required unity to the whole; and (2) if being is a whole, then being and the one—that is, the property of being one—cannot be identical. Given (1), the one must exist. Given (2), there are (at least) two things: being and the one. It is the second point that the Stranger emphasizes, for this is what does damage to the monists' position. It is the first point that damages the conception of composition with which the monists have been associated.

Consider again the *Parmenides*' puzzle. If composition is identity, a whole is a many as much as a one. In the *Sophist*, by contrast, the Stranger describes a whole as just one. At 245b1 this unified whole is described as being '*composed of* many parts' (ἐκ πολλῶν μερῶν). Contrast this with the characterization of the One in the second deduction of the *Parmenides*, the last in our series of puzzles. There Parmenides described the One as *both* the whole *and* the parts (145a3). As a result of this pattern of puzzle, the whole simply collapses into its parts. In the *Sophist*, by contrast, the Stranger describes a whole that appears to resist this kind of collapse into its parts. He does not here elaborate upon this conception, nor on the view of composition that underlies it. Nor need he, for the point of the argument of this horn of the dilemma is to show that such a whole can find no place in the monists' ontology.

It is the third and final step in the Stranger's argument that delivers this conclusion, what I called 'the blow'. A whole must be one. But such a whole cannot be the one, because what is truly one must be completely without parts.[97] What should we make of this latter assumption? Clearly, it is pivotal to the argument of the first horn of the dilemma. But why should the Stranger propose it? And, more importantly, why should the monists accept it? I take the Stranger first.

For the Stranger to propose that what is truly one must be completely without parts may seem problematic, at least if we take his argument to mark a departure from the *Parmenides*' puzzle. After all, if what is truly one has no parts, then a whole, it would seem, is not truly one. However, the Stranger cannot take this to imply that a whole is not one; the argument is explicit enough on this point. Rather, the Stranger's remarks thus far merely suggest two ways in which something might be one: by being a unified whole of parts, or, in the case of the one, by being a mereological atom; and the role of the latter one is to bring the required unity to the whole in question. There is still a sharp contrast with the *Parmenides*' puzzle, according to which a whole is a many as much as or instead of a one; and the only way of being just one is to be a mereological atom, the latter because a mereological atom, having no parts, is simply unaffected by the *Parmenides*' puzzle.

---

[97] Notice that the Stranger must here assume that the one—where this is the property of being one, that in virtue of which the whole is one—is itself truly one. Only thus could he infer that this one is completely without parts, and is thus distinct from the whole. This adds an additional complication to an already complex argument. And the argument seems to be weak at just this point. In what follows, I shall offer reasons why the monists might be brought to accept, first, that *if* the one in question is truly one, it is without parts, and, second, that they cannot nonetheless avoid commitment to the one. But this may yet leave it open to them to deny that the one in question is in fact truly one. To the extent that it does so, the argument is correspondingly weak. I am grateful to Lesley Brown for discussion of this point.

This then helps with the second question: why should the monists accept that what is truly one is completely without parts? From their point of view, it would clearly be better not to accept it, since it is this assumption that lands them with (at least) two things: the whole (that is, monist being) and also the one. If, however, such a view is taken to be a consequence of the Eleatics' own conception of composition—that is, that of the *Parmenides'* puzzle—the Stranger can put it forward as one of the Eleatics' own assumptions. On the puzzle conception, a whole is both many and one. The Eleatics may choose to emphasize that it's a many identical with one, but this does not detract from the fact that it is a *many*–one. According to the puzzle, the only thing that is just one is a mereological atom.

Notice that the way in which the Stranger puts this pivotal assumption encourages the thought that it is offered as one of the Eleatics' own assumptions. What he says, at 245c8–9, is this: 'According to the correct account (λόγος) what is truly one must surely be said to be completely without parts.' One might well suppose that the account in question is Eleatic. Later in the passage, in the argument of the second horn of the dilemma (B1), the Stranger asserts that, if being lacks something of itself, then 'according to this account, it will be not being' (245c5–6). Here, it seems very likely that the account involved is Eleatic.[98] Thus, one might suppose that, on each occasion when the Stranger refers to a conclusion as being the result of some account (λόγος), the account in question is Eleatic.[99]

Suppose, then, that the monists are themselves committed to the claim that what is truly one does not have parts. Must they also assume that there is such a mereologically atomic one, in addition to the whole that monist being has thus far been taken to be? They need not, but it will be at the cost of supposing that that whole is not, after all, one. Recall that the role of the one is to provide the required unity for the whole in question. According to the Stranger's argument, monist being, considered as a whole of parts, may, indeed must, be one; it must, that is, have the property of

---

[98] See e.g. Parmenides B8. 11 or B8. 33.

[99] There are three such occasions: 245a8–9, 245b1–2, and 245c5–6.

being one; and hence this one must be.[100] If the monists choose to deny the existence of this one, the *Parmenides'* puzzle will threaten. Neither version of the puzzle will help the monists' situation. If, as per the *Parmenides'* version, the whole that is monist being is many, then there is more than one thing. Alternatively, if, as per the monists' own preferred version, the many parts of being are simply swallowed up into it, there will be no real substance to the claim that monist being is a whole of many parts; that it is a whole at all. Rather, monist being will itself have turned out to be mereologically atomic. This option will be explored on the second horn of the dilemma.

The Stranger and the monists are thus in different positions as regards the assumption that what is truly one must have no parts. In breaking with the conception of composition that underlies the *Parmenides'* puzzle, the Stranger can allow *both* that a whole of parts is one and that the one of the monists is mereologically atomic. The point of his argument on the first horn of the dilemma is to show that the monists cannot have both. They cannot have the first—monist being identified as a whole of parts which is genuinely unified—without the second—a distinct and mereologically atomic one. And thus they cannot have both without pluralism.

They can, however, have the second—the mereologically atomic one—without the first. In this way, the Stranger's choice between two ways of being one—being a unified whole of parts or

---

[100] Here is where the Stranger's additional assumption—that the one in question is itself truly one—cuts in and creates difficulties for the argument. (Cf. n. 97 above.) The monists might accept the existence of the one, but deny that it is truly one and, in doing so, destroy the grounds for distinguishing it from the whole. However, further reflection on the *Parmenides* may yet help here. The monists' position may be compared to that of Socrates at the start of the *Parmenides*. If the Eleatics assume that a whole of parts is both many and one, and that only a mereological atom is just one, then, like Socrates, they may suppose that the unity of such a whole is problematic. This gives them a motivation not only to accept the existence of the property of being one, which is designed to secure the unity of a whole, but also to agree that this property of being one must itself be one in a different way from the whole; in a way that is immune to the *Parmenides'* puzzle. In this way, the monists might themselves be brought to agree that the one itself is one in such a way as to be mereologically atomic. However, I do not claim that the argument can, with certainty, be rescued this way.

being a mereological atom—becomes the means by which the monists are forced onto the second horn of the dilemma. The Stranger has argued that for the monists to suppose that monist being is a unified whole of parts is not compatible with the conception of composition underlying the *Parmenides'* puzzles. It would, however, be compatible with that conception for the monists to suppose that monist being is atomic. And this is the only route the monists have left, if they want to avoid ontological additions.

We now come to the argument of the second horn of the dilemma, to the assumption that being is not, despite Parmenides' words, a whole of parts, but is a mereologically atomic one. Again, pluralism threatens. Even if the monists deny that monist being is itself a whole, but admit that wholeness exists, they are again committed to there being (at least) two things: being and wholeness (B1). Their sole remaining strategy is simply to deny that wholeness exists (B2). Composition has no place in their ontology. I shall consider the Stranger's argument against this final proposal below. For now, consider the general thrust of the monists' dilemma as regards the nature of composition.

Composition is not innocent—or so the *Sophist* here suggests. Whether monist being itself is taken to be a whole of parts or whether it is simply the case that wholeness exists, the monists must add to their ontology. Against the monists, the strategy of this dilemma is clear, for the monists are committed precisely to denying the possibility of any addition to their ontology. And it is the monists' fanatical desire for ontological innocence that reveals why the Eleatics are the natural progenitors of the *Parmenides'* puzzle. Their desire to identify many with one is simply the converse of the *Parmenides'* pluralization of any composite one. So, conversely, the conception of composition that the Stranger exploits against them, in the arguments of the dilemma, marks a significant departure from the conception of composition involved in the *Parmenides'* puzzle.

Innocence and Unrestricted Composition

We have not yet exhausted all the aspects of the dilemma which make points about composition. Composition features prominent-

ly in the argument of the final stage of the second horn of the dilemma (B2). In the final stages of the dilemma, the monists have been
argued into the position of supposing not only that being is not
itself a whole of parts, but also that wholeness does not exist.
Against this the Stranger argues that, if this is so, the monists will
be unable to characterize monist being as being, or as having come
to be, or has having any quantity (245c11–d10).

They will be unable to characterize monist being as being,
because of an argument originally used in the first argument of
the second horn of the dilemma (B1), which remains in force.
There the Stranger had argued that, if being is not a whole—
there, on the assumption that wholeness nonetheless exists—
being will in fact lack something of being and, being thus lacking,
will be not being. Whatever the precise force of this argument, it
must be Eleatic in spirit, and thus *ad hominem*. The second stage
of the argument denies that wholeness exists. *A fortiori*, it
remains true that being is not a whole and is, once again, lacking
or incomplete.

The Stranger goes on to argue that the monists also cannot
claim that being ever became a being, for, he says, 'what came to
be has always come to be a whole' (245d4).[101] Nor can the
monists take being to have any quantity, for what is not a whole,
he argues, cannot have any quantity. If it is something of quantity—whatever quantity you like—it must, he argues, be a whole of
that quantity. In sum, whether the monists suppose that something is, has come to be, or is of some determinate quantity, they
are committed to something being whole. But the dilemma's earlier arguments have shown that the monists' minimal ontology
has no room for wholes. Here, and finally, the Stranger shows
that, without composition, they cannot have an ontology at all.

The arguments of this final stage of the dilemma are puzzling.
For my purposes, the last two, in particular, deserve closer attention. The Stranger here makes two claims. The first is that what
has come to be has come to be a whole. The second is that something of quantity is a whole of that quantity. At least apparently,

---

[101] I am grateful to Myles Burnyeat for advice on the translation of 245d4, where
the use of tenses seems both careful and pointed.

these claims suggest a view of composition that is somewhat surprising, given its context. Prima facie, the second—if not also the first—suggests that composition is utterly unrestricted. The second, after all, is perilously close to the claim that anything that has any quantity whatsoever is a whole.

Of course, if composition is ontologically innocent—if, that is, the relation of composition just is the relation of identity—unrestricted composition follows immediately.[102] Everything is identical to itself. Any number of things, however (apparently) unrelated, are identical to themselves. If one denies that composition is ontologically innocent, it does not follow that one need suppose that it is also restricted. But considerations of economy would speak in favour of restrictions. I have argued that the dilemma in effect denies that composition is ontologically innocent. Hence the surprise, if the arguments of this final stage of the dilemma do indeed deny that composition is in any way restricted.

One possibility is that the Stranger's arguments here should be interpreted as being *ad hominem*. Later in the *Sophist*, I shall argue, the Stranger provides arguments in favour of a restricted conception of composition.[103] Thus, if an unrestricted conception of composition is at work here, it seems likely to be that of the monists themselves. However, a second possibility is that appearances may simply mislead. Perhaps the Stranger's claims do not, after all, commit him to a lack of any restrictions upon composition. I suggest that, despite appearances, they do not.

Consider his first claim: that anything that has come to be has always come to be a whole. This, in itself, is a somewhat surprising claim. It suggests that anything that has come to be must be a whole. It thus rules out the possibility that a mereological atom might be something that has come to be.[104] But does the sugges-

---

[102] The view that composition is thus unrestricted is, of course, Lewis's view, discussed in Ch. 1. Lewis's own final position is not that composition *is* identity, but merely that it is like identity. The lack of any restrictions upon composition is one aspect of what he takes to be the analogy between composition and identity.

[103] I shall discuss these arguments in §3.4 below.

[104] Assuming, here as elsewhere, that a whole is something that has (proper) parts. (Cf. n. 30 above.) Note that a similar consequence may be drawn from Melissus B2, where Melissus argues that if (what is) came to be, it would have a beginning and end, for it would begin coming to be at some point in time and end doing so at another. As

tion that anything that has come to be must be a whole force an unrestricted conception of composition? There is a ready alternative. The Stranger may simply suppose that coming to be is subject to the very same restriction as is composition; thus the only things that come to be are wholes.

Next, then, consider his claim about quantity. What exactly is it that the Stranger claims here? Here's how one might read it: 'But nor could what is not whole be of any quantity whatsoever, because, being something quantified ($\pi o\sigma \acute{o}\nu$ $\tau\iota$ $\gamma\grave{\alpha}\rho$ $\check{o}\nu$), whatever quantity it is, it must be a whole of that quantity' (245d8–10).[105] Does this mean that any quantity you like is a whole of that quantity? It need not, for not every quantity is a *something* of quantity, or so the Stranger might suppose, for the notion of being a something is more restricted than this would suggest.[106] Now suppose, inspired by Lewis, I take the front half of one whole (a trout) and the back half of another (a turkey); what Lewis calls a trout-turkey and what an opponent of Lewis might rather suppose not to be a whole. Is the Stranger now committed to denying that a trout-turkey has any quantity? Not exactly. Rather, the point is that, if the trout-turkey is not a something, then there is nothing to say regarding 'its' quantity, since there is no 'it' about whose quantity one might ask.[107]

suggested in the commentary on this passage in Kirk *et al.* (1983: 394), it is difficult not to suppose that Melissus is imagining something coming to be a bit at a time. In this case, anything that comes to be will have parts, and, having finished coming to be, will be a whole of those parts. Perhaps the Stranger has this argument of Melissus or something like it in view; the argument will then be *ad hominem* in this respect at least.

[105] In the phrase $\pi o\sigma\acute{o}\nu$ $\tau\iota$ $\gamma\grave{\alpha}\rho$ $\check{o}\nu$ I propose taking the $\tau\iota$ not to modify $\pi o\sigma\acute{o}\nu$, but as the complement of $\check{o}\nu$.

[106] I owe this suggestion to Myles Burnyeat (personal communication). For the claim that being a something ($\tau\iota$) is restricted in scope, compare *Sophist* 237c10–e2, where the Stranger argues that one cannot apply $\tau\iota$ to not being, arguing not only that $\tau\iota$ must always be applied to some being, but also that it must be used of something that is one. The connection between being something and being one is grist to my mill, since the arguments of the dilemma have insisted that a whole is one, suggesting a comparable scope for 'something', 'one', and 'whole'. For discussion of the wider significance of the connections between being something and being one, see McCabe (1994, *passim*).

[107] Of course, I am not proposing that Plato wrote this passage with trout-turkeys or the like in mind. Nonetheless, a position such as Lewis's can be used to test the consequences of the Stranger's commitments.

Read thus, each of the Stranger's claims can be brought within the scope of a restricted conception of composition. This then allows for the following reading of the final stage of the dilemma overall. Prior to this final stage, I have argued, the arguments of the dilemma have shown that the monists cannot admit composition into their ontology without, from their point of view, unwanted ontological accretions. The final stage of the dilemma may now be taken to show that the monists cannot avoid such ontological accretions simply by denying composition altogether. The basic commitments involved in having an ontology at all—there being some thing or things that are, have come to be, and that have some quantity or other—bring a commitment to composition in their train. They do so, I suggest, not because the Stranger takes composition to be ubiquitous, with no restrictions whatsoever; but rather because he takes the kind of things that are, have come to be, and are of determinate quantity, to be subject to the same kind of restrictions as is composition.

The final stage of the dilemma has nothing to tell us about what such restrictions upon composition might involve. Taken together, the arguments of the dilemma are designed to show that composition cannot be ontologically innocent in the way the Eleatics must maintain. In doing so, they offer an alternative to the conception of composition that drove the *Parmenides'* puzzles and the *Theaetetus'* dilemma. In particular, they involve the claim that a whole is one thing—just one—composed of many parts. But the passage does not elaborate on this alternative. For the beginnings of an elaboration, we must return to the *Parmenides*, to the second and positive movement of the mereological undercurrent to the dialogue; to a passage again much resonant with the *Sophist*'s dilemma. First, however, the *Parmenides* tackles the logical core of its earlier puzzles: the thesis that composition is identity.

CHAPTER 3

A New Model of Composition

THE discussions of composition on which I have focused thus far have in common their exploration of an understanding of composition according to which a whole is identical to its parts. In these discussions, I have argued, this understanding of composition is there to be problematized, not endorsed. I now turn to those discussions of composition in which Plato responds to the problems he has posed and from which an alternative model of composition will be seen to emerge. The *Parmenides* as a whole maps out the framework for this movement from problem to solution, and itself lays the foundations for a new understanding of composition. In general, however, the discussions of composition from which this new understanding will be seen to emerge are marked by a departure from the abstract style of discussion of part and whole which is characteristic of the texts that I have thus far considered. Outside the *Parmenides* Plato's work on his own, alternative account of composition is found in his recurring interest in certain composing relations: relations such as mixing and combining. In discussions of these composing relations Plato will be seen to be responding to the problem—and the framework for a solution—that the arguments of the *Parmenides*, above all, have posed.

I begin with the *Parmenides*; with the second and positive movement of the mereological undercurrent to the dialogue as a whole. I shall then step back, so as to recover some of the broader context for these abstract discussions of part and whole and for the solution to the problem they have posed. Within this broader context, the outlines of a new model of composition will begin to emerge.

3.1 COMPOSITION: A *SUI GENERIS* RELATION

Everything, I take it, is related to everything as follows: it is either the same ($\tau\alpha\grave{\upsilon}\tau\grave{o}\nu$) or other ($\acute{\epsilon}\tau\epsilon\rho o\nu$), or, if it is neither the same nor other, it would either be a part of that to which it is thus related or be related as whole to part. (*Prm.* 146b2–5)

Here, part way through the *Parmenides'* second deduction, and with no great fanfare, is an important element of the material required for breaking the pattern of argument which I have explored in Chapter 2. In context, this premiss forms part of an argument to show that the One is both the same as and other than both itself and the Others.[1] But the premiss itself is free-standing, asserted independently of its surrounding context.

Parmenides here canvasses four possible relations: (I) *a* is the same as *b*; (II) *a* is other than *b*; (III) *a* is part of *b*; (IV) *a* is a whole of which *b* is part. His description of these four relations as the ways in which 'everything is related to everything' suggests that he takes these four relations to be universally instantiated. That is, he supposes that any (putative) pair (*a*, *b*) must stand in (at least) one of these four relations. Parmenides also appears to suppose that the relations (I)–(IV) exclude one another. Reading '*either* same *or* other' and '*either* part *or* whole' as exclusive disjunctions, it follows that relations (I) and (II) exclude one another, as do (III) and (IV). In the case of these two pairs of relations considered in relation to each other, the exclusion is explicit: if the pair (*a*, *b*) are so related that one is part of the other, then *a* is 'neither the same nor other' than *b*. Relations (III) and (IV) thus exclude each of (I) and (II). Combining these two aspects of his assertion, Parmenides may be understood as saying that any

---

[1] The 'Others', recall, is a collective name for whatever is other than the One.

(putative) pair (*a*, *b*) must stand in exactly one of the four relations (I)–(IV).

Given this understanding of Parmenides' assertion, we may now examine more closely the nature of each of these relations, beginning with relations (I) and (II). The relation '*a* is the same as *b*' is most naturally read as meaning that *a* is identical with *b*. What of the relation '*a* is other than *b*'? Is being other simply not being the same? If so, '*a* is other than *b*' will mean that *a* is not identical with *b*. However, given the exclusive character of the relations (I)–(IV), there are, in fact, three distinct ways in which *a* might not be the same as *b*: *a* might be other than *b*, but it might alternatively be part of *b*, or a whole of which *b* is part. Thus, '*a* is other than *b*' cannot simply mean that *a* is not identical with *b*. It must rather mean that *a* is not identical with *b* in such a way as to exclude the possibility of *a* being part of *b* or being a whole of which *b* is part. One way to construe this relation is to take '*a* is other than *b*' to mean that *a* is distinct from *b* in the sense of being disjoint from *b*.[2] If *a* is disjoint from *b*, then *a* is not identical with *b*, but nor is it a part of *b*, nor a whole of which *b* is part. Understood in this way, the four relations are properly exclusive. However, one possibility is omitted: *a* and *b* might overlap, but neither be part of the other. If *a* and *b* thus overlap, they are not disjoint, since they have a part in common. Alternatively, therefore, '*a* is other than *b*' must be taken to mean that *a* is distinct from *b* in such a way as to cover both overlap and disjointness. Only thus will it be plausible to suppose that the four relations are both exclusive and universally instantiated in the sense explained.[3]

Thus far, we have a merely negative characterization of the parthood relation, relation (III): a part is neither identical with

---

[2] Compare Barnes (1988: 263), although Barnes does not himself take a stand on the interpretation of the *Parmenides* passage; and contrast the rather different account of this passage in Kutschera (1995, §3.3.5). Discussion of whether or not a part is the same as or other than a whole was to have a long history of its own. See e.g. Aristotle, *Physics* I. 185b10–16 and Simplicius, *in Ph.* ad loc.; and Sextus Empiricus, *M* IX.335–8 with discussion in Barnes (1988: 259–68). For the connection between this discussion and Stoic thoughts on identity, see Sedley (1982).

[3] What is not clear is whether this is a plausible construal of 'being other'. Overlapping things may simply not fit within the schema proposed.

nor distinct from the whole of which it is part. This negative characterization has undoubted attractions. Consider, for example, the relation between my hand and (the whole of) me. My hand is not identical with me. (I have features my hand does not.) But it is clearly not (entirely) distinct from me either. (If I leave the room, you would not expect to find my hand remaining.) Is there anything positive we might say about this relation?

We might say that my hand is *partially identical* with me. Such a suggestion is made by David Armstrong and taken up by Lewis.[4] Armstrong's first example of partial identity is a case of overlap: two terrace houses share a common wall; they are partially identical in so far as they have a part in common. The part–whole relation may then be understood as a special case of the overlap relation and thus, on this view, as a case of partial identity.[5] Is this what Parmenides intends? It seems unlikely, since he has gone to such trouble to mark the part–whole relation off from the relations both of identity and of distinctness.[6] Armstrong, by contrast, takes the part–whole relation to be intermediate between cases of strict identity and strict difference (distinctness). Where Parmenides has set out four distinct, mutually exclusive relations, Armstrong's position would better be represented by indicating a single spectrum of relations whose extremes are (complete) identity and (total) distinctness. This, at least, is the way in which Lewis seems to take his position.

Armstrong's view suggests that parthood is to be understood in terms of identity, as a partial case of identity. The view that a part is partially identical to the whole of which it is part then leads all too directly to the view that (complete) composition is (complete) identity; it is thus, of course, that Lewis exploits it. If my hand is partially identical with me, it is natural to suppose that, if one simply takes ever greater portions of me, one comes closer and closer to complete identity with me. Identify my parts

[4] Armstrong (1978: ii. 37–9), taken up by Lewis (1991: 82–3).

[5] In Mereological systems, the relation of overlap may be taken as a primitive and parthood defined in terms of overlap. See e.g. the first system described in Simons (1987: 48–50).

[6] The difficulty of accommodating things that overlap within Parmenides' schema seems, if anything, to support a contrast with Armstrong. For Armstrong, overlap is, rather, a central case.

and you identify me.[7] In contrast, Parmenides rather suggests that the part–whole relation is itself an alternative, primitive relation, not to be understood in terms of its relation to the identity relation. And it is this divorce between the relation of parthood and the relation of identity that suggests a departure from the puzzle conception.

The *Parmenides'* puzzles have turned on a particular conception of the part*s*–whole relation; that the part*s*–whole relation is identity. Parmenides' assertion, at 146b2–5, is rather concerned with the part–whole relation; he denies that this relation is identity. It by no means follows from the denial that a part is identical to its whole that the part*s* are not identical to the whole.[8] But if the part–whole relation is treated entirely separately from the identity relation, if, for example, the part–whole relation is not understood as partial identity, then it seems unlikely that one will construe the part*s*–whole relation as (complete) identity.

Parmenides' separation of the relation of parthood from that of identity may also be contrasted with the Mereological conception of parthood. What is at issue here is a contrast in strategy, not inconsistency as such. Mereologists do not themselves suppose that the part*s*–whole relation is itself the relation of identity. Even Lewis, despite the way in which he describes his view, in the end withdraws from this position, endorsing only an analogy between the relation of composition and that of identity. However, Mereologists do suppose that constitution is a criterion of identity. This view is enshrined in the Mereological axiom of extensionality; that objects with the same parts are identical. This interconnecting of composition and identity is the reason why some Mereologists have found it natural to define identity in terms of parthood or some other, related mereological primitive.[9] It is also crucial to the Mereological understanding of

---

[7] This thesis is, of course, close cousin to the Mereological axiom of extensionality, on which more below.

[8] Lewis, for example, would accept this; cf. Lewis (1991: 83).

[9] Three of the Mereological systems described in Simons (1987, ch. 2), define identity in terms of their chosen mereological primitive: systems CI, E, and AE, as outlined on pp. 48–52. For a critical appraisal of the way in which such definitions of identity load the dice in favour of Mereological assumptions, such as the axiom of extensionality, see Johnston (1992, esp. §II).

improper parthood—according to which everything is an (improper) part of itself—as the relation of being part of or *identical*.[10]

The Mereological conception of parthood, no less than the full-blown thesis that composition is identity, involves pursuit of a strategy of interlinking parthood and identity. In contrast, I suggest, Parmenides' strategy of distancing the part–whole relation from the relation of identity marks an important step towards a departure both from the puzzle and from the Mereological conception of parthood. On this view, my hand is not partially identical with me (except in the trivial sense that it is identical with a part of me, namely itself); it is, simply, a part of me.

Perhaps this bald claim is unsatisfactory. Surely there is more that can and should be said about this primitive relation? In context, of course, this is not Parmenides' focus. Equally, so far as I can see, nowhere in the *Parmenides*—or, for that matter, anywhere else in Plato—do we find an account of, for example, the logical properties of the part–whole relation of the sort this question might suggest. However, in an argument of the third deduction, Parmenides does have something more to say about the converse relation, relation (IV): that of being a whole for.[11] And what he says confirms that we have broken with the pattern of the puzzles thus far.

3.2 UNITY AND STRUCTURE

Consider what has been true of wholes throughout the negative movement of the mereological undercurrent to the *Parmenides*. By the Pluralizing Parts Principle, a whole is a many as much as, or instead of, a one. What unity a whole has is either derivative (as at the start of the puzzle series, where Socrates sought to secure the unity of a whole through its relation to the form One) or irredeemably paradoxical (as at the end, where no such resource was

---

[10] For the way in which this understanding of improper parthood relates to the axiom of extensionality, see Simons (1987: 112).

[11] I take this label from Barnes (1988: 244). *a* is a whole for *b* *iff b* is a part of *a*.

available). The puzzles have given no content to the claim that the whole (the many parts) is/are one, nor, for that matter, to the claim that the many parts (the whole) are/is many. (Conceptions of plurality come into focus in the later deductions; I shall discuss them below.) In an argument of the third deduction Parmenides will argue that a part cannot in fact be part of a many, but must be part of something one. This, the third, and the remaining deductions contain the positive movement of the mereological undercurrent to the dialogue.

The Argument: Parmenides *157b7–c8*

The argument that concerns me is found right at the beginning of the third deduction. At the start of the third deduction Parmenides sets out to consider what follows for things other than the One, the Others, if One is. He argues that, although the Others must be other than the One, they have a share of One. The Others are a whole(s) of parts,[12] and both whole and part must, he argues, have a share of One. My concern is with his argument to show that a whole must have a share of One.

First, consider the overall shape of his argument:

Then should we say in what way things other than the One must be affected, if One is?—We should.—Since, then, they are other than the One, neither is the One the Others; for they would not be other than the One.—True.—Nor indeed are the Others completely deprived of the One; rather they have a share of it in some way.—In what way?—In this way: the things other than the One are other, I suppose, because they have parts; for if they did not have parts, they would be completely one.—True.—But parts, we say, are of that which is whole.—We do.—But the whole of which the parts are parts must be one thing composed of many ($\check{\epsilon}\nu$ $\check{\epsilon}\kappa$ $\pi o\lambda\lambda\hat{\omega}\nu$); for each of the parts must be part, not of a many, but of a whole. (157b7–c8)

---

[12] Is each of the Others a whole of parts, or are they (collectively) one whole of parts? At the beginning it looks like Parmenides will argue for the first (note the plural $\check{\epsilon}\chi o\nu\tau a$ at 157c3; the others have parts, that is, they all—distributively—do). But he seems to conclude with the latter (see 157e4–5). The argument will make play with the question of whether the Others should be taken collectively or distributively at various points, not always happily.

Parmenides' argument is not yet complete, but the passage I have quoted suffices to reveal the overall shape of his argument.

Parmenides seeks to show that the Others, although they are other than the One, have a share of the One in some way. To this end, he argues as follows. (1) The Others, since they are other than the One, must have parts. (2) Since the Others have parts, these parts must be parts of a whole, for 'part' and 'whole' are correlative terms. (3) A whole is one. Thus (4) the Others have a share of the One because, having parts, they are a whole of parts, and a whole is one.

Taken on its own, Parmenides' first claim may seem all too familiar. The Others, being other than the One, must have parts; otherwise, he suggests, they would be completely one. Parmenides must here assume that to be completely one is to be without parts; to be a mereological atom. And this assumption may seem familiar, since the *Parmenides'* puzzles have repeatedly assumed that only a mereological atom could be (just) one. However, this need not mean that Parmenides is still in thrall to this pattern of puzzle. Notice that, given (3), Parmenides must here deny that this is the only possible way to be one. Indeed, the direction of his argument demands that he do so. The thought that there are two ways in which to be one should be familiar (to us) from the discussion of the monists in the *Sophist*. I shall return to it below.

If we take Parmenides' argument as a whole, the contrast with the pattern of earlier arguments is immediate and striking. Consider, for example, the opening argument of the first deduction, which I discussed in §2.3 above. There Parmenides had argued that, both on the grounds of having parts and on the grounds of being a whole, the One would be many *and not one*. Here, by contrast, the fact that the Others, having parts, are a whole is precisely his grounds for declaring them to have a share of the One. His break with the pattern of earlier arguments is only confirmed by the additional argument that Parmenides provides in support of his conclusion that the parts of the Others, being parts of a whole, are parts of something one. This additional argument runs directly counter to the direction of the puzzles, denying that a part might be part of a many, rather than of something one.

Parmenides argues as follows:

If something were part of a many in which it were, then it would be part of itself, which is impossible, and of each one of the others, since [it is part] of all of them (πάντων). For if not part of one, it will be [part] of the others except that one, and thus it will not be part of each one, and if not part of each one, it will be part of none of the many. But it is impossible for something which is part of no one of all of them to be a part or anything else of those things of none of which it is a part.—So it appears.—Therefore a part is not part of the many, nor of all of them (πάντων), but of some single form (μιᾶς τινὸς ἰδέας) and some one thing which we call 'whole', one complete thing created out of all the parts (ἐξ ἁπάντων ἓν τέλειον γεγονός); that is what a part is part of.—Certainly.—Then if the Others have parts, they have a share of both the whole and One.—Yes.—Then the things other than the One must be one complete whole which has parts.—They must. (157c8–e5)

Parmenides here offers a *reductio ad absurdum* of the notion that a part might be part of a many. Suppose, contrary to fact, that a part were part of a many. There are, Parmenides suggests, two ways in which this might be thought to occur. A part might be part of all of the many including itself. Alternatively, a part might be part of each one of the many except for itself.[13] Parmenides derives absurdity from each proposal: from the first, that a part would be part of itself;[14] from the second, that a part, contrary to the initial hypothesis, would in fact be part of none of the many.

---

[13] I take this to be the force of the situation envisaged at 157d3: 'For if not part of one, it will be [part] of the others except that one.' Of course, what Parmenides says here requires only that a part not be part of *one* of the many, not specifically that it not be part of itself. But the place of this proposal in his argument as a whole supports the interpretation I propose. On the first alternative that Parmenides considers—that a part is part of all of the many—what proves impossible is precisely that a part should be part of itself. In order to evade this consequence, the envisaged opponent must suppose that the part which is part of a many is part of all of the many except itself. Thus, when Parmenides moves from the impossibility of a part being part of all of the many (including itself), on the grounds that it cannot be part of itself, to arguing against the possibility that a part is part of all of the many, save one, it is natural to identify the one of which it is not part as the part in question.

[14] Parmenides, of course, is not working with the technical notion of an improper part; nor would we expect him to. For 'part', understand 'proper part'; nothing is a proper part of itself.

Prima facie, both parts of the argument are fallacious—the same fallacy in each case.[15] In the first part of the argument Parmenides appears to argue fallaciously from the assumption that a part is part of all of the many to the conclusion that a part is part of each of the many (and thus of itself). But the diagnosis of this fallacy depends on the assumption that, when Parmenides supposes that a part is part of all of the many, he takes 'the many' collectively; it is part of all of them, taken collectively. In context, such an assumption is illegitimate.

Consider what the argument sets out to prove: that what a part is part of—a whole—must have a share of One; that the Others are not entirely devoid of unity. Parmenides' counterfactual supposition that a part is rather part of a many must be an alternative to the claim that a part is part of something somehow one. The many in question, therefore, must not have a share of One; they must be devoid of unity, a bare plurality.[16] Such a many cannot be taken collectively, for this would be to take them as somehow one. The many can here only be taken distributively.[17] Thus, to be part of all is to be part of each. Think of the argument in the terms of the *Theaetetus* dilemma. Given the context, there is no one thing—all of it ($\tau\grave{o}$ $\pi\hat{a}\nu$)—that a part could be part of; rather a part is part of all of them ($\tau\grave{a}$ $\pi\acute{a}\nu\tau a$), where 'they' are the many parts. A part, then, is here supposed part of a plurality across which it must be distributed. Thus Parmenides' references to all the parts are in the plural ($\pi\acute{a}\nu\tau a$) (157d2, d8).

On the assumption that the many in question is a bare plurality, the first part of Parmenides' argument proceeds, without fallacy, to its conclusion. Suppose a part, p, is part of such a many. It must be part of each of the many. But p is itself one of the many, of each of which it is a part. Thus p is part of itself, as well as of each of the others. But this is absurd, for nothing is part of itself. So far, so good. What of the second part of the argument?

---

[15] Cf. Allen (1983: 267) and M. L. Gill (1996: 87–9). I have been persuaded by Gill that the second part of the argument is harder to rescue than I had first thought, on which see below.

[16] The coherence of such a notion is discussed in later deductions, on which see below.

[17] This is both Allen's (1983) and M. L. Gill's (1996) solution to the apparent fallacy.

Suppose, instead, that p is part of each of the many except for itself, since nothing can be part of itself. Again, Parmenides derives absurdity: if p is not part of one of the many, it is part of none of the many. Again, the argument appears fallacious. Parmenides starts with a claim about one of the many—that p is not a part of it—and concludes with a claim about all of the many—that p is part of none of them. Same fallacy; now in reverse. Here, however, the fallacy is harder to remove; it may be impossible.[18]

In the first part of the argument the apparent fallacy lay in the move from all the many to each of the many; and the argument was rescued on the grounds that, in context, 'all' must be taken distributively and so is in fact equivalent to 'each'. The same must be true of the 'all' of the second part of the argument. Here, however, the fallacy lies in the move from one of the many to each or all of them. And it is not true that if something is not part of one of them, it is part of none of them, even if we take 'them' distributively. For it might, as Gill suggests, be part of some of them.[19]

Perhaps Parmenides supposes that the idea that one could isolate and identify some of the many falls victim to problems similar to the earlier mistaken claim that one could take all of them collectively. The argument must assume that, if we can identify some of the many, we must take these some distributively. But this does not remove the fallacy. Perhaps, however, the argument calls into question the very idea that one could isolate one of the many and leave the rest, these some. Parmenides will, after all, go on to argue, not only that the whole that a part is part of must have a share of One, but also that each part, being one part, must have a share of One. If, then, the argument imagines a many, which not only cannot be taken collectively as one, but whose members cannot themselves be assumed to be one, the attempt to draw a distinction between one of the many and the rest begins to look incoherent.

I do not claim that the second part of Parmenides' argument can, with certainty, be rescued in this way. Perhaps Parmenides makes a mistake. The difficulty of getting to grips with a bare

---

[18] So, M. L. Gill (1996: 89).   [19] Ibid.

plurality of the kind in question is, I take it, part of his point. But, in fact, his conclusion can be shown to follow, even without the second part of his argument.[20] Suppose that our part p is indeed part of the rest of the many, but not of itself. Then p is not one of the many of which it is part. There is clearly something odd about this situation (remembering that a whole has been described as 'that from which no part is absent', 137c7–8). Further, this situation will hold for each of the many's putative parts. Suppose we take this putative many—the original 'many' less p—and consider another of its parts; call this part p^*. p^* cannot be part of all of the many, on pain of being part of itself, just as before. Then, is p^* too part of the rest of the many, excluding itself? But we can simply repeat the argument, for another part, until there are none left. Thus no part will be one of the many of which it is part; and no many will include any of its parts. The moral is clear, and it comes from the first part of Parmenides' argument: a part cannot be part of a many, one of which it is. But such would be the consequence of the identification of a whole with its many parts.

Parmenides' argument is difficult, but his break with the pattern of the puzzles is clear. First, and negatively, is the claim that a part cannot be part of a many, nor of 'all of them', where 'they' are the parts of a whole. But the puzzles have turned on the claim that a whole is a many, as well as, or instead of, a one. And the thesis that a whole may be identified with 'all of them'—where 'they' are its parts—was the core of the *Theaetetus* dilemma, as we saw in Chapter 1. Speaking positively, Parmenides offers instead an alternative account of what it is to be a whole: to be one thing composed of many; a single form; one complete thing created out of all the parts.

How do the negative and positive aspects of Parmenides' conclusion fit together? If a part cannot be part of a many, must it then be part of a whole of the sort that Parmenides here describes?[21] There is, I think, no direct route from the negative

[20] Cf. M. L. Gill (1996: 89).

[21] Allen (1983: 267) suggests that at least the proposition that a whole is one thing composed of its parts could have been taken to be true by definition. Perhaps in another context that would be true, but not in light of the earlier puzzles. This much, however, the argument does secure. But Parmenides here says rather more than this about what such a whole must be like.

to the positive. A whole must be one, and it must have the many as parts. Parmenides describes such a whole as being complete, and as being a single form. As yet, these characterizations are somewhat vague; I shall discuss them below. They are what Parmenides offers by way of giving some content to this notion of a whole that is one, not many. There may be alternative ways to characterize a whole. But, in the light of his argument, Parmenides would no doubt demand that any alternative characterization be sufficiently robust to ensure that a whole is genuinely one and not in any danger of collapsing into many. And this demand may be cashed out in the terms in which the problem of composition was originally set up. Unlike Lewis, and despite being the original Eleatic, Plato's Parmenides here sees no virtue in the claim that composition is ontologically innocent.

A New Ontology

Recall the other context in which we have seen an Eleatic—the Eleatic Stranger—take issue with his ancestry: the discussion of the monists in the *Sophist*. There too, I argued, we were presented with a whole that was just one and that resisted collapse into its many parts. There, too, such a whole was described as one thing *composed of* many (ἐκ πολλῶν, *Sph.* 245b1, *Prm.* 157c6) in contrast to the characterization of the One in the second deduction of the *Parmenides* as *both* one *and* many, *both* the whole *and* the parts.

According to the Stranger's argument in the *Sophist*, I argued, such a whole not only may, but must, be one. In our *Parmenides* passage, too, Parmenides argues that a whole must be one, or at least that a part cannot be part of a many. The point is confirmed by the (incredibly brief) reference to part and whole in the fourth, and subsequent, deduction. Parmenides begins this fourth deduction (159b2 ff.) by arguing that the One and the Others are entirely separate. In contrast to the third deduction, then, Parmenides here denies the Others a share of the One. He concludes, in consequence, that the Others are neither wholes nor parts (nor one nor many) (159d6). In the third deduction the Others have a share of the One in so far as they are a whole of parts. Conversely, in the fourth deduction, since the Others do not have a share of the One, they cannot be a whole of parts. The fourth deduction is less constructive in its discussion of composition, but it confirms the moral of the third deduction nonetheless. Wholes of parts must be one.

But wholes of parts are not *truly* one, or so both the *Sophist* and the third deduction of the *Parmenides* appear to suppose. Only a mereological atom can be truly one, although this, of course, precisely does not detract from the claim that a whole of parts is (must be) one. The claim that only a mereological atom can be truly one was, recall, a crucial step in the Stranger's argument against the monists. Being could, he argued, be a unified whole. But being, considered thus, could not be identical with 'the one', for what is truly one does not have parts. Our *Parmenides* passage has the same argument, but in reverse. Since, *ex hypothesi*, the Others are other than the One, they must have parts, for if they did not have parts, they would be completely one.[22]

Both passages offer two (exclusive) ways in which something can be one: by being a unified whole or by being a mereological atom. Both therefore offer an alternative to the ontology of the *Theaetetus* dilemma or of the earlier passages of the *Parmenides*. In the *Theaetetus* dilemma and throughout the negative movement of the mereological undercurrent to the *Parmenides*, we were presented with an ontology made up of mereological atoms (ones), paradoxical many-ones, and bare collections (manys). Here, by contrast, we are offered a choice of ones: unified wholes or mereological atoms. The third deduction of the *Parmenides* does not say very much more than the *Sophist* about the nature of such unified wholes, but what little it does say is worth considering.

---

[22] Recall that in the *Sophist* the Stranger appeared simply to assume that 'the one itself' is truly one (§2.5, n. 97). Here, in the *Parmenides*, Parmenides seems to assume both that the One is itself completely one and that it alone can be so. These assumptions are certainly puzzling, as indeed, in general, is this talk of being truly or completely one. But I shall not be pursuing these issues here. My interest is the unity of a whole, and not the (apparently special) character of the One.

The Language of Wholeness

Consider Parmenides' characterizations of what a whole must be like, as argued in the passage of the third deduction discussed above. A whole must be one thing, composed of many, that is, of all its many parts (ἐκ πολλῶν, ἐξ ἁπαντῶν). It is created as something one and complete out of all its parts (ἐξ ἁπαντῶν ἓν τέλειον γεγονός). It is, he says, a single form (μία τὶς ἰδέα). What should we make of these characterizations?

We have already seen that Parmenides' emphasis on the fact that a whole is *composed of* its many parts—and is not simply indifferently characterizable as *both* the whole *and* the parts—is a clear departure from the conception of a whole to be found in the *Parmenides'* puzzles. A whole is composed of many, but is not identified with the many that compose it; hence a whole, here, is just one, not also (or, rather) many. Such, too, is the effect of his description of a whole as something *created* one and complete out of all the parts. The reference to creation also relates to the issue that I have identified as being at the heart of Plato's discussions of composition thus far: the question of innocence. Creation, of course, is the bringing into being of something new. As in the *Sophist*, composition is here portrayed as something ontologically committed.

A whole is created one and *complete*. The reference to completeness reinforces the thought that a whole must, as at least a necessary condition, be made up of *all* its parts. But the adjective here translated as 'complete' (τέλειος) can also carry evaluative connotations of perfection.[23] I shall argue, later, that Plato's less abstract discussions of composition, outside the *Parmenides*, do indeed suggest that there is a normative aspect to his account of composition.

The remaining item among Parmenides' characterizations of a whole is perhaps the least perspicuous of them all. A part is part, not of many, nor of all, but of *a single form* (μία τὶς ἰδέα, 157d8). We have met this characterization of a whole before, to rather different effect. When, in the *Theaetetus* dilemma, Theaetetus was

---

[23] See LSJ, s.v. τέλειος.

offered an alternative to the identification of a syllable with its letters, and, later, of a whole with all its parts, he was offered the suggestion that a syllable and, later, a whole might be 'some single form' (μία τὶς ἰδέα).[24] In the context of the *Theaetetus*, however, and as a result of the thesis that composition is identity, it was argued that such a syllable could not have parts at all; it must be a mereological atom. Likewise, the application of the suggestion to the case of a whole collapsed under pressure. In our *Parmenides* passage, by contrast, the 'single form' describes precisely a whole as distinct from an atom.

What does the phrase 'a single form' suggest, when used in the more positive context of the *Parmenides*?[25] We might start by reflecting on the difference between the two 'ones' we are offered: a mereological atom and a unified whole, the single form. The whole has many parts; the mereological atom has no parts. Thus, a single form is internally complex in a way that a mereological atom is not. But the phrase 'a single form' suggests further that there is a certain unified character to this internally complex whole; it has, one might say, a certain structural integrity. And structure, I suggest, is central to this characterization of a whole, although the notion of structure itself will require considerable examination.[26]

For the present, a comparison with Aristotle may be instructive. Consider the following entry in Aristotle's philosophical lexicon (*Metaphysics* v), under 'whole' (ὅλον): 'In the case of a quantity which has beginning, middle, and end, those for which position (θέσις) makes no difference are called "a totality" [literally, "all of it", πᾶν]; those for which position does make a difference are called "whole" (ὅλον)' (1024a1–3). For an elaboration of

---

[24] For the suggestion as applied to a syllable, see *Theaetetus* 203c5–6, and cf. 203e3–4, again reminiscent of our passage, where it is suggested that a complex (syllable) might be 'some single form *created* out of them [its elements]' (ἐξ ἐκείνων ἕν τι γεγονὸς εἶδος). This latter formulation is taken up and briefly proposed as a description of the whole at 204a8–9.

[25] It would, I think, be a mistake to connect the phrase 'a single form' with middle-period discussions of forms, despite the apparent verbal connection. After all, such forms were explicitly described in the *Phaedo* as being incomposite, whereas here the term 'form' is explicitly ascribed to something composite, as a way of describing what a composite—a whole—must be like.

[26] For which, see Ch. 4, esp. §4.1.

the role of 'position', we may refer to the entry under 'disposition'[27] or 'arrangement' (διάθεσις): 'Disposition is the ordering (τάξις) of what has parts with respect to place, capacity, or form (εἶδος); for there must be some position (θέσις), as indeed the name "disposition" makes clear' (1022b1–3). By definition, then, in Aristotle, a whole is something whose parts have a certain position or ordered arrangement, in accordance with some principle of structural organization, be it spatial or otherwise.

In a passage of *Metaphysics* VII. 17—a passage with numerous resonances with the *Theaetetus* dilemma—Aristotle identifies the organizational principle of (at least, natural) wholes as (Aristotelian) form (εἶδος).

. . . the syllable is not its letters—'B and A' is not the same as 'BA'—nor is flesh fire and earth (for these—the flesh and the syllable—no longer exist, when decomposed, but the letters exist and the fire and the earth); the syllable, then, is something, not just the letters—the voiced and the unvoiced—but also something else (ἕτερόν τι), and flesh is not just fire and earth, or the hot and the cold, but also something else (ἕτερόν τι)[28] . . . (1041ᵇ12–19)

This 'something else' is not a further part of the whole (cf. 1041ᵇ25–7), but is rather its nature (φύσις) and principle (ἀρχή) (1041ᵇ30–1); and this, although Aristotle does not here explicitly use the term, is form (εἶδος).[29]

In Aristotle form is responsible for the organizational structure that is central to the identity of a whole as such. And in making a connection between form, structure, and composition, he is at one with his teacher (no doubt, while having his own distinct views about the nature of the kind of structural organization that form imports, about the relation between form and structure, and about the metaphysical status of form). What is implied, I

---

[27] I use the translation 'disposition' to preserve the connection, immediately apparent in Greek, between this term and the term 'position'. In context, it should be understood as used in English to refer, for example, to the disposition of furniture in a room, and not as used in psychology or the philosophy of action.

[28] Cf. *Tht.* 203e4–5, 204a9.

[29] For the connection between 'nature', 'principle', and (Aristotelian) 'form', see e.g. Aristotle, *Physics* II. For discussion of this passage of *Metaphysics* VII. 17, see Bostock (1994: 244–7); Burnyeat *et al.* (1979: 155–8); M. Frede and Patzig (1988: ii. 319–23); and Scaltsas (1985).

am suggesting, by the *Parmenides'* characterization of a whole as 'some single form' is that structure is essential to the constitution of a whole. Structure, recall, was precisely what the *Theaetetus'* examples of composition appeared, conspicuously, to lack; and it was absent too from the conception of parts as measures that dominated the *Parmenides'* series of puzzles.

Perhaps this seems a lot to extract from a single phrase. But then the *Parmenides* does not give us a lot to go on. Outside the *Parmenides* we shall find Plato discussing composition in less ruthlessly abstract terms. In these more concrete—but also less direct—passages, I shall argue, there is a considerable amount to be gleaned by way of positive suggestions about the nature of structure and its centrality to the composition of a whole. For now, let us complete our discussion of the positive movement of the mereological undercurrent to the *Parmenides* and reflect on the progression of the dialogue's discussions of composition considered overall.

3.3   BARE PLURALITIES

The mereological undercurrent to the *Parmenides* has a definite shape, over the course of the dialogue. First, there is the repeating (and escalating) pattern of the puzzle series, culminating in the second deduction. In the third deduction this pattern is broken and we are presented with an alternative account of the nature of a whole. The pivot by which the transition from negative to positive movement is brought about is the passage at 146b2–5, discussed above, which distinguishes the part–whole relation from the relations of distinctness and, more importantly, identity.

The positive movement of the mereological undercurrent is much less dense than was the negative movement. Aside from the argument of the third deduction, which establishes the alternative conception of a whole, there is little direct discussion of part and whole in the remainder of the dialogue. There is a brief reference to composition, in the fourth deduction, as we have seen. But this simply confirms, without adding to, the

argument of the third deduction. The four remaining deductions—the fifth to eighth—contain no discussion of part and
whole whatsoever.[30] The final deductions thus add nothing to
the positive account of composition developed in the third
deduction and indirectly confirmed in the fourth. But nor do
they detract from this account. Arguably, the absence of discussion of part and whole is in fact a consequence of the argument
of the third deduction.

Recall the moral of Parmenides' argument in the third deduction. A whole of parts, he argued, must have a share of the One; it
is impossible for a part to be part of anything other than a whole
of this sort. He also argued that each of the parts of a whole
must have a share of the One, in so far as each is one part
(157e5–158a7). The last four deductions of the *Parmenides*, in
contrast to the first four, begin from the assumption that the One
is not. If both a whole and each of its parts must have a share of
the One, and the One is not, then, it follows from the argument
of the third deduction that neither the One nor the Others—the
subjects of the fifth and sixth, and of the seventh and eighth
deductions, respectively—can be a whole or a part. The arguments of these final deductions neither assert nor deny that they
are. But the absence of any discussion of part and whole is entirely consistent with the results of the third deduction.[31]

There is, however, a passage in these final discussions that
bears on an aspect of the original puzzle that has been otherwise
largely ignored. Let us return for a moment to the very first of the
puzzles, presented in the conversation between Socrates and
Zeno at the start of the dialogue proper. There, as in the very last
of the puzzles, a whole of parts—there, Socrates himself—was
presented as being both one and many—many, in virtue of having many parts. But Socrates claimed to be unconcerned about
this state of affairs (somewhat naively, as it turns out). He

[30] The word 'part' ($\mu\acute{\epsilon}\rho o\varsigma$) occurs once, in the final deduction, at 166a4, where
Parmenides simply states that what is not has no parts.

[31] M. L. Gill (1996: 104–9), argues that, in general, the third deduction is the most
constructive of them all, and that the third and fourth deductions are somewhat
bracketed off from the others in this respect. The overall shape of the discussion of
composition seems to me to support this, at least as far as the dialogue's interest in
composition is concerned.

claimed to be unconcerned, providing, that is, that his situation could be defused by the fact of his standing in some relation to the forms One and Many, and providing the same kind of puzzle did not recur at the level of forms. In order to prevent the recurrence of the puzzle at the level of forms, Socrates had to suppose that the form One is just one and not also many—as such, it must, I argued, be a mereological atom; and he had to suppose that the form Many is just many and not also one; the form Many is thus a bare plurality. What could such a plurality be like?

An argument in the seventh deduction gives us Parmenides' best shot at saying what such a plurality must be like, for here he attempts to characterize the Others as a plurality of precisely this sort. This is what he has to say about the nature of the Others, in the absence of the One:

> Then each of the Others is other than each other as multitudes (κατὰ πλήθη).[32] For they cannot be other than each other as one, since One is not. Rather, each, as it seems, mass (ὄγκος) of them is unlimited in multitude (ἄπειρος ... πλήθει); and if someone were to take what seems to be smallest, then, suddenly, as though in a dream, in place of what seemed one there appears many, and in place of what seemed smallest appears something enormous in relation to the chopped up pieces of it. (164c7–d4)

Parmenides' attempt may be an achievement, as far as thought-experiments go. The attempt to give the Others determinate characteristics on this basis, however, is not a success. Thereafter, each of the characteristics that he ascribes to the Others have only the appearance, not the reality, of holding,[33] including their having (only) the appearance of being one or of having any determinate number (*arithmos*). A plurality of this kind, it seems, is barely coherent, if at all.[34]

---

[32] Appropriately, given the context, the word here translated 'multitude' (πλῆθος) is considerably more vague about numerical quantity than the word 'many' (πόλλα) and hence can mean 'mass', in the sense of a mass of people. See LSJ, s.v. πλῆθος I.

[33] See the use of δόκειν, φαίνεσθαι, and cognates in this deduction.

[34] Perhaps this is why there is little discussion of the plurality end of the problem within the dialogue as a whole, because Plato supposes that a bare plurality of this sort is simply incoherent. Certainly, plurality, no less than composition, turns out to be parasitic on the One. For Socrates, should he reflect on the position from which he began, this would mean that he could have his mereologically atomic one—I do not say a form One—providing he now allows that this is not the only way for something to be one; he must, however, give up entirely his conception of plurality, form or not.

It was, of course, of such a bare plurality that the argument of the third deduction denied that a part could be part. And the third deduction had its own attempt at characterizing such a plurality, in discussing the nature of the Others before—or, independently of—their having a share of the One.

Since things that have a share of the oneness of a part and things that have a share of the oneness of a whole are more than one,[35] must not these things that have a share of the one themselves be unlimited in multitude (πλήθει ἄπειρα)?—How so?—Let us consider it in this way: isn't it the case that things that get a share of the one, at the time when they get a share of the one, are neither one, nor have a share of the one?— Evidently so.—Then it is as multitudes (πλήθη), in which the one is not present?—As multitudes, indeed.—Well, then, if we were to wish to take away from such [multitudes], in thought, the smallest possible, mustn't that which is taken away be a multitude and not one, since it does not have a share of the one?—It must.—Thus, whenever we consider just by itself the nature different from the form, however much of it we see, won't it always be unlimited in multitude?—Certainly. (158b5–c7)

That this is precisely not what a part is part of is confirmed by what Parmenides goes on to say.[36]

Whenever each part becomes one part, they then have a limit (πέρας) in relation to each other and to the whole, and the whole in relation to the parts.—Indeed.—It then follows for things other than the One that, as a result of the combining (κοινωνεῖν) of themselves and the one, as it seems, something different (ἕτερόν τι)[37] comes to be in them, which provides a limit in relation to each other; but their nature in themselves is without limit (ἀπειρίαν).—So it seems. (158c7–d6)

Parmenides' characterization of what happens when the Others do have a share of the One—when, that is, they are a

---

[35] Here, I follow Gill's and Ryan's translation in M. L. Gill (1996, ad loc.).

[36] Here I am indebted to the discussion in M. L. Gill (1996: 90–1), which alerted me to the connections between this passage and the argument earlier in the deduction.

[37] This phrase may be compared with Aristotle's use of the same phrase in *Metaphysics* VII. 17, 1041^{b}17, 19, on which see above, §3.2 n. 28 and text there. As in Aristotle, and unlike the *Theaetetus*, where the same phrase is used to different effect, the phrase here indicates the *Parmenides*' new, positive conception of a whole, comparable to the earlier description of a whole as 'a single form'.

whole of parts—confirms the moral of his argument earlier in this deduction. Composition—the making of one thing out of many—involves limit in the relations the parts have with each other and with the whole; composition, that is, involves structure.[38]

3.4 RESTRICTIONS UPON COMPOSITION

Composition is not ontologically innocent, so both the third deduction of the *Parmenides* and the discussion of the monists in the *Sophist* agree. And, in doing so, they reject the thesis that composition is identity on which the puzzles depended. What, then, of the question of restrictions upon composition? If composition is identity, then composition is no more restricted than is identity. In Lewis the lack of any restrictions on composition went hand in hand with his conviction that composition is ontologically innocent. Restrictions upon composition do not follow from a denial that composition is ontologically innocent. But considerations of economy will favour such restrictions. I raised this issue earlier, when discussing the *Sophist* passage. And I suggested that, despite the misleading impression given by certain aspects of the passage, the argument with the monists is consistent with a view of composition as in some way restricted. There, however, the *Sophist* had nothing to say about what such restrictions might involve and did not address the question of restrictions on composition directly.

The *Parmenides* does not address these questions directly either. Here too, however, the view of composition outlined in the third deduction seems out of step with the view that composition is unrestricted. Parmenides has argued that composition centrally involves parts and whole standing in certain structural relations to one another. But this claim would surely be trivial if structure were to be found in any many you like. And, of course, the point of his argument was to deny that a part could

---

[38] The language of limit and its lack recurs in the *Philebus*. I shall discuss the significance of these terms in relation to the imposition of structure in that context below, in §4.3.

be part of a many; a part could only be part of something one in the requisite sense. He cannot suppose that any and every collection of many could count as one in the requisite sense, remembering that Plato's problem of composition is not a puzzle about counting; it is not a question of whether we could, as a matter of fact, count any collection of many you like as one for some purpose or other.[39]

Thus far, however, all this may just be speculation. As I have said, neither the *Parmenides* nor the discussion of the monists in the *Sophist* deals directly with the question of restrictions on composition. There is, however, another passage of the *Sophist* that does deal directly with this question, or so I shall argue. It also leads us away from the thus far abstract character of discussion of part and whole, to be found in the *Parmenides*, to recover some of the broader context of the very first passage we looked at, the *Theaetetus* dilemma.

Rules for Combining

First, the *Sophist*. The discussion of the monists in the *Sophist* formed one part of the Stranger's and Theaetetus' joint investigation into the things that had been said by other theorists about the nature of being. Prima facie, this investigation goes in a circle. It begins with a discussion of the views of certain dualists—'all those of you who say that all things are hot and cold or some such pair' (243d8–9). It ends—after the discussion of monism and of the views on the quality of being of certain 'gods' and 'giants' (246a4 ff.)—with the Stranger and Theaetetus appearing to propose a dualism of their own: 'saying that being—all there is—is both, both everything that is unchanging and everything that changes' (249d4–5). The Stranger proceeds to subject this thesis in turn to a repetition of the argument he had used against the original dualists. And so their investigation into being concludes in apparent despair: they are, it seems, no less confused about being than discussion earlier in the dialogue had shown them to be about not being.

[39] As in Ch. 1, I use the term 'collection' simply as a convenient way in which to refer, in the plural, to many things.

Their discussion, however, has not been entirely in vain. The Stranger takes the fact of their equal confusion about being and not being to hold out the prospect of joint illumination: the achievement of some measure of clarity about one will bring equal clarity about the other (250e5–251a3).[40] And the Stranger's confidence bears fruit. Hereafter the discussion takes a constructive turn from which it does not falter in the remainder of the dialogue, culminating, after various twists and turns, in the achievement of the dialogue's overall goal: the identification of the sophist through the definition of his art, sophistry. First, however, there is one further band of theorists to join the party, generally referred to as 'the Late Learners'.

ELEATIC STRANGER. Let us say in what way we call the very same thing—whatever it may be—by many names.

THEAETETUS. What do you mean? Give an example.

ES. We speak of man, surely, in naming him many things, ascribing to him colours and shapes and sizes, virtues and vices; in all these and countless other cases, we call him not only man, but also good and indefinitely many other things; and in the case of other things too, by the same account, thus supposing each to be one in turn we call it many and by many names.

THT. That's true.

ES. Hence, I suppose, we have provided a feast for the young and for those of the old who come to learning late. Straight away, they get their hands on the objection that it is impossible for the many to be one or the one many, and they clearly delight in not allowing us to call man good, but rather the good good and man man. You have come across people who enthuse about such things often, I suppose, Theaetetus, sometimes elderly men who have marvelled at such things through their poverty of intellect and think themselves to have discovered something tremendously clever.

THT. Indeed.

ES. Then, in order that our discussion may be addressed to all those who have ever made any claim about being, let the questions we now put be addressed to these people as well as to the others with whom we were talking before. (*Sph.* 251a5–d3)

The Stranger here raises a puzzle about language—about calling the same thing by many names. And the Late Learners'

---

[40] This claim is what Owen called 'the Parity Assumption' (Owen 1971).

difficulty is a difficulty about language, in particular, about predication, or so it appears.[41] But they must, the Stranger says, be included in the discussion, if it is to encompass 'all those who have ever made any claim about being' (251c8–d1). The Late Learners' difficulty about language must, then, go along with a claim about being. If we look at what the Stranger says about their position, it is not hard to see what that claim must be: the claim that 'it is impossible for the many to be one or the one many' (251b7–8). And this claim is familiar: it is the claim that gave the puzzles of the *Parmenides* bite, which Socrates sought to temper by respecting it, but only for the case of forms; and it is the claim with which, as we have seen, the Eleatics are, in Plato, most often associated.

Recall, once more, the report in Simplicius of Eudemus' characterization of Zeno's position.

Eudemus says in the *Physics* '. . . they say that Zeno said that if anyone would demonstrate to him what the one is, he would be able to speak of the things that are. He was puzzled, it seems, because each perceptible thing may be called many both predicatively and in virtue of having parts, whereas the point may be supposed to be nothing . . .'. (Simplicius, *in Ph.* 138. 30–139. 1 = Eudemus fr. 37a)

Here there are two grounds on which a one might turn out to be many: its having many properties or its having many parts. In the *Parmenides* these two grounds were run together, by treating the properties of something as parts of it (property-parts) and by taking parts (of any kind) to pluralize. Since the Late Learners have qualms (at least) about predication—which involves the ascription of properties—their claim about being seems likely to have affinity with the first of Zeno's grounds for pluralization. Since Plato has treated this puzzle as grounded in the general problem about composition, it seems likely that any response to the Late Learners' difficulty will have implications for his discussion of composition. And so, I shall argue, it does.

---

[41] There is an issue about what, more precisely, the Late Learners' difficulty might be. Do they allow identity statements—'man is man'—and simply rule out predicative statements—'man is good'? Or would even this much linguistic pluralism be too much for their taste, preferring simply that we utter monadically 'man' or 'good'? I do not need to decide this issue here and have attempted to preserve the ambiguity of their thesis in my translation.

The Stranger's immediate response to the Late Learners' difficulty, and the start of his lengthy constructive response to all of the difficulties thus far encountered, comes in the form of a discussion of the question of whether all things, no things, or some things only may be said to mix or combine (251d5–252e8). The discussion makes explicit mention of being, change, and rest (given the significance of these three items in the preceding discussion), but its scope is absolutely general. Here is how the Stranger begins:

Then shall we not fasten being to change or rest, nor anything to anything else, but rather take them to be unmixed (ἄμεικτα) and thus incapable of having a share of each other in our assertions (λόγοι)? Or shall we gather them all together in the same, as being capable of combining (ἐπικοινωνεῖν) with each other? Or shall we suppose that some can and some cannot? Which of these shall we say that these people choose, Theaetetus? (251d5–e1)

The structure of the subsequent argument is clear, even if many of its details are not. We are presented with three exclusive and exhaustive options: (1) no things are capable of combining; (2) all things are; (3) some things are and some are not. The first two options are ruled out, to establish the third. How, though, should we understand these options? What exactly does the argument establish?

Just as it was clear that the Late Learners had a problem (at least) with predication and with the ascription of properties, so it is clear that the question of whether and how things combine has implications for predication and for the ascription of properties. First, whether and how things combine has implications for whether and how one thing has a share of or is affected by another. This seems to be the implication of Theaetetus' contribution to the refutation of the second option, that all things are capable of combining, when he says that, if this were the case, 'change itself would be completely at rest and rest itself in turn would change' (252d6–7). Second, this in turn has implications for the linguistic combinations we use to express the fact that one thing does or does not have a share of another. This seems to be the implication of the self-refutation ascribed to those who deny the possibility of combination under option 1. Thus the Stranger says:

They are compelled to use 'being' about everything, and 'separate', 'from the others', and 'by itself', and countless other things; being powerless to prevent this, to prevent them fastening together in their speech, they need no one else to refute them, having the proverbial enemy within to oppose them, carrying it around wherever they go, sounding out from down below just like that strange chap Eurycles. (252c1–9)

Combining or mixing per se should not, however, be straightforwardly identified with whatever relation(s) are involved in one thing having a share of another. Rather, the capacity to combine or mix is presented as a necessary condition of one thing having a share of another. Thus, if nothing can combine with anything else, then we must suppose 'things to be unmixed' (point 1), 'and thus to be incapable of having a share of each other' (point 2) (251d6–8).[42] The capacity to combine or mix should thus be understood as a more general ontological capacity to combine to form some composite or other.

Recall that the Late Learners' difficulty over predication had its roots in a claim about being: that the many cannot be one, nor the one many. We should expect, then, that any response to them should itself take off from a counter to this claim about being. This I take to be the function of the argument about things' capacities to combine: some manys can combine into a one; conversely, some ones can be formed from the combination of some manys. And the argument is absolutely general. In what follows, the Stranger provides a range of diverse examples of domains of things in which it is true that some things can combine and some things cannot.

His first example is the domain of letters: some letters combine to form syllables, whereas some do not. Likewise, musical sounds: some may be put together to form a chord or a melody,[43] some may not. The reference in the original argument to change

---

[42] Perhaps it is also a sufficient condition, since Theaetetus clearly supposes that, if all things can combine, change will rest and rest will change. As we shall see, however, terms for combination have a much wider scope than could plausibly be construed as involving references to one thing having a share of another. One thing having a share of another is thus, at most, a species of combination.

[43] It is not clear to me which of these best captures the composite in question here; perhaps both?

and rest is expanded into a general discussion of the possibilities for combination between kinds (γένη).[44] Later still the Stranger will discuss the permissible combination of terms which make up a statement (λόγος). The range of applications of the original argument and the return of the familiar example of letters and syllables confirm that things' capacity to combine may be understood, in general, as their capacity to join together to compose something.

With this in mind, consider again the three options presented: (1) no things are capable of combining or mixing; (2) all things are; (3) some things are and some things are not. The first asserts that no group of things ever compose anything. Composition vanishes. The second asserts that any group of things you like may compose something. Composition is ubiquitous. The third asserts that some things are capable of composing something, but others are not. Composition, that is, is subject to certain limitations or restrictions. By ruling out the first and second options, and endorsing the third, the Stranger argues that composition is indeed restricted.

Of course, the Stranger makes no mention of part and whole here. Neither here nor elsewhere in what I take to be positive discussions of composition shall we see a return to the direct and abstract style of discussion of part and whole we found in the *Parmenides*. I shall return to a consideration of the language the Stranger here chooses to describe composition, and to the examples of restricted composition which he discusses. First, however, let us recover something of the wider context of this, more concrete, but less direct style of discussion by returning to the *Theaetetus* and going back to school.

Composition, Expertise, and Language

The third and final part of the *Theaetetus* took off from a dream, central to which was the Asymmetry Thesis—the thesis that there is an epistemological asymmetry between elements

---

[44] Combinations of kinds might be described as 'states of affairs', following Heinaman (1983), with the proviso that such states of affairs will be types, not tokens as in modern discussions.

and complexes: elements are unknowable, complexes are knowable. This epistemological asymmetry goes along with another asymmetry. Recall that Socrates' dream is offered as an elaboration of Theaetetus' third proposed definition of knowledge as true judgement with an account (λόγος). According to the dream, elements are unknowable, because they have no account, but only a name.[45] Complexes, by contrast, do have an account and are thus knowable; their account is 'woven together' (συμπλέκειν) from the names of their constituent elements, 'just as the [complexes] themselves are woven together' (202b3).

The dream theorist's characterization of elements bears comparison with the way in which, in the *Sophist*, the Late Learners will be said to characterize everything.[46] And it runs into the same kind of reflexive difficulties in the attempt to describe the position. Thus:

Each of [the elements] can only be named; it is not possible to say anything else of it, either that it is or that it is not. That would mean that we were adding being or not being to it; whereas we must not attach anything, if we are to speak of that thing itself alone. Indeed we ought not to apply to it even such words as 'itself' or 'that', 'each', 'alone', or 'this', or any other of the many words of this kind; for these go the round and are applied to all things alike, being other than the things to which they are added . . . (201e2–202a6).[47]

In addition, the *Sophist* will later pick up on the dream's suggestion that an account (λόγος) is a 'weaving together of names' (ὀνομάτων συμπλοκή) (202b4–5).

[45] That there are certain unknowable things, which have no account, had also been a feature of the theory Theaetetus half-recalled, which gave him his third definition. See 201d2.

[46] I do not intend to enter into the question of which, if any, historical figure may be the real 'author' of the dream; nor, likewise, into the question of who, if anyone in particular, the Late Learners may be. I think it perfectly possible that Plato made them both up.

[47] There is an unclarity regarding what is refused in refusing to add being to an element, which parallels the unclarity regarding the Late Learners' position (see n. 41 above). Does this rest on the impossibility of describing an element as being *something else* (having some property or other) or simply on the impossibility of using any term other than its name, so that one could not say of it, for example, ' "X" is its name'? For this point, see n. 52 to the Burnyeat–Levett translation in Burnyeat (1990, ad loc.).

The dream's epistemological Asymmetry Thesis is subjected to two refutations. The first, the dilemma, I have already considered at length;[48] it provided my first example of puzzles deriving from the thesis that composition is identity, and the most explicit statement of the thesis to that effect. The conclusion of the second refutation contradicts the conclusion of the first, maintaining that knowledge of elements and complexes is not symmetrical—as the dilemma arguments had concluded—but that, contrary to the dream, elements are in fact more knowable than the complexes they compose. Like the dilemma, and unlike the dream, this second refutation supposes that both elements and complexes are in fact knowable; but it supposes that knowledge of elements is both prior and more decisive than knowledge of complexes. The refutation proceeds on the basis of an argument from experience, from Theaetetus' experience of being at school.

SOCRATES. . . . wouldn't you more easily believe somebody who made the contrary statement [to the Asymmetry Thesis], because of what you know of your own experience in learning to read and write?

THEAETETUS. What kind of thing do you mean?

SOC. I mean that when you were learning you spent your time just precisely in trying to distinguish, by both eye and ear, each individual letter in itself so that you might not be bewildered by their different positions in written and spoken words.

THT. That's perfectly true.

SOC. And at the music-teacher's, wasn't the finished ($\tau\epsilon\lambda\acute{\epsilon}\omega s$) pupil the one who could follow each note and tell to which string it belonged—the notes generally being admitted to be the elements in music?

THT. Yes, that's just what it amounted to.

SOC. Then if the proper procedure is to take such elements and complexes as we ourselves have experience of, and make an inference from them to the rest, we shall say that the elements are much more clearly known, and the knowledge of them is more decisive for the mastery ($\tau\grave{o}$ $\lambda\alpha\beta\epsilon\hat{\iota}\nu$ $\tau\epsilon\lambda\acute{\epsilon}\omega s$)[49] of any branch of study than knowledge of the complex. And if anyone maintains that the complex is by nature knowable and the element unknowable, we shall regard this as tomfoolery, whether it is intended to be or not. (206a1-b10)

[48] See §1.6 above.

[49] For 'mastery', one might instead read 'finished grasp' to bring out the repetition of $\tau\epsilon\lambda\acute{\epsilon}\omega s$, translated by 'finished' above.

The argument from experience makes two claims: one about the nature of learning, the other about the nature of expertise. The two claims are linked, for the argument takes the order of learning to indicate the order of knowledge and the mark of expertise. (It need not be this way. Consider Aristotle, who takes learning to begin from what is more knowable to us and to culminate in what is more knowable by nature. For Aristotle, then, the order of learning is the reverse of the order of knowledge.[50]) Thus, the beginner in spelling begins with the task of learning to identify and distinguish each individual letter. And the mark of the 'finished' pupil, in music or in spelling, is simply the realization of this task, having knowledge of each individual note or letter.[51] Indeed, knowledge of the elements of a subject is the (more 'decisive') mark of expertise, the mastery of the branch of learning in question. The Greek term here translated 'finished'—the finished pupil, the mastery or finished grasp of a branch of learning—has the sense both of having completed and of having perfected one's ability in the relevant domain, as indeed can be true of the term 'finished' in English.

In what sense, however, could such a pupil be described as finished? In what sense could knowing one's ABC count as the completion—even perfection—of one's attempt to learn to read and write, let alone as the mark of expertise? This argument from experience marks a departure from the epistemology of the dilemma, but it does not seem entirely to have emancipated itself from the dilemma's ontology. Consider what was characteristic of Socrates' examples of composition in the dilemma: the pointed absence of any reference to structure.[52] Likewise, the argument from experience is, at best, silent about how one builds up from one's grasp of the elements of a domain—individual letters or notes—to an understanding of the complexes they compose; and about the part played in expertise by an understanding of the

[50] See e.g. *Physics* I. 1, 184ᵃ16–21; *Metaphysics* VII. 3, 1029ᵇ3–12.

[51] As Myles Burnyeat points out to me (personal communication; and cf. his 1990: 209–10), individual letters are here envisaged as things that occupy different positions in different words. But the focus of learning, as here described, remains on the individual letters, so that one will not be 'bewildered' when one comes across them in the context of words (206a7–8).

[52] As discussed above, in §1.6.

permissible relations between the elements of a domain, those combinations of letters that make up syllables or words. At worst, the argument continues to suppose that there is nothing more to knowledge of a complex than knowledge of the elements that compose it, and simply gives this view a different epistemological spin from the arguments of the dilemma.[53]

The worst-case scenario gains some support from the second and third accounts of 'account' (λόγος) that Socrates goes on to propose, in an attempt to further their understanding of the original proposal that knowledge may be defined as true judgement together with an account. (His first proposal is simply that to add an account to one's judgement is just to express it in words, a proposal quickly dismissed.) Socrates' second proposal is that knowledge of a complex might be achieved when, in conjunction with a true judgement about it, one can provide an exhaustive list of its elements; what Hesiod accomplishes in saying that 'one hundred are the timbers of a wagon' (207a3–4),[54] whereas Socrates and Theaetetus could, Socrates suggests, do no better than list its macro-parts—'wheels, axle, body, rails, yoke' (207a6–7)—thus revealing their deficient understanding of wagons. Exhaustive knowledge of what something is made up of, it is implied, is all that is involved in knowing the thing.

This proposal fails, not because of a recognition that knowledge of the parts of a wagon, however fine-grained, tells you nothing about how those parts are put together, but because parts like wheels and axles—parts that are themselves composite, like the syllables of a word—turn up in different complexes, in both wagons and cars, say. But someone might make mistakes about parts of this sort: they might, for example, correctly identify the first syllable of Theaetetus' name as The, but mistakenly suppose that The is also the first syllable of the name Terence; alternatively, and this is the version that Socrates illustrates, they

[53] For a more optimistic appraisal, see Burnyeat (1990: 209–12). Contrast also Fine (1979, esp. 385–7), who argues that knowledge is here presented as the ability to identify and interrelate the elements of a domain. I agree with Fine that an 'interrelation model' of this kind will be central to Plato's response to the problems here posed, but I do not agree that such a model is being presented here.

[54] Quoting *Works and Days* 456.

might correctly identify The as the first syllable of Theaetetus' name, but suppose that Theodorus' name begins with the syllable Te (207e7–208a3).[55] Such a person, Socrates and Theaetetus agree, cannot be said to know the first syllable of Theaetetus' and Theodorus' names; and cannot, in consequence, be said to know either of their names.[56]

The third proposed account of 'account' picks up on this worry about repetition and similarity between different contexts, and supposes that to give an account of something might be to include mention of some mark that is unique to the object in question. But Socrates continues to propose that a rough and ready, if inadequate, model of an account of Theaetetus would be a list of his parts (and properties): being a human being, having a nose, eyes, and mouth, etc. (209b4–6). And again, the inadequacy lies not in a lack of sensitivity to the way in which Theaetetus' parts are arranged, but in a failure to give a sufficiently fine-grained account of Theaetetus' parts, where being fine-grained now involves taking account of other contexts; I must be able to identify the precise snubness of nose that is a feature of Theaetetus and Theaetetus alone, distinct from that of his looka-like Socrates, for example (209c4–7). This third proposal also fails, but again, not because of any challenge to the ontology on which it appears to be based. The dilemma arguments have problematized that ontology; but the *Theaetetus* has no alternative to offer.

The conception of composition that dominates the final part of the *Theaetetus* thus has consequences both for the conception of understanding and of the nature of expertise that the dialogue presents and for its account of the way in which one might express such understanding in language. Its accounts of 'account' (λόγος) and its epistemology are both reflected in and a reflection of the ontology of the dilemma.[57] In turn, epistemology and language

[55] Both versions are outlined at 207d3–6, but only the latter is illustrated. The Greek counterparts of The and Te differ, when spoken, only in aspiration.

[56] For a discussion of this conclusion—and the accounts of 'account' in general—see Burnyeat (1990: 213–34).

[57] It should come as no surprise to find Plato supposing that the nature of understanding and of explanation in language—the giving of accounts—are themselves reflections of the way things are.

are two of the contexts in which, in the *Sophist*—the *Theaetetus'*
dramatic successor—Plato will put to work his emancipation
from that ontology,[58] an emancipation achieved both in the
Sophist itself, in the discussion of the monists, and in the third
deduction of the *Parmenides*. Epistemology and language are thus
two of the contexts to which I shall look to learn more about his
alternative view of composition and about the significance of
structure.

Letters, Syllables, and the Combination of Kinds

Like the *Theaetetus*, the *Sophist* too has something to say about the
nature of expertise, and something interestingly different from
what is suggested by the *Theaetetus'* description. Immediately following the argument that some things are capable of combining
with one another, but some things are not—the argument discussed above—the Stranger goes on to consider two particular
instances of this general claim: the combination of letters and of
(musical) sounds.

ELEATIC STRANGER. Since some things are willing to do this [to
    combine] and some things are not, they will be affected in just the
    same way as the letters of the alphabet; for some of these do not fit
    together with each other and some do fit together (συναρμόττειν).
THEAETETUS. Of course.
ES. And the vowels, more so than the others, run through all of them
    like a bond, so that without one of these [the vowels] it is impossible
    for one of the other letters to fit together with another.
THT. Indeed.
ES. Then, does everyone know which are capable of combining with
    which, or does the person who is going to do this properly require a
    skill (τέχνη)?
THT. He requires a skill.
ES. Which one?
THT. The science of letters (ἡ γραμματική).

---

[58] By this I do not mean to suggest that Plato ever subscribed to the view that composition is identity, *in propria persona*; nor, for that matter, to deny this. But so far as
I can see, wherever that view is at work, the view is problematized, not endorsed.
Equally, the frequency with which it is discussed suggests that Plato took consideration of it to be important.

ES. Again, isn't it the same as regards sounds of high and low pitch? Isn't the one who has the skill to know which blend and which do not musical (μουσικός), whereas the one who does not know is unmusical?

THT. Yes.

ES. And we shall find the same to be true of other skills and the lack of them.

THT. Of course. (252e9–253b7)

Having generalized his point to include all sciences, the Stranger proceeds to apply it to the greatest science of all, philosophy, whose business it is to understand the combination of kinds. There follows a compressed and difficult description of the science of philosophy (253d1-e2), whose interpretation will not concern me here.

Whatever the science—be it in the domain of letters, of music, or of kinds—what is distinctive about expertise, the Stranger argues, is knowledge of the ways in which the elements of the domain combine and the ways in which they do not. This is in stark contrast to the picture that emerged from the *Theaetetus*, where expertise was said to consist in knowledge of the elements, taken individually, with no mention of the need to understand the rules for their combination. The examples—knowledge of letters and of musical sounds—are common to both dialogues.

In the *Theaetetus*, I argued, the account of expertise was constrained by the ontology of the dilemma and its account of composition. So too the *Sophist*'s alternative account suggests a new ontology is at work. Nor should this surprise us. The discussion of the monists offered an alternative to the account of composition on which the *Theaetetus*' dilemma depended. And the account of expertise portrayed above is presented as a direct corollary of the *Sophist*'s argument that composition, in general, is restricted. Restrictions upon composition are incompatible with the dilemma's view of composition as identity, since the identity relation is not at all restricted. It remains, then, to consider what can be said about the view of composition implicit in the dialogue's description of the combination of letters, of sounds, and of kinds.

First, a red herring, or so I shall argue. When talking of the combination of letters, the Stranger draws attention to the role of vowels. Vowels, he suggests, have a special role in the combination of letters; they run through all the other letters like a bond, such that, without one of the vowels, other consonant letters cannot fit together at all. Further, when he turns to the description of the combination of kinds, there is some suggestion that there may in turn be certain kinds that play a role in the combination of kinds analogous to that of vowels. At 253b8–c3 the Stranger sets out three questions, correct investigation of which is said to require the science of philosophy: (1) the question of which kinds combine with one another and which do not; (2) the question of whether there are some kinds that run through all the others and hold them together so that they are capable of mixing together; (3) the question of whether there are other kinds that 'traverse wholes' (δι' ὅλων, 253c3) and are responsible for their separation.[59] Question 2 asks whether there are vowel-like kinds.

The comparison of vowels to a 'bond' (δεσμὸς, 253a5) might suggest that vowels (and, by association, vowel-like kinds) have the following role in composition. They might be taken to be the agents of composition in much the way in which a particularly sticky toffee, placed in a bag of sweets, might bind other sweets to itself, and, through itself, to each other. So, Moravcsik suggests that vowels are like the cement between two bricks. And vowel-like kinds—which, in common with other commentators, he takes to include the kinds Being and Other—are said to have an 'ontologically ordering role'.[60] In Moravcsik's image, when one kind, X, combines with another, F, such that X may be said to have the property of being F, this may be represented as follows:

---

[59] 'Separation' here translates διαίρεσις, in place of the more usual 'division', because it is here contrasted not to 'collection' (συναγωγή), but to 'mixing together' (σύμμειξις). Cf. Gómez-Lobo (1977: 38).

[60] Moravcsik (1992, ch. 5, with app. 2). Gómez-Lobo (1977) takes the kinds Being and Other to be vowel-like kinds, having a special role to play in combinations. So, with reservations, does Trevaskis (1966). Despite stressing the absence of textual evidence, Trevaskis concludes that vowels are responsible for combinations and that the kinds Being and Other play special roles in the combinations and separations among kinds, merely deeming it unfortunate that Plato 'omitted to say so in words' (1966: 116).

X is F = X – (connector, i.e. Being) – F. Vowels, on this conception, are thus directly responsible for composition.

Such a view, however, is mistaken, as attention to the precise
way in which the Stranger describes the role of vowels, and of the
putative vowel-like kinds, will show. Of vowels, the Stranger
says: '[the vowels] run through all of them [the other letters] like
a bond, so that without one of these [the vowels] it is impossible
for one of the other letters to fit together with another' (253a4–6).
As regards the putative vowel-like kinds, the Stranger suggests
that there may be some kinds: 'which pervade all (διὰ πάντων)
and hold them together (συνέχειν) so that they are capable of
mixing together' (253c1–2). In both cases, vowels and vowel-like
kinds are identified as things that hold the other letters or kinds
together so that they are *capable* of combining with one another
(of fitting or mixing together). Vowels, that is, operate as
necessary—but not sufficient—conditions for the combination
of letters and kinds; they do not themselves bring about such
combination.

The Stranger has a rich vocabulary in which to describe composition: he talks of things fitting together (συναρμόττειν), mixing together (συμμείγνυσθαι), and of cognate verbs, as well as of
their harmonizing (συμφωνεῖν) and communing (κοινωνεῖν).
These relations describe what vowels make possible for other
letters, not what vowels themselves accomplish.[61] Where
Moravcsik describes vowels as acting like some kind of cement,
we might instead take our cue from Ryle and think of phonetics.[62] The point is not that vowels in some sense form syllables; it
is rather that consonants cannot be sounded without at least one
vowel.[63]

[61] Another point of language may be of interest here: the Stranger suggests that
putative vowel-like kinds might 'hold things together' (συνέχειν), using a verb that
will later be used precisely for the relation between a mere string of names or of verbs
in contrast to the relation involved in the composition of a properly interwoven sentence (261e1, 262c1). Little, however, could rest on this point alone.

[62] Ryle (1960) famously argues that Plato's frequent mention of letters and syllables almost exclusively refers to spoken letters and syllables. His point is somewhat
overstated, on which cf. Gallop (1963). Nonetheless, there is something to be gained
from thinking of phonetics here.

[63] Cf. Ryle (1960: 434–5). Note that, in the *Theaetetus*, consonants are thus
referred to as 'mutes' (ἀφώνα), 203b2.

Likewise, if there are vowel-like kinds—and there is some textual evidence that there may be[64]—an analogous point may be
said to apply. The kind Change, for example, cannot be taken on
its own, but must be taken in combination with other kinds. In
particular, if the kind Change is to combine with other kinds, it
must both be and be distinct; that is, it must be the same as itself
and different from the rest. Precisely the burden of the greater
part of the discussion of the combination of the 'greatest kinds'—
and of the fuss about how many they are, resulting eventually in
their numbering five[65]—namely, Change, Rest, Being, Same,
and Other—is to establish such individuating conditions.[66] In
the sense of being necessary conditions for combination—but in
this sense only—the kinds Being, Other, and, I would add, Same
are clearly likely candidates for the putative vowel-like kinds of
253c1–3.[67] However, Plato never clearly says as much. Further, if
this view of the role of vowels is right, then, for my purposes,
attention to it is indeed a red herring, for it has little to offer by
way of elaboration on the view of composition at work here.
Instead, we must concentrate on what can be learned from the
account of what is involved in understanding the combination of

[64] First, of course, there is the fact that the Stranger offers this as a possibility to
be investigated by the philosopher's science, at 253c1–2. Second, towards the end
of his discussion of the combinations available to the kinds Change, Rest, Being,
Same, and Other, the Stranger states that they have shown that the kinds Being and
Other run through all the others (διὰ πάντων) (259a5); earlier, the same claim had
been made explicitly for the kind Other, at 255e3–6, inasmuch as all the kinds have
a share of the kind Other. These two echoes of the phrase 'running through them
all' (διὰ πάντων), the phrase used of the putative vowel-like kinds of 253c1–2, are
certainly striking. As far as I can see, however, there is no textual basis for the
rather more elaborate claims of Gómez-Lobo (1977) to the effect that Being and
Other are vowel-like kinds that have distinct roles as regards the combination and
separation of kinds.

[65] *Sophist* 253^b8 ff. For the fuss about how many they are, see e.g. 254e2–255a2.

[66] On which, cf. McCabe (1994, ch. 8, §2).

[67] The kind Same should be included, I think (as does Moravcsik 1992, ch. 5),
because it too 'runs through all the others' inasmuch as it, like the kinds Other and
Being, is something of which all kinds have a share. Against this, it might be objected that, at 259a4–6, it is only Being and Other that are identified as having been
shown to run through everything (on which see n. 64 above). But the reason that it is
these two kinds that are specifically named is surely that it is precisely these two kinds
whose combination with each other and with everything else is of particular relevance to the overall project of finding the sophist.

letters, sounds, or kinds, and from the language the Stranger chooses to describe composition.

First, epistemology. We have already seen that, in the *Sophist*, in sharp contrast to the *Theaetetus*, the mark of the expert in any domain is the ability to know which of the elements of the domain combine and which do not. This characterization follows the argument to show that composition must be restricted. And it underlines the restricted character of composition; it is a matter of expertise to know which elements combine and which do not only if it is not the case that elements combine without any restrictions whatsoever, in any combinations you like. What, then, is the basis for the constraints upon combinations within a domain?

The constraints are based, I suggest, upon the presence of certain structural relations between the elements of a domain; in phonetics, say, the presence of certain structural relations between the English phonemes 'k', 'æ', and 't',[68] such that they can be combined to form the syllable 'kæt', but fail to form a syllable when ordered 'tkæ'.[69] In knowing which of the elements of a domain combine and which do not, the business of the expert is precisely to have an understanding of such structural relations. I shall have more to say on this when it comes to considering the kind of examples of structure the *Sophist* suggests. For now, the description of expertise that the *Sophist* presents can be seen to imply, first, that composition is restricted and, second, that it is restricted on the basis of the presence or absence of certain structural relations between the elements of the domain.

What, then, of the Stranger's vocabulary for composition? Aside from the general term 'combination' (κοινωνία), which is used to cover a variety of examples, he talks, as we have seen, of

[68] Representation of phonemes of English here follows the International Phonetic Alphabet, as given in *The Pocket Oxford Dictionary of Current English*, 7th edn., ed. R. E. Allen (Oxford: Clarendon Press, 1984).

[69] And contrast the phonemes 'k', 't', 'z', which cannot be combined at all. Which contrast is at work here? That between 'k'-'æ'-'t' and 't'-'k'-'æ'? Or that between 'k', 'æ', 't' and 'k', 't', 'z'? The stress on knowing *which* combine and *which* do not may suggest the latter rather than the former. But the former is at least implied, since to know of the phonemes 'k', 'æ', 't' that they can be combined is to know, *inter alia*, that they combine in the order 'k'-'æ'-'t' and not in the order 't'-'k'-'æ'.

things 'mixing together' (συμμείγνυσθαι) (of kinds); of their 'fitting together' (συναρμόττειν) (of letters); of their blending together (συγκεράννυσθαι) (of sounds); and, later, of the 'weaving together' (συμπλέκειν) of names and verbs. Such language is, no doubt, metaphorical, but the metaphors involved have two common themes. First, once again, the existence of a composite seems to depend on the existence of certain structural relations between the elements of which it is composed. Each of the Stranger's terms for composition describe an operation or activity upon the elements of a domain: combining, blending, mixing, etc. Taken literally, such operations describe, if anything, how one might produce a composite—take two kinds and mix them together; but this, I take it, is not the Stranger's meaning. Instead, as metaphors, his terms tell us something of the nature of a composite already formed: the existence of a composite depends on the action of its parts upon each other; on their internal structural relations.

In choosing terms for composition that describe operations on the elements of a domain, the Stranger's language further suggests that the resulting composite could not exist without the performance of these operations. This brings us to the second feature of his metaphors: composition is characterized as being creative; a composite is something new, arising from the action of its parts upon each other. So, to pursue his own metaphors, if I mix or blend two colours, a new, third colour results.[70] Likewise, if I fit together the pieces of a jigsaw, a picture emerges. Note: I do not suggest that the Stranger here implies that composition *is* a matter of fitting together, or blending, the parts of a whole. Rather, his use of metaphors to capture the relation of composition tells us something more general about what composition is like.

---

[70] We should, however, be cautious about use of the English term 'mixture', which can as readily apply to a mixture of sand and sawdust, in which the original components remain unaltered. Perhaps the best way to understand the *Sophist*'s use of the verb 'mixing together' (συμμείγνυσθαι) is by reference to Aristotle's use of the noun 'mixture' (μίξις), e.g. in *GC* 328ᵃ6, ᵇ23, where a 'mixture' is sharply contrasted with a loose assemblage of elements of the sand and sawdust type, and where, for example, Bogaard (1979) instead prefers the translation 'chemical combination'.

Formally speaking, the view of composition that emerges from consideration of the epistemology of the *Sophist* and the terms that the Stranger chooses to describe composition is a precise match for that of the third deduction of the *Parmenides*. Composition is restricted. It is ontologically committed or creative. And composition centrally involves the existence of certain structural relations between the parts of a whole.

The *Sophist*'s discussion is less explicit, and less precise, than that of the *Parmenides*. This is because, first, the *Sophist* is not directly concerned with composition, at least not to the same extent as the *Parmenides*.[71] The *Sophist*'s explicit goal is the identification of the sophist, as distinct from both the statesman and the philosopher (216d2–217b3 with 218b6–c1). In the passages on which I have focused here, in which the combination of letters, sounds, and kinds is discussed, the Stranger's predominant interest is the nature of expertise regarding each of these domains.[72] Second, and in consequence, the picture of composition that emerges from the *Sophist*'s discussion must be extrapolated from the direct discussion of the epistemological and, as we shall see, semantic concerns that provided the context for its dramatic predecessor's, the *Theaetetus*', own more direct discussion of parts and wholes.

It is now time to see what flesh can be put on this, thus far, rather sparse account of composition, by considering what, more directly, can be said about the nature of structure and its centrality to composition.

---

[71] And, in the *Parmenides* too, composition is but one central theme.

[72] This focus persists right up until the discussion of the combination of the greatest kinds, and is, I think, the explanation of why it has proved so hard to understand exactly what is going on in the compressed description of the philosopher's science at 253d1–e2; contrast, for example, the different interpretations of Cornford (1935, ad loc.); Gómez-Lobo (1977); and Moravcsik (1992, ch. 5, app. 2). I myself think it is a mistake to try too hard to unravel exactly what is being claimed about the *objects* of the philosopher's science—the various ones and manys and their interrelations; the emphasis here is squarely on what the philosopher knows or understands. As in the rest of the account of the nature of expertise, the moral, at least, is relatively clear: the business of the philosopher is to understand the structural relations between the elements of his domain, whatever they may be. See, now, McCabe (2000, ch. 7, §4), for an interpretation of the passage based on its epistemic character.

CHAPTER 4

Composition and Structure

I BEGIN this chapter with some general considerations about structure and about the role it might be thought to play in the constitution of a whole. It will be useful to have a general framework within which to locate the various Platonic discussions on which I shall focus in the remainder of this chapter.

4.1 TWO WAYS OF THINKING ABOUT STRUCTURE

First, then, some general considerations about structure. I focus, in particular, on the different ways in which one might answer the following general questions. The first concerns the role, if any, that is played by structure in the constitution of a whole. In particular, is structure essential to the constitution of a whole? Are wholes essentially structured? The second concerns the relation between the parts of the whole and the structure of the whole they compose?[1] In particular, are the parts identifiable independently of the structure of the whole they compose? Or is structure essential to the identity of the parts of a whole, no less than to that of the whole itself?

---

[1] Structure is not itself a *part* of the whole, as Aristotle saw. See *Metaphysics* VII. 17, 1041^{b}12–33 and cf. §1.1.

A believer in unrestricted composition such as Lewis supposes that structure is not in any way essential to the constitution of a whole, and, *a fortiori*, that the parts of a whole are identifiable independently of any structure belonging to the whole which they compose. Lewis, that is, answers both of the questions above in the negative. I have already suggested that Plato, in contrast to Lewis, takes structure to be in some way essential to the constitution of a whole. However, there are (at least) two possible ways in which he might do so. Distinguishing these two possibilities, in general, will help to clarify the view which I shall subsequently attribute to Plato.

In what follows, then, I shall consider two different views according to which structure is essential to the constitution of a whole. Each of these views answers the first of our questions above in the positive. They differ in their answers to the second question. The first view continues to suppose, with Lewis, that the parts of a whole may be identified independently of the structure of the whole they compose. The second view denies this. I shall further suggest that the first is vulnerable to objection in a way the second is not.

I shall associate the difference between the two views in question with the difference between two possible ways of talking about structure in relation to a whole. According to the first way of talking, structure is something a whole *has*. According to the second way of talking, structure is rather something a whole *is*. While these different ways of talking do not themselves force a choice between the two contrasting views in question, each is, I suggest, more naturally associated with one than the other. What is important about the contrast between these two ways of talking is the way in which the first, unlike the second, leaves open the possibility of driving a wedge between the structure of the whole and both the whole and its parts. It is this possibility that leaves room for objection.

In exploring these various ways of thinking and talking about the relation between structure and whole, it will be helpful to have an example to work with. Thus, suppose that you are organizing a dinner party. There are eight guests—four men, four women—and you are to seat the guests so that they alternate by gender. Starting from one of eight chairs around a round table, you seat the guests clockwise in the following sequence: first a man, then a woman, then a man, then a woman, etc. The resulting configuration seats every man between two women and every woman between two men. 'Sequence' and 'configuration' are terms closely connected to structure. The seating arrangement of the dinner party here described may be taken as an example of structure.

Notice that the seating arrangement is something abstract, in the sense that it can be considered, and represented, independently of the particular components involved in its construction. One could code the instructions for producing just this structure into a machine, producing a seating arrangement programme such that, on entering the names and genders of your guests, the programme will generate the requisite seating arrangement. Notice, too, that the seating arrangement is something repeatable; it can be realized by any party of eight people (or indeed, of any even number), exactly half of whom are women.

With this example to hand, consider, first, the ways in which one might answer the first of our general questions, given above. Is structure essential to the constitution of a whole? This is the question to which both of the views I shall consider answer yes, and to which Lewis answers no. I begin with Lewis. According to a believer in unrestricted composition such as Lewis, structure has no role to play in the constitution of a whole. Of course, given unrestricted composition, the eight guests of our example do compose something, as does any collection of things. But the way in which these guests are arranged, in the example, has no bearing on the fact of their composing something. The whole which the guests compose exists entirely independently of their being so arranged. As such, it continues to exist even after they have ceased to be so arranged; when, for example, the party has broken up, and the guests have dispersed and are on their way home.

In contrast to Lewis, each of the views that I shall consider rather supposes that structure is essential to the constitution of a whole. If we apply this to our example, then the guests may be said to compose something—a dinner party, let's say—when, and only when, they are arranged in the way described above. The views differ, as I have said, in their answers to the second of the general questions, given above. According to the first, while structure is essential to the constitution of a whole, the structure in question is not, as such, essential to the parts of the whole. Thus, applied to our example, there will be nothing about being a guest that requires that one be seated in an arrangement of this sort. The parts—the guests—may thus be identified independently of the structure of the whole they compose. According to the second, structure is no less essential to the parts than to the whole. Thus, applied to our example, guests will be essentially things that are seated in this way. The parts—the guests—are thus not identifiable independently of the structure of the whole they compose.

These two contrasting views may each be associated with one of the two different ways of talking about structure mentioned above. According to the first, structure is something that the whole and the parts may be said to *have*, where talk of 'having' sits well with the independence of the parts from the structure that they (collectively) have. According to the second, structure is something a whole of parts *is*. Here, the identity of the parts is determined only in the context of the structure of which they are part. The difference this makes may now be considered in light of our example.

According to the first way of thinking, structure is something a whole has. Thus, one might think of the eight guests of our example as collectively having a certain structural property, being seated in a certain arrangement, say. This will be a property of a rather special sort. It is a property that no one of the guests has individually, and that is not obviously a simple summation of properties each of them does have individually. (Contrast their collectively having the property of weighing 72 stone.)[2] On this first way of thinking, structure is something ascribed to components already given: the guests. There are eight guests, independently identifiable, and, collectively, they have a certain property. While having this property is supposed essential to

---

[2] Armstrong (1978: ii. 70–1) distinguishes two types of structural property. What I here call a 'structural property' would be what he calls a 'relationally structural property'.

these eight guests composing a whole, it is not essential to the guests as such. Once the party has broken up, the guests will cease to have this property and will instead have a series of other, rather less coordinated, properties, according as they are dispersed and on their way home.

According to the second way of thinking, structure is rather something that a whole is. And the parts of such a whole cannot be identified independently of the structure of which they are part. Thus, in our example, we now suppose that the guests cannot be identified independently of the seating arrangement of which they are part. Guests are, let us say, 'structure-laden'. Our structure—the seating arrangement—writes a prescription for certain components—an even number of guests, exactly half of whom are women—to sit in the places prescribed by the structure (give or take the leeway required for different possible ways of realizing the structure with any one even-numbered party of the requisite sort). To think of the people involved as 'guests', on this view, is already to think of them in terms of their capacity to occupy a place within the seating arrangement. Indeed, for the purposes of the seating arrangement, one can think of them only in these terms;[3] the only characteristics required to identify them for the purposes of the structure are their genders. The guests occupy positions within the structure.[4] Rather than supposing that the guests collectively instantiate a certain structural property, on this model, that which the guests (collectively) compose—the dinner party—*is* (an instance of) the structure. When the party breaks up, this (token of the) structure dissolves.[5]

[3] The example is no doubt somewhat forced in this respect, since the notion of 'guest' is a richer notion than that of occupying a place in the seating arrangement of a dinner party and there are, in any case, various different arrangements in which guests might be seated. No matter: my interest here is in mapping out the alternatives, not in defending the application of one or other to the example as such.

[4] Talk of 'positions' suits the example. It is also influenced by the terminology employed by mathematical structuralists in thinking about structure in works that I have found helpful in my own reflections upon the nature of structure. More on this below. For similar talk, cf. also Rescher and Oppenheim (1955), which, in turn, is taken up by Simons (1987, §§9.2, 9.5–7).

[5] The structure-laden character of parts on this way of thinking of structure raises an important question about what happens to the components of a structure, once the structure no longer exists. More on this below.

Each of these two contrasting views assumes, *ex hypothesi*, that the guests may be said to compose something when, and only when, they are arranged in the way the example requires. However, the first seems vulnerable to a charge of special pleading in this respect in a way the second is not. Notice that, on the first way of thinking about the seating arrangement example, structure appears to be something of an afterthought. Structure, on this way of thinking, is something ascribed to components already given: the guests. And it is this feature of this way of thinking that makes the question of the structure a given set of components may have look less than integral to the question of what is involved in their composing something. After all, before we even consider the structural arrangement of the eight guests—which, on this view, is the structural property that they collectively have—we must already be able to take our components collectively, to consider them as (some kind of) whole, for this is the bearer of the property in question.

It is because this first way of thinking about structure makes the structure of a given set of components look like something added after the fact of their being taken together that this view seems vulnerable to the following kind of objection. According to this view, our eight guests compose something—a dinner party—when, and only when, they collectively instantiate a certain structural property. But mightn't this look like special pleading? Why suppose that they only compose something because on this occasion they collectively instantiate this special structural property, as opposed to the rather less coordinated property they collectively instantiate once the party has broken up and they are on their way home? As far as 'taking together' goes, the situation in fact looks entirely parallel in both cases: the guests collectively have one property at one time and another, albeit less interesting and harder to specify, property at another. But this, one might suppose, is indeed a matter for ideology, not ontology.[6]

Next, then, consider the second way of thinking about structure, according to which structure is not something a whole has, but something it is. Here, the parts of the whole—the guests—are themselves things whose identity is determined only in the

[6] For the contrast, see §1.6 n. 82 and text there.

context of the structure of which they are part. The guests occupy positions within the structure. And the guests are things that are essentially such as to occupy the various positions of this structure. They are, as I have put it, 'structure-laden'. Thus, the 'taking together' of the guests occurs only within the context of the structure they compose.

Does this alternative make any difference when it comes to thinking about the relevance of structure to an account of composition? One might think that it does not. One might think that the charge of special pleading can be raised again, just as before. When the party breaks up, one might say, while this structure dissolves, another, less coordinated and harder to specify, structure comes into being—the party-breaking-up structure. Why privilege one over the other, ontologically speaking? Now, it is not my purpose here to defend the existence of dinner parties and seating arrangements; this is only an example. However, the apparent analogy between the two charges of special pleading is, I think, only superficial.

According to this second way of thinking about structure, wholes are structures. In our example the dinner party is (an instance of) the structure in question, the seating arrangement. And this structure is no less essential to the parts of the whole than to the whole itself. Given this view, if we then ask what, if anything, is to be said about the situation once the party has broken up, we are faced with a different question from before. Where before, appeal to structure could be made to seem somewhat secondary, a matter of the property of the parts of the whole when taken together in one way, but not in others, here structure is built into the identity of both parts and whole. Thus, the question now is simply: *what* structures are there? In particular, is there a party-breaking-up structure, in addition to the dinner party structure whose existence has been assumed at least for the purposes of the example?

No doubt, the question of what structures there are needs an answer. One might approach it in rather the way in which, for example, Armstrong approaches the question of what properties there are.[7] The question becomes analogous to the question of

---

[7] Armstrong (1978, *passim*).

why one might think that there is a property of being aquamarine (whatever one thinks of the ontology of properties) whereas there is not a property of being neither blue nor green, nor of being my favourite colour. As in the case of properties, one possible answer is that one recognizes as structures only those structures that science discovers.[8] But however one answers this question, the question is now independent of that of the place of structure within an account of composition.

Of the two ways of thinking about structure that I have distinguished, the first, I have argued, is vulnerable to a charge of special pleading in a way the second is not. But the second way of thinking is not without problems of its own. If the parts of a structure are 'structure-laden' in the way described—if, that is, they get their identity only in the context of the structure of which they are part—then the parts will only exist for as long as the structure itself exists. This creates the need for an account of the relation between that which comes to be part of a structure and the part which it becomes. I shall not have much that is positive to say on this matter; but the problem should certainly be noted.[9]

One final point of clarification as regards this second way of thinking is also in order. I have associated this second way of thinking with the claim that wholes are structures. But there is an ambiguity in the reference of the term 'structure' that can be brought out by considering our example once again. In this example the candidate whole is the dinner party; thus, on this view, the dinner party is itself a structure. However, the term 'structure' may also be used to apply to the seating arrangement of the dinner party; indeed, I myself described this seating

---

[8] So, Armstrong (1978: ii. 8): 'What properties and relations there are in the world is to be decided by total science, that is, the sum total of all enquiries into the nature of things.'

[9] In this regard, it is also worth noting that a similar view is found in Aristotle; this despite his worry about the differential survival of parts and whole to which I earlier referred (§1.6, pp. 43–4 and §1.6 n. 81 and text there). Aristotle supposes that (at least) certain parts of, for example, an animal cease to be what they are, except in name, when the animal dies; thus, the hand of a corpse is only homonymously a hand (see e.g. *Parts of Animals* 640^{b}35–641^{a}6 and cf. *Metaphysics* 1035^{b}24–5). In the case of such parts, the parts cannot—at least not straightforwardly—survive the dissolution of the whole.

arrangement as an example of structure when first setting up the example. This ambiguity of reference is harmless, provided we are clear about the relation between these two referents of the term 'structure'. The dinner party is (an instance of) a structure; the seating arrangement is the structure of which it is an instance, abstractly conceived. In order to reflect this difference between the two referents of 'structure' and the relation between them, one might—and sometimes I will—talk of the structure *of* a structure or whole; and I will sometimes talk of the structure or whole that such structure is the structure of as being something structur*ed*. But one should not be misled by these ways of talking into neglecting the difference between the two alternative ways of thinking about structure that I have distinguished.

Both of the alternatives that I have considered seek to make structure essential to the constitution of a whole. However, they differ in the way in which they do so. In the second, and not in the first, structure is no less essential to the parts than to the whole. The first such approach is exemplified by Van Inwagen. Van Inwagen supposes that some things (some simples) compose something when, and only when, they are caught up in the activity of a life.[10] Thus, a certain kind of biological arrangement is here made essential to the constitution of a whole. But Van Inwagen does not also suppose that the parts of such a whole (the simples) cannot be identified independently of their involvement in a life.

In contrast, it is the second of these alternative approaches, according to which wholes are structures, whose parts are structure-laden in the way I have proposed, that will be most conducive to an understanding of Plato's views about structure and the role it plays in the constitution of a whole. To the extent that such parallels are possible, it is also the approach most consistent with Plato's own linguistic practice. Recall the positive, but incredibly abstract, account of a whole that we found in the third deduction of the *Parmenides* (in §3.2 above). A whole, it is said, is 'some single form' (μία τις ἰδέα, 157d8). What this implies, I suggested, is that a whole has a certain structural integrity. But

---

[10] Van Inwagen (1990, §9).

Parmenides does not say anything literally translatable as the claim that a whole *has* structure. If I am right to connect 'form' with structure, what Plato has Parmenides say is not so much that a whole *has* structure, as that it *is* a structure.

In what follows, I shall examine three different works in which, I shall argue, Plato may be seen to be presenting an account of composition and of structure which is in line with this approach on points of substance as well as of language. I begin with what can be extrapolated from the *Sophist*.

4.2 THE *SOPHIST*: A FIRST PLATONIC EXAMPLE OF STRUCTURE

Recall that the *Sophist* has made it the mark of expertise to know which of the elements of a given domain combine and which do not. An expert, the *Sophist* argues, must know the rules for combining the elements within the domain of their expertise. The *Sophist* provides four examples of such domains: the combination of letters or phonemes, of musical notes, of kinds, and, finally, the combination of words into a *logos* or statement.[11] I shall take my example from this latter domain.

The *Sophist* returns to a conception of *logos* that is found in the dream theory of the *Theaetetus*: that a *logos* is something 'woven together' out of its constituents (cf. *Tht.* 202b4–5). However, the context in which it does so is substantially different. Where the dream theorist had supposed that a *logos* was woven together simply of names (ὀνόματα), the *Sophist* makes it something woven together of a name (ὄνομα) and a verb (ῥῆμα). In doing so, it recognizes that there is a certain syntactic complexity to well-formed sentences, unlike mere strings of names. In this, I suggest, it reaps the benefit of the *Sophist*'s departure from the ontology of the final part of the *Theaetetus*, which refused to recognize complexity of any sort, allowing the *Sophist* to recognize that complexity

---

[11] *Logos* is a much broader term than 'statement'. The *Sophist* passage that will concern me is clearly focused on the constitution of meaningful statements, as the examples will show. However, in places the translation 'speech' or 'discourse' might be equally appropriate. In general, I shall leave the term untranslated.

is built into the nature of things, including the language we use to describe them. It is this ontological aspect that I shall be seeking to capture, rather than the account of language itself as such.[12]

The central passage with which I shall be concerned is *Sophist* 261d1–262e1. The passage begins and ends in a way that makes clear its connection with the dialogue's earlier discussions of combination. Thus the Stranger begins: 'Well, then, just as we investigated regarding kinds ($\epsilon\check{\iota}\delta\eta$) and letters ($\gamma\rho\acute{\alpha}\mu\mu\alpha\tau\alpha$), let us investigate in the same way in turn regarding names ($\grave{o}\nu\acute{o}\mu\alpha\tau\alpha$)' (261d1–2). The question to be investigated regarding names is: 'whether they all fit together with one another, or none do, or whether some will and some will not' (261d5–6; cf. 251d5–e1). The passage ends with the assertion that the combination of elements in language is just as restricted as is the combination of elements in other domains; only some combinations of terms make a *logos* (262d8–e1).

Within the context of the dialogue as a whole, our passage is part of the final push to capture the sophist.[13] In order to catch the sophist, it was necessary to show, contrary to Parmenides' dictum (triumphantly reprised at 258d2–3), that not being is. And the lengthy preceding discussion of the communion of kinds has indeed, the Stranger concludes, shown exactly this. But our sophist is a resourceful fellow—to Theaetetus' despair (see 261a4–b4). Even if he concedes that some of the kinds ($\epsilon\check{\iota}\delta\eta$) partake of not being, he may yet seek to deny that such unreality is a feature of language as well. The sophist may seek, that is, to keep the question of language entirely separate from that of ontology.

This is the explicit reason for their investigation into language that the Stranger gives the young and, no doubt, now somewhat tired Theaetetus when he expresses incomprehension at this new topic (260b4–5). Immediately beforehand, however, we

---

[12] The *Sophist*'s account of language has been well discussed elsewhere. See e.g. Ryle (1960) and Denyer (1991, ch. 9).

[13] The stages of the argument required to do so are carefully itemized at 260e3–261a3. Our passage contains the account of the nature of *logos* required to enable us to see its 'communion with not being' (e5–6) and thus to demonstrate the possibility of false *logos*, swiftly accomplished in 262e3–263d5. The compossibility of false thought ($\delta\iota\acute{\alpha}\nu\iota\alpha$), belief ($\delta\acute{o}\xi\alpha$), and appearance ($\phi\alpha\nu\tau\alpha\sigma\acute{\iota}\alpha$) is shown by tying the accounts of thought, belief, and appearance to this account of *logos* (263d6–264b4).

have rather been reminded of the deep roots the question about language has in our ongoing investigation into ontology. In particular, we have been reminded of our old friends the Late Learners. It must be they who are the target of the Stranger's savage condemnation in 259d9–e6:

ELEATIC STRANGER. Indeed, my friend, to try to separate off (ἀποχωρίζειν) everything from everything else is unreasonable (οὐκ ἐμμελές), being, amongst other things, the mark of a completely uncultivated (ἀμούσου) and unphilosophical person.
THEAETETUS. Why is that?
ES. To separate (διαλύειν) each thing from everything is the utter destruction of all *logoi*; for we come to have *logos* by reason of the kinds weaving together with each other (διὰ τὴν ἀλλήλων τῶν εἰδῶν συμπλοκήν).

The Stranger's language here is carefully chosen. Someone who seeks to separate everything from everything else is, literally translated, 'discordant' or 'out of tune' (οὐκ ἐμμελές) and hence 'unmusical' (ἄμουσος).[14] As we shall see, the structure endemic to music is a recurring example of the structure such a person is set to deny. And, in talking of 'separating' (διαλύειν), the Stranger uses a verb found in Herodotus in opposition to διαπλέκειν for the twin actions of twining and untwining.[15] Here, it contrasts with the cognate term συμπλοκή, or something 'woven together', anticipating the account of *logos* itself as something woven together of name and verb.

The Late Learners, we may recall, had a problem with language. They certainly denied the possibility of predication; they may also have denied the possibility of any linguistic complexity whatsoever. But this linguistic problem was a consequence of their position about being. It was they who denied that anything combines, and who, as such, were late inclusions in the dialogue's previous roll-call of all those who have ever taken any position about being.[16] Language itself, however, may be taken as an illustration

[14] 'Unmusical' is a literal translation of the word translated as 'uncultivated' in the passage quoted, as 'discordant' and 'out of tune' are possible literal translations of the phrase there translated as 'unreasonable'.
[15] Herodotus 4. 67; see LSJ, s.v. διαλύειν.
[16] See 251c8-d3 and discussion above, in §3.4.

of the point about being; indeed, the Stranger will take it to be one among the kinds of being (260a5–6). And the Late Learners' position about being will come back to haunt them, when applied to language itself. If *nothing* combines with anything else, then nor do the components of language. But then the Late Learners will simply refute themselves, when they attempt to state their position, as the Stranger reminds us (260a6–b2; cf. the explicit self-refutation of 252c2–9).

If we are to have any conversation about language at all, we must first have surmounted the problem about being. Just as the Late Learners' problem with language was a consequence of their position on being, so, conversely, the Stranger's ensuing investigation into language must build on the ontological progress he has made. As he says, in the passage quoted above, we have *logos* 'by reason of the kinds weaving together'. There is some question as to what precisely he means by this.[17] But the least that he means is that the possibility for combination among kinds in being is a precondition upon the possibility of language. And at least one reason why this is so, as the self-refutation of the Late Learners has shown, is that the combination of terms involved in the construction of language is itself one case of the kind of ontological combination whose possibility the Late Learners had denied, and which the discussion of the combination of kinds was to rescue. It is as such that I shall exploit it in seeking to extrapolate from the discussion of language a first Platonic example of structure.

What follows is nowhere explicit in the ontology of the *Sophist* itself. But it is, I suggest, an ontological corollary of some of the key developments of the *Sophist*.

---

[17] Denyer (1991: 160–4) proposes that the components of *logoi*—names and verbs—should themselves be taken to be kinds. At 260d6–8 the Stranger does talk as if *logos* in general—where it seems most natural to take him to mean speech or discourse as a whole—might be a kind, or at least he puts such a suggestion into the mouth of the sophist. However, Denyer's proposal for the components of *logoi* does not sit well with passages, such as 261d1–2, in which combination between the components of *logoi* is listed as an arena for combination distinct from the combination of kinds. Regarding the components of *logoi*, then, it seems better to suppose that their combination—like the combination of kinds—is one example of the ontological combination whose possibility the Late Learners denied.

Syntactic Space

The question before us, then, is whether all terms in language fit together (συναρμόττειν), whether none do, or whether some do and some do not. Schooled by the preceding discussions of the combination of letters, notes, and kinds, Theaetetus correctly infers that some terms will fit together and some will not. But the fact that Theaetetus has learnt a general rule, and here applies it, does not yet show that he genuinely understands the point being made, as soon becomes clear. Consider his response to the Stranger's paraphrase of the answer he has given.

ELEATIC STRANGER. Perhaps you mean this: that some, being said in sequence (ἐφεξῆς) and indicating something (δηλοῦντά τι), fit together, whereas some, which indicate nothing through being continuous (τῇ συνεχείᾳ μηδὲν σημαίνοντα), do not fit together.
THEAETETUS. What do you mean?
ES. Precisely what I thought you were supposing when you agreed. (261d8–e4)

In considering the combination of terms in language, we are not just considering what sequence of words can, as a matter of fact, come out of your mouth, but what forms a *logos*, something meaningful. The notion of 'fitting together', as described by the Stranger, has two aspects: (i) a syntactic aspect—that of sequence; and (ii) a semantic aspect—that of meaning. Meaning will here be made dependent upon syntax.[18] Only syntactically well-formed sentences are meaningful; simply stringing together a series of terms one after the other will not do. Thus the notion of 'fitting together', as described by the Stranger, is itself already a syntactic notion and cannot be understood independently of the syntactic distinctions he is soon to make. But this was not what Theaetetus

---

[18] Too much so perhaps, for one might think that one could have a syntactically well-formed sentence that fails to mean anything. In this case, syntactic criteria will simply be necessary, but not also sufficient, for meaning. The passage appears to run the two together. The Stranger does succeed, however, in distinguishing meaning from truth. The sentences 'Theaetetus sits' and 'Theaetetus flies' are both meaningful, because they are well-formed and about something, namely Theaetetus (see 262e5–6 for the importance of the latter). But the second is false, because it says things 'other than the things that are' about him (263b7).

had had in view. In tracking the initial discrepancies between the Stranger's and Theaetetus' understandings of what has been said,[19] the dialogue reinforces the fact that the fitting together of the elements of language is explained only in and through the account of the syntactic criteria for well-formed sentences. Each application of the general rule about restricted combination is context-specific. One understands the combination of the elements of a specific domain only by understanding the structure of that domain. For the discussion of language, this requires that Theaetetus be given a short lesson in syntax.

Central to this lesson is the syntactic distinction between name (ὄνομα) and verb (ῥῆμα). There are, the Stranger says, two kinds of 'vocal indicators' (τὰ τῇ φωνῇ δηλώματα, 261e5–6): names and verbs. Verbs indicate actions;[20] names the things that perform actions. A string of verbs—such as 'walks runs sleeps'— does not constitute a *logos*, and nor does a string of names—such as 'lion deer horse'. Rather, a name and a verb must be woven together to constitute a sentence. Thus 'man learns' is the Stranger's example of the first and most basic of sentences. Note that word order is not the point here: first 'man', then 'learns'. Such word order is a feature of English sentence construction; in Greek, however, the translation of 'man learns' could be written as either μανθάνει ἄνθρωπος or ἄνθρωπος μανθάνει, that is, with the name and verb in either order. The Stranger's point is rather to distinguish the naming function of nouns and the saying function of verbs.[21] A noun indicates the person or thing of which something is asserted. A verb gives the sentence its assertoric force. Only when name and verb are woven together do we have a unitary sentence that says something—or 'accomplishes something', as the Stranger puts it (262d4). A list of names or verbs, or a single name or verb, have no assertoric force.[22]

---

[19] Cf. also 262b1–3.

[20] 'Action' must have a fairly broad construal here, as shown by the list in 262c2–5.

[21] So, Ryle (1960, esp. 442–3 and 448–9), to whose discussion of this passage I am indebted.

[22] No doubt, this is all far too simple. In Greek, for example, the naming function of nouns can be dealt with by the endings of verbs. And not all nouns are names. Further, one could, as Denyer does, devise notations in which lists of names, or even a single name, are in fact able to express truths or falsehoods, by assigning the saying

How, ontologically speaking, might we understand the composition of such a sentence? Drawing on Plato's syntactic intuitions, let me offer the idea of a 'syntactic space' as a first Platonic example of structure. A syntactic space should be thought of as having 'slots' for a name and a verb that define the function of name and verb; they are, as it were, name-shaped and verb-shaped respectively. In the sentence we have been considering, these slots are occupied by 'man' and 'learns' respectively. The syntactic space is the structure of a well-formed sentence such as 'man learns', abstractly conceived.

Central to Plato's syntactic intuition is the thought that names and verbs are not, as such, separable; they are separable only in the sense that a name could occur with other verbs or a verb with other names. Ryle saw in this a foreshadowing of Frege's characterization of verbs, or predicative expressions generally, as being 'incomplete' or 'unsaturated'. In Ryle's paraphrase, a verb 'flourishes gaps or lacunae around it, namely lacunae for such other expressions as would, with it, constitute an integral statement'.[23] The comparison with Frege is useful, but it is not clear that there is quite the community of interests between Plato and Frege that Ryle suggests. In particular, the lacunose character that Frege attributed to verbs or predicates is here applied to names as well. At least, the passage gives no indication that verbs are somehow special in this respect. This broader characterization might be expressed algebraically by saying that the components of the sentence 'fa' are '$f(\ )$' and '$(\ )a$' respectively (reading '$(\ )$' to indicate a gap, and taking nouns, like verbs, to be unsaturated expressions). Neither 'f' nor 'a' can be taken in isolation. Ontologically speaking, one might express this inseparability of name and verb by saying that the distinction between name and verb is already premised on the existence of a syntactic space. 'Man' and 'learns'

function to the order in which the names are written or the typeface in which they are printed. See Denyer (1991: 152–6). But such complications do not substantially affect the point at issue. Such sentences are themselves complex unities in the relevant sense, involving two distinct syntactic functions, the two that the Stranger here assigns respectively to names and verbs. Nor do I think Plato can be unaware of the oversimplification this involves, since the passage itself is littered with (meaningful) sentences that do not follow the simple model.

23 Ryle (1960: 448).

are woven together when each 'slots into' its respective role as marked out in syntactic space, and a complex unity, the sentence 'man learns', comes to be.

How should we think about such syntactic structure? First, syntactic structure of this sort is clearly something abstract, in the sense that it can be considered independently of its components, here 'man' and 'learns'. It can be considered independently of its components, not because it is itself a further component. Rather, it is independent of its components in the sense that it could be occupied by a different name and/or verb. As such, a syntactic space—as, indeed, its components also—will be something repeatable. The sentences 'man learns' and 'millipedes crawl' are instances of the same syntactic type. In these respects a syntactic space is comparable to the seating arrangement of the dinner party in my earlier example (§4.1 above).

Next, then, recall the two alternative ways of thinking about structure, discussed above (§4.1). According to the first, structure is something a whole has. Such structure is applied to components already given. As such, the parts of a whole may be identified independently of the structure of the whole they compose. According to the second way of thinking, wholes are structures. Here, structure is no less essential to the parts of a whole than to the whole itself. Parts get their identity only in the context of the structure of which they are part.

Which of these alternatives best represents the syntactic case, in the light of the *Sophist*'s discussion? The second, I argue. The passage clearly suggests that the components of language are themselves 'structure-laden', as I have put it. Names and verbs, because of the unsaturatedness of such expressions, are themselves syntactic entities. The description of name and verb as *fitting together* is a syntactic description. Hence, Theaetetus could have no genuine understanding of the combination of elements in language until he had a grip on the syntactic criteria for well-formed sentences. Structure, one might say, is an irreducible feature of sentences. Sentences are (instances of) syntactic structures.

Structure and Science

Within the *Sophist* the irreducibility of structure is reflected in Plato's account of science or expertise. The proper object of science is not individual letters, names, or verbs; it is not the elements of a compound as such. It is rather the ways in which the elements of a given domain do and do not combine. And to study the ways in which, for example, names and verbs combine, is to study the topography of syntactic space. Of course, the Stranger's lesson in syntax falls far short of conveying such expertise. He has considered only what he describes as the 'first and least' of sentences (262c6–7). But he has illustrated a fundamental aspect of syntactic structure. And, just as, in the *Theaetetus*, the epistemology—in the account of learning and expertise—was a corollary of the dialogue's problematic ontology, so the new epistemology of the *Sophist* is a sign of the change in the underlying ontology.

Consider, for comparison, the account of structure and of the science of structure to be found in the work of modern mathematical structuralists. Mathematical structuralism is the view that mathematical objects—such as numbers, or even sets—are positions in patterns or structures.[24] Resnik defines a structure—or, in his preferred usage, a pattern—as follows: 'a pattern is a complex entity consisting of one or more objects, which I call *positions*, standing in various relationships (and having various characteristics, distinguished positions and operations)'.[25] Notice that, in Resnik's characterization, the complex entity *is* the structure; structure is not something that the objects involved *have*. Indeed, the objects—or positions—of the structure are identified in terms of the structure. So, Resnik again: 'A position is like a geometrical point in that it has no distinguishing

---

[24] See e.g. Resnik (1975, 1981, 1982, 1988); and Shapiro (1983, 1989). It is not my intention to enter into the debate as to the merits or demerits of this position as a philosophy of mathematics; I have no expertise in this area. My intention is rather to make use of the various insights provided by these authors into the nature of structure, independently of the question of the role structure may play in mathematical ontology.

[25] Resnik (1981: 532).

features other than those it has in virtue of being *that* position in the pattern to which it belongs.'[26] The positions of such structures are, as I have put it, 'structure-laden'.[27]

Interestingly, from the point of view of comparison with Plato, in the work of mathematical structuralists both linguistic and musical structure are frequent illustrative examples of the notion of structure involved. And Plato's own notion of structure will turn out to have closer connections with mathematics than has thus far been clear. For now, however, consider the way in which Resnik attempts to characterize an epistemology for mathematics to correspond to his structuralist view: 'Characterizing a pattern consists in describing it in abstraction from its instances and in isolation from its connections with other patterns. Given this, to characterize a pattern is to say that it has such and such positions which stand in such and such relationships to each other.'[28] Since the identity of the objects of the patterns is determined by their relation to other objects or positions in the patterns to which they belong, the mathematician first describes the pattern, and it is in terms of this pattern that individual mathematical objects are studied.

Now consider the epistemology of the *Sophist* once again. Names and verbs may be considered as positions in syntactic space. According to the *Sophist*, the proper object of the expert or scientist is to study the ways in which names and verbs—the relevant positions—do and do not combine, i.e. to study the relationships in which they stand to one another. What I have described as studying the topography of syntactic space corresponds well to the way in which Resnik characterizes the mathematical study of patterns. In the *Sophist*—as, in mathematics, for Resnik—structure is the proper object of science, and it is so

---

[26] Resnik (1981: 532).

[27] Talk of geometrical points might seem to spoil this analogy, since points have no internal complexity whatsoever. Indeed, elsewhere Resnik describes individual mathematical objects as 'structureless entities which occur in structures' (1982: 95). However, in describing such objects as 'structure-laden', I do not mean to refer to any internal complexity they may or may not have, but rather to highlight the fact that their identity is determined only in the context of the structure; they are those objects that the structure determines, and hence are structure-laden.

[28] Resnik (1988: 408).

because structure has now been made a basic and irreducible item in its ontology.

Of course, this first Platonic example of structure is something I have extrapolated, rather than simply extracted, from the text of the *Sophist*. For more explicit, but also more complex, Platonic examples of structure, I turn now to two dialogues which, in their different ways, each gives structure a central place in their metaphysics: the *Philebus* and *Timaeus*. Both dialogues are difficult, and I shall not attempt to provide a comprehensive interpretation of either dialogue. I begin—without prejudice to any question about their relative dating—with the *Philebus*.

4.3 THE *PHILEBUS*: STRUCTURE AND CONTENT

There are two aspects to the analysis of wholes conceived as structures in the way I have described. First, structure: in the Platonic example I extrapolated above, the structure of a well-formed sentence, abstractly conceived; what I have called a syntactic space.[29] Second, each such whole—structure—must have some *content*: the content of a syntactic space is the (syntactic) entities that occupy positions within it, terms such as 'man' and 'learns'. Content is tied to structure, as I have said: thus, the components of a well-formed sentence are 'structure-laden'; 'man' and 'learns' are themselves syntactic entities. No less so, structure is tied to content. This relation between structure and content is implicit in the description of the structure of a well-formed sentence as '*syntactic* structure'. If the domain of content in question were different—if, for example, we were instead to consider the composition of phonemes into syllables, or musical notes into tunes—the nature of the structure in question would be different also. It was for this reason that Theaetetus' ability to

---

[29] Recall that, even on the view that wholes are structures—the view that, I argue, Plato endorses—one can talk of the structure *of* a structure or whole, and of the whole that such structure is the structure of as being structured, on which see §4.1. However, this should not be taken to imply that structure is either a part or a detachable property of the whole in question.

apply the general rule—that some elements combine and some do not—to the components of language did not, in itself, make him an expert on language. Structure and content are not separable, in the sense of being separate components to be fitted together in the way in which one might fit together the pieces of a jigsaw. But they are, in analysis, distinct—if interconnected—aspects of the constitution of a whole. Wholes, we might say, are *contentful* structures.

A twofold analysis of precisely this sort is, I shall argue, at the centre of the *Philebus*' metaphysics. The passages that are central to the presentation of this ontology are the two passages that discuss the constitution of things in terms of limit and unlimited (16c5 ff. and 23c4 ff.). The interpretation of both passages is vexed, as is the question of the relation between them.[30] I shall begin with the second passage and work backwards.

Limit and Unlimited in the Analysis of Mixtures

Central to the ontology of the *Philebus* is an account of the metaphysical ingredients of composites—or mixtures, as they will here be called. The *Sophist* has made us familiar with use of the language of mixing (σύμμειξις) and blending (κοινωνία)—both of which return here—in talk of the composition of structured wholes. In the *Philebus* the context of both of the passages concerned with limit and unlimited confirms that we have reason to expect once again to be concerned with the constitution of complex wholes.

The *Philebus* opens in the midst of an ongoing dispute as to the competing claims of pleasure and intelligence to be the good. At the start of the dialogue it is agreed that Protarchus will defend the claim of pleasure, on behalf of Philebus, the recalcitrant figure from whom he takes the argument over. Socrates, in turn, will defend the claim of intelligence. But the conversation is quickly diverted—or so it seems—into a general discussion of one and many, followed by a lengthy discourse on method, the

---

[30] See e.g. the various discussions of D. Frede (1993) and, at considerably greater length, (1997); Gosling (1975); McCabe (1994, ch. 8, §§6–9); Meinwald (1996, 1998); Sayre (1983); Striker (1970).

first of the passages framed in terms of limit and unlimited. The discussion of one and many is inaugurated by Protarchus' initial denial and subsequent grudging acceptance that pleasure—and, Socrates concedes, also intelligence—has some internal complexity. Like shape and colour, in Socrates' examples, pleasure, though one in kind (γένει . . . ἕν, 12e7), may yet have different parts (μέρη, 12e7), and thus pleasures—and intelligences—may differ from one another in any number of ways. Here, then, is our first indication that we shall have reason to be interested in the constitution of complex wholes.

The principle (λόγος) to which Protarchus has thereby agreed, Socrates claims, is naturally such as to amaze (14c7–8): 'For that the many are one or the one many are amazing statements, and it is easy to dispute with one who posits either of them' (14c8–10). Such amazement at the suggestion that one thing is many or many things one may put us in mind of the Late Learners; in the *Sophist* this was precisely what they denied could be so (*Sph.* 251b5–c6). And we may note that Socrates will shortly suggest that it is an inevitable result of language (λόγοι) that the same thing becomes both one and many (15d4–8), where language is precisely the thing with which the Late Learners had such difficulty.[31] More strikingly still, however, disputes about many being one or one being many may remind us of the Eleatic-inspired puzzles of the *Parmenides*. So they do Protarchus, it would appear, since he immediately offers one version of the Zenonian worry about ones being many: that one thing—himself—might also be many in virtue of having many opposing properties (14c11–d3). Socrates himself offers its twin—just as he had in the *Parmenides*: that one person might also be many in virtue of having many limbs and parts (14d8–e4; cf. *Prm.* 129c4–d2).

While Socrates denies that these are the kinds of puzzle that concern him here, it is not, we may note, the form of the puzzle he objects to, but, first and foremost, its object in the two examples

---

[31] In the *Sophist* the 'feast' of puzzles that this provides is one for both young and old (251b5–6), although it is the old—the Late Learners—who are given top billing. In the *Philebus*, by contrast, Socrates concentrates on its effect on the young (15d8–16a3), much to Protarchus' chagrin.

before us: they involve the kind of one that comes to be and per-
ishes (15a1–2). Second, the kind of puzzle Protarchus has illustrated is, Socrates says, 'familiar'. Most literally, the term he
uses—δεδημευμένα—describes this kind of puzzle as one that has
been 'made public'. This can carry connotations of its being
somehow vulgar or hackneyed; so, Frede translates the term by
'commonplace'.[32] But it can also mean 'published', and so, of
course, it has been, in the *Parmenides* itself.[33]

Why spend so much time reminding us of a puzzle, only to tell
us that this is not quite what he has in mind to discuss? Perhaps
it is because the puzzles, as they were presented at the start of the
Parmenides, and as they are here recalled, are just that: puzzles.
The puzzle gets to the problematic identification of one with
many and then stops, with its apparent paradox complete. Both
the *Parmenides* and *Sophist* had taken such puzzles seriously—
despite Socrates' claim that they are considered 'childish and
easy'; here too, they are 'an excessive impediment to arguments
[or: statements, λόγοι]' (14d7–8). But both the *Parmenides* and
Sophist had also progressed some way beyond such puzzles to the
more serious challenge that they provoke: the attempt to give an
account of the constitution of complex unities that allows for a
non-paradoxical sense in which many can be united into one and
one made up of many. It is, of course, just such an understanding
of complex unities that the *Philebus* now appears to require, in
light of Socrates' and Protarchus' agreement about the internal
complexity of pleasure and intelligence.

The question of how these one–many problems prepare us for
the introduction of the method that follows is a complex issue that
I shall not attempt to unravel here.[34] But the complex allusion to

---

[32] D. Frede (1993, trans. ad loc.).   [33] See LSJ, s.v. δημεύω II.

[34] Since Socrates' objection to the puzzles that he and Protarchus have offered is
not to their form, but to their application to particulars, we at least have reason to
expect the puzzle about composition as applied to imperishable 'ones' (see 15a1–2) to
be of some importance in what follows. It is then an open question what becomes of
the puzzle as applied to particulars if and when a solution is found for its application
to imperishables; whether, for example, the resolution of the puzzle at this level carries implications for one's response even to the 'childish' version of the puzzle. Of the
abundant literature on the one–many problems of the *Philebus*, Meinwald's interpretation of the passage as a whole (see Meinwald 1996; and cf. also her 1998) also

the *Parmenides* does suggest at least one task for the ontology ahead: to continue the progress made in the *Parmenides* and *Sophist* on giving an account of the constitution of the kind of complex unities that both pleasure and intelligence have turned out to be.

Next, then, consider the context of Socrates' later fourfold classification of beings, the second passage framed in terms of limit and unlimited. It is inaugurated by Socrates' recollection of a dream, which seems, at least initially, to have taken the course of the dialogue off on a different track once again. Socrates' dream provides him with a swift argument to the effect that neither a life of pleasure alone, nor of intelligence alone, but a life mixed of both, must be the good life (20b6–22e3). In light of this argument, the contest between pleasure and intelligence with which the dialogue opened becomes a contest for second, rather than first, prize; first prize goes to the good mixed life. It is agreed that second prize will go to whichever of pleasure and intelligence is responsible ($a\H{i}\tau\iota o\varsigma$) for the good of the mixed life (22c6–23a5).[35]

Despite appearances, however, the analysis of the complexity of pleasure and intelligence required by the context of the earlier passage turns out not to have been abandoned at all; it has simply been postponed. The contest for second prize clearly demands a detailed understanding of the ingredients of the mixed life, provided by the lengthy analysis of pleasure and intelligence in 31b2–59d9. First and foremost, however, what is required by the new appraisal of the dialogue's contest is an understanding of the constitution of mixtures, both in general and of the winning mixture—the good life—in particular. It is Socrates' fourfold classification that provides this general understanding. By the time we

places special weight on the part–whole puzzle, although I find her subsequent attempt to identify this as one of the questions directly asked in 15b1–8 ultimately unpersuasive. The interpretation of the vexed passage at 15b1–8 is one of the most troublesome issues for the understanding of the sequence of this passage as a whole; I here avoid attempting to decide the number and nature of the questions there posed. For discussion, see, among others, the works cited in n. 30 above.

[35] 'Responsible' or 'culpable' are core meanings of $a\H{i}\tau\iota o\varsigma$. For discussion of the significance of this, when reflecting on ancient discussions of causation, see M. Frede (1980).

reach this second passage, the identity of the specific composite that will ultimately be in question has become considerably more complex than before; the complex entities with which we began, pleasure and intelligence, are now among the ingredients of this whole. But the general interest in the constitution of complex wholes has, if anything, only been reinforced. We will do well to remember that this is its context in our attempt to understand the fourfold classification that Socrates presents.

Two features of Socrates' account of limit and unlimited seem to me crucial for its interpretation. First is the fact that the conjunction of limit and unlimited constitutes a mixture, a member of the third kind or class. This is something that Socrates simply builds into his initial presentation of the three kinds—unlimited, limit, and the mixture of them both. And it is a feature of the relation between the three kinds of which the dialogue repeatedly reminds us. So, Socrates' initial invitation to divide 'all the things that now are in the universe' into two—unlimited and limit—is immediately turned into a threefold division—unlimited, limit, and the mixture of the two (23c4–5). It is as if, as soon as one has the kinds limit and unlimited in view, one has also their combination. And this third kind—the mixed class—is introduced simply as 'some one thing mixed together of both of these', i.e. limit and unlimited (23d1).

The course of the discussion itself suggests that we do not have an adequate understanding of either unlimited or limit until we have understood the way in which they combine to form mixtures of the third kind. In particular, we do not even attempt to gather the kind of limit into one and give it a unitary description until we are ready to consider it in the context of the mixtures to which it contributes (25d5–9).[36] For this reason it will be important in our interpretation of both limit and unlimited to keep, as it were, thinking back from the mixtures they compose.

The second important feature of Socrates' characterization of limit and unlimited is the fact that both, in different ways, are characterized in relational terms. Consider, first, Socrates' introduction to the members of the unlimited kind:

[36] Cf. here D. Frede (1997: 191–3), who rightly emphasizes this point.

SOCRATES. Consider, first, whether you could ever conceive of any limit regarding hotter and colder, or is it that the more and less reside in these kinds, and, for so long as they (jointly) inhabit ($\dot{\epsilon}\nu o\iota\kappa\hat{\eta}\tau o\nu$) them, they (jointly) do not permit ($\dot{\epsilon}\pi\iota\tau\rho\epsilon\psi\alpha\dot{\iota}\tau\eta\nu$) any end ($\tau\dot{\epsilon}\lambda o\varsigma$) to come to be; for if an end has occurred these two ($\alpha\dot{\nu}\tau\dot{\omega}$) have been ended also.

PROTARCHUS. You're absolutely right.

SOC. But, we say, the more and less are always present in hotter and colder.

PROT. Certainly.

SOC. Then the argument indicates to us that these two ($\tau o\dot{\nu}\tau\omega$) always have no end, and, being both without end ($\dot{\alpha}\tau\epsilon\lambda\hat{\eta}$), they both become absolutely without limit ($\dot{\alpha}\pi\epsilon\dot{\iota}\rho\omega$). (24a6–b8)

Notice that both members of the unlimited class and characteristics of these members come in pairs: 'hotter *and* colder'; 'the more *and* less'—and not, note, 'the more and the less'.[37] (See also the list of paired members of the unlimited class at 25c8–11.) Notice, too, the preponderance of duals in this passage, that means by which, in Greek, one can indicate that one is referring jointly to a pair and to the activity or characteristics of a pair, an effect that I have tried to preserve in my translation. The fact that members of the unlimited class come in pairs suggests that we should be thinking of their characteristics in terms of relations between two items.

The relational character of the unlimited might be thought simply to fall out of the use of comparatives as examples: hotter and colder are always hotter or colder than something. However, as others have noted,[38] this will not account for all the examples that Socrates gives during the course of the passage. These include non-comparative terms—such as 'high and low', 'quick

---

[37] The lack of a second definite article in the phrase $\tau\dot{o}$ $\mu\hat{\alpha}\lambda\lambda\dot{o}\nu$ $\tau\epsilon$ $\kappa\alpha\dot{\iota}$ $\hat{\eta}\tau\tau o\nu$ indicates that we should take 'more and less' conjointly, not severally. As D. Frede (1997: 189) points out, this use of a shared article applies only to Socrates' references to this characteristic of members of the unlimited and not to his list of paired members, to which separate articles are given. But this does not detract from the fact that the members of the unlimited are, throughout the passage, listed in pairs. It may simply indicate a further feature of this characteristic of the pairs, that the terms 'more' and 'less' are inextricably intertwined in their application to pairs of this sort: e.g. if x is more hot than y, y is less hot than x.

[38] e.g. D. Frede (1997: 187).

and slow' (26a2)—although these terms still have a relational component. But they also include 'frosts and heatwaves' (26a6), terms that have no such intrinsically relational character. By contrast, my suggestion is that the relational character of the unlimited is rather a function of the fact that its members are given, throughout the passage, as opposing *pairs*. It is not so much that the paired terms are themselves relational terms, as that, by putting them in pairs, they are related to each other; to anticipate, they are related to each other as marking out a domain of content on which limit may be imposed.[39] Recall, again, that we should keep in mind that both unlimited and limit are here introduced by way of an analysis of the constitution of members of the third kind, their mixture.

A second aspect of Socrates' introduction to the unlimited kind is worthy of note: the connection that Socrates establishes between having no end (τέλος) and having no limit (πέρας). What we have here is, in effect, a little argument built around the connection between these two terms. Any pair jointly inhabited by the pair more and less are thereby prevented by the joint operation of more and less from having an end. Conversely, where an end occurs, so the occupation by this pair—more and less—is destroyed. Since, then, it is agreed that the pair more and less always inhabit the pair hotter and colder, we may infer that this pair have no end. And, from the fact that they have no end, Socrates infers that they are absolutely without limit.

The term 'end' (τέλος) has a number of senses. It can mean the cessation of something: the end of a battle or of a life. But it can also mean that which constitutes the completion of something: its result or product. Somewhat later Socrates will characterize pleasure—in so far as it is (generically) unlimited—as 'belonging to the kind that in and of itself neither has nor will have either beginning, middle, or end' (31a8–10). Having a 'beginning, middle, and end' has been a standard description of a whole, in both the *Parmenides* and *Sophist*.[40] Conversely, the association which

---

[39] Perhaps Socrates chooses comparatives as examples at first, so that Protarchus may more easily understand the point about 'more and less' in the absence of the full account of all three kinds: unlimited, limit, and their mixture.

[40] See e.g. *Prm.* 137d4–5, 145a5–7; *Sph.* 244e6.

Socrates forges between being without end and being without limit, and the characterization of the unlimited as what has neither beginning, middle, nor end, may be taken to indicate that the members of the unlimited are paired constituents that, in and of themselves, do not constitute a whole. I suggest, however, that they do constitute the domain in which determinate wholes can be wrought, but only by the imposition of limit.

Next, then, consider the way in which Socrates introduces the class of limit. As is to be expected, if, as I have suggested, we are encouraged always to think of both unlimited and limit in terms of the role they play together in the constitution of mixtures, members of the class of limit are introduced by directly relating and contrasting them to the members of the unlimited class: 'Then things which do not admit these [i.e. more and less and their kin], but admit all the opposites of these—first, equal and equality; after equal, double and every ratio of number to number or measure to measure—we would seem to do well in reckoning all of these in the class of limit' (25a6–b3).[41]

Here, quite clearly, we are dealing with relational items: equal and double are equal to and double of something; ratios of number to number and measure to measure are explicitly relational. There is an air of deliberate sequence about Socrates' list here: *first* equal, *after equal* double. I suggest that both the appearance of sequence and the relational character of the members of the sequence can best be captured by supposing that, by 'equal' and 'double', Socrates refers, respectively, to the two first whole-numbered ratios: equal is the ratio of 1:1; double the ratio of 2:1. Thereafter, Socrates simply generalizes from this.[42]

If we now put members of the unlimited and limit class side by side, what we have, it seems, is this: (i) a domain of pairs of characteristics[43]—the unlimited—in which the more and less

---

[41] As D. Frede notes (1997: 190–1), Socrates' description does not in fact make clear whether equal, double, etc. are members of the class of limit or simply characteristics thereof. I follow Frede in supposing them to be its members.

[42] Contrast Sayre (1987: 56).

[43] And/or things characterized. While the majority of Socrates' examples seem to be characteristics, some—frosts and heatwaves—might be better thought of as things characterized. It is not clear to me that we need favour one of these options to the exclusion of the other in the interpretation of this passage.

constantly reside; which, in and of themselves, have no deter-
minate quantity ($\pi \acute{o} \sigma o \nu$)[44] (for this, see 24b10–c6); and which, in
and of themselves, do not constitute a whole; and, on the other
hand, (ii) a domain of numerical ratios—1:1, 2:1, etc. In conjunction, these are to create the members of the third kind, mixtures of unlimited and limit.

Let us now see if we can begin to make some sense of all of this
by means of an example. Suppose I am running a bath and turn
on the hot and cold taps. Ignore, for the moment, any bath that
may result. If we are to understand the nature of the unlimited,
we must think of it as something that, together with limit, will
constitute a mixture of the third kind, but that, in the absence of
limit, must be considered in abstraction from any mixture it may
compose. For the present, then, think only of the two streams of
running water, one hot, one cold.

The water from the hot tap is hotter than the water from the
cold tap; conversely, the water from the cold tap is colder than the
water from the hot tap. By picking opposing pairs—hot and cold,
hotter and colder—this will always be the case. Not only that:
since hot and cold fall at different ends of a single spectrum,[45]
that of temperature, each paired constituent will always be related to each other by certain opposing pairs of relations. The water
from the hot tap will always be both more hot and less cold than
the water from the cold tap, while the water from the cold tap will
always be both more cold and less hot than the water from the hot
tap (cf. 24c3–6). If this were not the case one would not have the
pair—hot and cold water—at all; one would simply have water of
a uniform temperature of some degree or other.

There are, of course, any number of amounts by which the hot
water may be hotter than the cold water and, conversely, the cold
colder than the hot—1 degree hotter and colder, 2 degrees hotter

[44] The fact that members of the unlimited have no determinate quantity may also
relate to their lack of completeness or wholeness. Cf. the association between wholeness and quantity in *Sophist* 245d8–10 and my discussion of this passage above, in
§2.5.

[45] Note, however, that one need not thus identify the members of the unlimited
with such spectra or continua. For a defence of a continuum interpretation, see
Gosling (1975: 196–206); for objections to such an interpretation, see D. Frede
(1997: 187–8).

and colder, etc., and this is sticking with whole-number differences. But the two streams of water are still hotter and colder than each other all the same. For so long as I am simply running water—and not thinking about the kind of bath I would like to result—it is to all intents and purposes irrelevant which of the indefinite number of ways in which they might differ in temperature I have produced. Following Frede, I take this to be the sense in which the unlimited pairs 'always likewise advance and do not remain' (24d4–5).[46] The hot and cold waters will be just as much more and less hot (or cold) than one another and in just the same way no matter what points on the temperature scale mark the difference between them. Thus, as a pair, hot and cold cannot be tied to any specific fixed degree of difference between them.

The characterization of members of the unlimited in terms that suggest that they are somehow in process may also be a function of the fact that we are here considering the ingredients—the hot and cold water—that will go to make up a mixture—a bath—but that, in the absence of limit, cannot do so yet. Just as there is an indefinite number of amounts by which the hot and cold water might be hotter and colder than one another, so there is an equally indefinite number of combinations of hot and cold water I could thereby produce. I could not begin to list them all, no matter how fine-grained my system of measurement might be. However, the vast majority of these hot and cold water combinations will either be too hot to get into or too cold to want to soak in for long. In the end, the water I am running is supposed to produce a bath; but again, if all I have is hot and cold water, and no thought for the particular combination I wish to result, I shall not have a bath as yet.

Now, therefore, think about the production of the perfect bath.[47] I still need hot and cold water. But not any old combination will do. Upon the indefinite range of variations of hot and cold streams of water I must impose some determinate quantity,

---

[46] D. Frede (1997: 188–9). Unlike Frede, however, I take it to be important to think of the unlimited as involving *paired* ingredients.

[47] There are some strongly normative assumptions at work here; more on this below.

a quantity determined not by any intrinsic feature of the hot and cold waters themselves, but by the nature of the product I wish to result. What I need is so many parts of hot water to so many parts cold. Notice that this, too, is relational: a ratio of hot parts to cold parts. It is not that I need such and such an amount of hot water and such and such an amount of cold. After all, a perfect bath can be more or less deep. This ratio is something I impose on the hot and cold waters with which I run my bath from without. What it creates, in combination with the hot and cold waters, is water in a determinate ratio of hot and cold, a bath.[48]

Notice that one cannot have more or less of the ratio x parts hot to y parts cold—not in the same dimension of measurement, at least; one could, of course, have a greater or lesser volume of water in just this ratio. Hence, members of the class of limit do not admit these characteristic features of the unlimited, being 'more and less'. It is in this sense that the imposition of a limit 'puts a stop' to the continual advancement of the more and the less (24d5). It is not that the hot water that goes into my bath is no longer hotter than the cold or the cold colder than the hot. However, in so far as these are features of the water in my bath, their mutual relations are fixed by the ratio of hot to cold required to produce the perfect bath, and remain so, for so long as they constitute a bath. And they are relations of fit, rather than of contrast: just the amount of hot to go with just this amount of cold; just the amount of cold to go with just this amount of hot. So, the class of limit contains those things that 'stop opposites differing from one another and, by introducing number, make them commensurate (σύμμετρα) and harmonious (σύμφωνα)' (25d11–e1). Notice again the relational terms. In the context of the mixture they compose, the opposing pairs are made *com*mensurate and harmonious, or in *con*cord, in terms of their relation to each other.

----

[48] One might ask: why do I need both hot and cold water at all? Why not simply run one of the taps and keep the water at a steady temperature, the ideal? My example, of course, is chosen to reflect features of Socrates' account, in which limit is imposed upon paired unlimited components. However, I take it that the objection would, in any case, simply push the analysis one stage back. All that it would do is put the perfect bathwater—in the perfect ratio of hot to cold—inside the tap.

Limit and unlimited are jointly necessary for the constitution of a whole. The imposition of limit may destroy the characteristic features of the unlimited, but that does not mean that the unlimited, as such, is not present in the whole. I will not have a *bath*, as such, to get into, until I have hot and cold waters in the requisite ratio. But I cannot bathe in a ratio. Just as earlier I said, of structure, that it must always have some content or other, so, here, there must be something on which measure is imposed. What the measures are imposed upon—and what measures are imposed—is determined only in light of the mixture they compose. So, members of the class of unlimited and members of the class of limit may be fully identified, as I have said, only by thinking back from the mixtures they compose.[49] But, by giving separate treatment to unlimited and limit, Socrates provides a twofold analysis of the nature of mixtures. Limit captures structure; unlimited the content in which such structure is found; and the mixtures themselves are contentful structures.

Limit and unlimited are the twin ingredients in the *analysis* of mixtures. But that is not because members of each of these kinds are both parts of any mixture. Rather, it is members of the unlimited that are parts, but here conceived in the absence of structure. Strictly speaking, 'parts', so conceived, are not parts at all, if parts are structure-laden in the way I have proposed (on which see further below). Thus, the parts of my bath—were such talk appropriate—would be not hot and cold water, but just the right amount of hot water and just the right amount of cold. The difficulty of identifying parts independently of the structure of the whole they compose is precisely the point. So, too, limit and unlimited can only be understood in relation to each other.

If members of the unlimited are parts, conceived in the absence of structure, members of the class of limit are the structure of these parts, abstractly conceived. The association between limit and structure is relatively easy to grasp. It is the characteristics of the unlimited that are harder to understand. This, I suggest, is because the unlimited is something essentially negative in

---

[49] And, in particular, what ratios are involved—and so the identification of the class of limit—is dependent on the nature of the mixtures they are to compose. Again, cf. D. Frede (1997: 191–3).

character; even its name is privative—that which has an absence of limit (is ἄ-πειρον). I suggest that the nature of the unlimited—and the difficulty of describing it—is a corollary of what I have described as the 'structure-laden' character of the parts of contentful structures of the sort here described.

Consider a passage from close to the end of the dialogue. At the end of the dialogue, and once the analysis of the ingredients of the good, mixed life is complete, Socrates vividly enacts the mixture of the good life itself (61b11 ff.). In doing so, he puts to work the general account of mixtures provided by his fourfold classification of beings.[50] He also makes his most explicit statement as to what is essential to the constitution of any mixture or blend:

Any blend (σύγκρασις) which does not have measure (μέτρος) or the nature of proportion (σύμμετρος) in any way whatsoever, of necessity destroys both its ingredients and, primarily, itself. A thing of this sort is truly no blend at all, but a kind of unblended disaster, a real disaster for the things which acquire it. (64d9–e3)

Measure and commensurability are here explicitly said to be essential to the constitution of a mixture, that is, of any complex whole. Without these, Socrates says, no mixture can exist. And it is for this reason that terms for measure and commensurability feature prominently in the list of prizewinners in the dialogue's final evaluation of the good of the mixed life (66a4–d4). According to his earlier, more general account of mixtures, measure is what is imposed by members of the class of limit upon members of the class of unlimited so as to constitute a mixture. Thus, each member of the mixed class, that is, each mixture, is there described, most generally, as 'a creation into being (γένεσιν εἰς οὐσίαν)'—a phrase to which I shall return—'resulting from the *measures* (μέτρα) produced through limit' (26d8–9). Measure and commensurability are bywords for structure. Structure is here made essential to the constitution of a whole.

There is no whole without structure; this is the core of Socrates' claim. But then there are, strictly speaking, no parts either. The absence of measure, Socrates claims, destroys a

---

[50] I have discussed the relation between the closing stages of the dialogue and the earlier fourfold classification in greater detail elsewhere, in Harte (1999).

whole's *ingredients* as well as itself. Why should this be so? The ingredients are destroyed only if the ingredients get their identity only in the context of the whole they compose. Properly speaking, parts come only in the context of the requisite structure, and hence are 'structure-laden'.[51] Socrates' characterization of the unlimited represents an attempt to describe the content such parts provide for the whole in the absence of the requisite structure. We have seen such an attempt before, in the deductions of the *Parmenides*.[52] One passage is well worth quoting again, here. It was, in fact, the first passage in which we came across the terminology of limit and unlimited, and it speaks directly to the interpretation of the unlimited I am suggesting here.

Whenever each part becomes one part, they then have a limit (πέρας) in relation to each other and to the whole, and the whole in relation to the parts.—Indeed.—It then follows for things other than the One that, as a result of the combining (κοινωνεῖν) of themselves and the one, as it seems, something different comes to be in them, which provides a limit (πέρας) in relation to each other; but their nature in themselves is without limit (ἀπειρίαν).—So it seems. (*Prm.* 158c7–d6)

Members of the unlimited, we may recall, are what, in and of themselves, cannot constitute a whole. But they cannot be excluded from our account of the constitution of mixtures nonetheless.

Socratic Mixtures

Socrates provides three examples of mixtures of limit and unlimited, although they are only sketchily described: health, music,

---

[51] As I have said (§4.1), this way of thinking about parts is not without difficulties. If parts exist only for so long as the structure of which they are parts exists, we need an account of the relation between that which comes to be part of a structure and the part which it becomes. (Of course, in so far as Plato focuses on the composition of imperishable types, no such question arises. But, in so far as one thinks that he could—or would—offer the same account of the composition of perishable tokens, an answer is called for.) The following example may help to illustrate the kind of distinction required. If I get the wrong mix of egg, flour, sugar, etc., then I will fail to produce a cake. I will still have egg, flour, etc.—the 'ingredients', in the more usual sense, of my cake. But I will not have the parts of the cake, for example the slice I planned to have with my coffee.

[52] See the discussion of bare pluralities in §3.3 above.

and good climatic conditions.[53] First, then, consider what he has to say about the nature of health: 'Isn't it the case that, in sickness, the right combination of these gives rise to the nature of health?' (26a7–8) By 'these', Socrates may refer, in particular, to the right combination of members of the class of limit, mentioned immediately beforehand, in 25d10–e2; i.e. to the requisite numerical proportions involved in the constitution of health. Alternatively, by 'the right combination of these' he may refer to the need for the right combination of limit and unlimited, whose mixture, in general, was invited at 25d2–3. The effect is much the same either way. Take the paired unlimited components relevant to both disease and health—perhaps, hotter and colder, and wetter and drier (the latter being added to the list at 25c8). Put these paired unlimited components in the requisite proportions, whatever they may be. The right combination of these, Socrates says, creates the nature of health.

Notice that we are here concerned with the constitution of health in general; its nature. Health is a complex whole, constituted by some system of mathematically expressible relations between such elements of the body as are affected by the more and the less as applied to the physical constitution of the body. Health, in general, is a harmonious and commensurate blend of these elements. Likewise, in his second example, Socrates portrays music as a blend of limit and unlimited, constituted by some system of mathematically expressible relations between the more and the less pertinent to music, listed here as the pairs high and low, fast and slow. 'And in the case of high and low, fast and slow, which are unlimited, isn't it the occurrence of these same things within them that both produces limit and establishes the whole of music as absolutely complete ($\tau\epsilon\lambda\epsilon\acute{\omega}\tau\alpha\tau\alpha$)?' (26a2–4). The reference to 'completeness' or 'perfection' ($\tau\epsilon\lambda\epsilon\acute{\omega}\tau\alpha\tau\alpha$) picks up the point that only through the imposition of limit can the unlimited constituents of music constitute a whole. This is the second time in the dialogue in which Socrates has referred to the example of music; the science of music is one of the examples chosen to

---

[53] Socrates refers to 'the seasons and all such fine things' (26b1). It seems best to understand this as referring to an overall conception of the ideal climate. Cf. D. Frede (1997: 198).

illustrate the method described in the first passage that talks of limit and limited. I shall return to this example in discussion of the method. Socrates' final example is that of climate:

SOCRATES. And occurring in winter storms and heatwaves, [these same things] take away what is too much and unlimited, and produce something balanced and at the same time commensurate (τὸ . . . ἔμμετρον καὶ ἅμα σύμμετρον).
PROTARCHUS. Indeed.
SOC. And out of these, when the unlimited things and the things which have limit are mixed together, we get the seasons and all such fine things, do we not?
PROT. Of course. (26a6–b4)

Where the introduction of limit was earlier described as making the unlimited opposites 'commensurate and harmonious' (σύμμετρα . . . καὶ σύμφωνα) (25e1), so that which the mixture of limit and unlimited produces is described as 'something balanced and commensurate'. Again, relational notions predominate, both in the fact that the unlimited components of such a mixture continue to be given in pairs and in the characterization of the harmonious relations between these components that result from the imposition of limit.

Socrates characterizes these and all members of the third, mixed class in general terms as each being 'a creation into being (γένεσις εἰς οὐσίαν) resulting from the measures imposed by limit' (26d8–9). As Frede notes, the term 'being' (οὐσία) is not idle here.[54] The moral, as at the end of the dialogue at 64d9–e3, is that, without measure—that is, the structure which limit provides, there is no being, only the unstructured morass of unlimited elements; to use my own example once again, without the right proportion of hot and cold water I do not have a bath at all. Note the strength of the normative assumptions at work here. A bath is either a proper bath or no bath at all.[55] I shall have more

---

[54] D. Frede (1997: 195–7).

[55] Is what constitutes the perfect bath the same for all? This seems a highly implausible claim about baths; but this is only an example. Applied to Plato's examples, this is the question of whether he has a 'one size fits all' approach to health, the ideal climate, and, perhaps most importantly, the good life. I shall not be discussing this question.

to say on this below. Socrates' use of the term 'creation' here is also important. As elsewhere, it indicates that composition is something creative; composition creates something new, which was not there before. The unlimited components of a mixture provide the content in which structure is found, but they do not constitute anything considered on their own.

Notice that each of Socrates' examples of mixture—health, music, and good climatic conditions—is the object of a science: medicine, music, and meteorology. Like the *Sophist*, the *Philebus* has a considerable amount to say about the nature of scientific expertise, most notably in the notoriously opaque account of the method (16c5–17a5), described as a gift from the gods to man, and subsequently illustrated by a series of examples, whose interpretation is scarcely less difficult (17a8–18d2). This is the first of the passages within the dialogue that talk of limit and unlimited. As in the *Sophist* also, the epistemology of the method is the corollary of an underlying ontology. And it is explicitly presented as such in the description of the god-given method, although this feature of the description of the method has not always been given the attention it deserves. I shall suggest that herein lies the clue to the relation between this passage and Socrates' subsequent analysis of the constitution of mixtures.

Recall, for a moment, the *Sophist*'s account of science or expertise. According to the *Sophist*, the mark of expertise is to know which of the elements of a given domain combine and which do not. And to know this, I have argued, is to know the structure of the relevant domain. One can, however, think of such structure on both a large and a small scale. Consider, for example, the study of the phonetics of the English language. On a small scale, one may think of an example of the structure of such a domain, a particular legitimate sequence of phonemes that may combine together, such as: k-æ-t. Such an example would be the equivalent, in phonetics, of the example of syntactic structure provided by the *Sophist*, the sentence 'man learns'. Alternatively, one may think of the structure of such a domain as the entire domain of permissible relations between any two or more of the elements of the domain, that structure of which the sequence k-æ-t is a part. It is such large-scale structure that is the object of the expert's study.

In the *Philebus*, I shall argue, it is with the constitution and study of such large-scale scientific domains that the god-given method is principally concerned. I begin with Socrates' account of the method and the question of the relation between this and his subsequent analysis of mixtures.

Epistemology and Ontology: Socrates' 'Method' and his Fourfold Classification

Consider how Socrates' description of the method begins:

There is a gift of the gods to men, as it seems to me, at any rate, thrown down from the gods by some Prometheus together with brightest fire; and the ancients, being better than us and living closer to the gods, handed down this saying: that the things which are always said to be are made up of one and many (ἐξ ἑνὸς . . . καὶ πολλῶν), and have limit (πέρας) and unlimitedness (ἀπειρίαν) naturally together within them. (16c5–10)

This much of the ancients' saying is pure ontology:[56] things are made up of one and many, and have limit and unlimitedness jointly within them. And the subsequent method is presented as a necessary corollary of this ontology, of the fact that things are ordered (διακεκοσμημένοι) in this way (16c10–d1). Thus Socrates continues:

Since, therefore, things are ordered (διακεκοσμημένων) in this way, assuming that there is always, in each case, a single form (μίαν ἰδέαν) for everything, we must search for it—for we will find it, it being there; then, if we grasp it, after one, we must look for two, if they are such, and, if not, three or some other number; and each of these ones must in turn be investigated in the same way, until, respecting the initial one, one sees not only that it is one and many and unlimited, but also how many it is. For one must not ascribe the character of the unlimited to the plurality until one sees its total number, which lies between the unlimited and the one, and then, at that point, one may let go each one of them all into the unlimited. (16c10–e2)

---

[56] Cf. here Sayre (1983: 119–21), who also stresses the ontological character of this section of Socrates' remark.

The ancients begin with a claim about the constitution of things, but it is desperately brief. Where, then, must we turn for an elaboration of this ontology? Not to the *method*, as such; to the procedure for finding one, and, after that, two, and so on. Rather, the elaboration of the ontology here described awaits, I argue, the analysis of the constitution of mixtures in Socrates' subsequent fourfold classification of beings. But this is a claim that requires defence.

The relation between Socrates' fourfold classification of being and the passage describing the god-given method has been the subject of much dispute.[57] The two terms 'limit' (πέρας) and 'unlimited' (ἄπειρον) occur in both passages, inviting comparison between them. Limit and unlimited are, as we have seen, two of the four kinds or classes that Socrates enumerates in his fourfold classification of all beings; third being the mixture of the two, fourth the cause of their mixture. In the earlier passage the two terms first occurred together in the ontological preface to the method (16c10), quoted above. The term 'unlimited' also occurs several times on its own in the subsequent characterization of the method (16d6, 7, e1, e2, 17a2). Despite these linguistic affinities, however, commentators on the dialogue have failed to agree on an understanding of 'limit' and 'unlimited' common to both passages, or indeed on whether the search for such a common understanding is even appropriate.[58]

The difficulty arises, I suggest, because commentators on the passage have, by and large, been looking for an understanding of limit and unlimited common to the fourfold classification of beings and the god-given *method*. But the only earlier occurrence of both the term 'limit' and the term 'unlimited' comes not in the account of the method as such, but in the ontological remarks that preface the method: the claim that the things that are always said to be are made up of one and many, and have both limit and

[57] See e.g. the discussions of Gosling (1975); D. Frede (1997); Meinwald (1998); Striker (1970).

[58] For example, both Gosling (1975: 186) and Meinwald (1998: 167–8) take a desideratum of any interpretation of the two passages to be that their use of 'limit' and 'unlimited' be consistent. In contrast, Striker (1970, esp. 80–1) and D. Frede (1997: 202–5) argue that the two terms have fundamentally different uses in the two passages.

unlimitedness jointly within them. It is to this brief ontological passage that Socrates must refer when he begins his presentation of the fourfold classification with a reference to what has been said before:

SOCRATES. All the things that now are in the universe, let us divide them in two, or, if you will, into three.
PROTARCHUS. Can you say on what principle?
SOC. Let us take up certain things from our previous statements.
PROT. Which?
SOC. Didn't we say that the god had demonstrated the unlimited (τὸ ἄπειρον) to belong to the things there are and also limit (τὸ πέρας)?
PROT. Certainly we did.
SOC. Then let us posit these as two of the kinds and as a third some one mixed together out of both of these. (23c4–d1)

In the preface to the method it was in fact 'the ancients'—but by the agency of 'some Prometheus'—who handed down the saying about the limit and unlimitedness occurring in things. But, in the passage quoted, Socrates clearly refers directly to something that was earlier said and something that Protarchus recognizes. And I can see no other passage to which he can refer than the brief ontological passage prior to the statement of the god-given method. No less clearly it is the pair—limit and unlimited—as mentioned in this ontological preface that are taken as two of the four kinds or classes in the fourfold classification of beings.[59] This may in turn help to explain why Socrates there simply assumes that limit and unlimited mix together, as he does in positing their mixture as yet a third kind. After all, the ancients

---

[59] This passage is the clearest reference back to the earlier passage, and the hardest to square with an interpretation in which the two terms do not stably refer. Socrates also refers to the need for different weapons, some of which, however, may be the same (23b6–9), for the discussion to come. This passage may also be intended to link the subsequent fourfold classification to the earlier passage; if so, however, the way in which it does so is much less clear. One might, following Frede, take his reference to weapons (βέλη, 23b8) and a contrivance (μηχανή, 23b7) to have methodological import. Thus, D. Frede (1997: 203–5) takes the fourfold classification to be itself a (partial) application of the god-given method as earlier described. This is certainly an attractive suggestion, but it does not, in itself, preclude the identification of a use of the terms 'limit' and 'unlimited' common to both passages; nor, *pace* Frede, does it diminish the impression given by the clear back reference at 23c4–d1 that there will be such a common use.

had spoken of the pair as 'naturally *together*' (σύμφυτον, 16c10) within things. By contrast, the assumption of a fourth kind, the cause of the mixture, receives a retrospective justification at 26e2–5, through Socrates' and Protarchus' agreement that everything that comes to be has an agent responsible for its doing so (an αἰτία).[60]

This much, but scarcely any more, can be drawn from a consideration of the ontological preface to the method to which Socrates refers at the start of his fourfold classification of being. As far as the project of comparing the ontology of the two passages is concerned, therefore, and, in particular, of identifying a shared understanding of the two terms 'limit' and 'unlimited', there is little to go on. The ontological preface does not attempt to elaborate upon the ontological claims it makes. And, as I have said, the subsequent characterization of the god-given method is presented as a consequence of this, thus far sparsely described ontology, but it is not itself an elaboration of that ontology. What, then, of the question of the relation between the two passages? There is no real purchase for a question about the relation between the understanding of the two terms 'limit' and 'unlimited' in each passage, since the first passage does no more than mention the two in the ontological preface.[61] A question does remain as to the relation between the understanding of the terms 'limit' and 'unlimited' as elaborated in Socrates' fourfold classification and the occurrence of the term 'unlimited' in the characterization of the *method*. This, however, is simply one aspect of a more general question as to how to interpret the correspondence between the epistemology of the method and its underlying ontology. This question applies just as much to the relation

---

[60] Or, perhaps better, an explanation or reason for its doing so. For the connection between the notion of responsibility and the terminology for causation, and for a distinction between the thing responsible (αἴτιος) and the reason or explanation (αἰτία), see M. Frede (1980). Although not ideal, I shall continue to refer to this fourth kind as that of 'cause'.

[61] This is not to say that one may conclude that the terms are used in *different* ways in the two passages; the back reference at 23c4-d1 speaks strongly against this. Rather, my suggestion is that, in the first passage, the two terms are not *used* at all, but merely mentioned; an explanation of their intended use awaits the discussion in the second passage.

between the ontological preface to the method, in 16c9–10, and the characterization of the method, in 16c10–e2, as to the relation between the method and the fourfold classification of beings. It may be considered by way of discussion of Socrates' examples of the method.

The God-Given Method and its Examples

It is no accident that the god-given method is presented as a necessary consequence of the way in which things are ordered or arranged (διακεκοσμημένοι, 16d1). As in the later passage, structure will here be made essential to the constitution of the kind of complex wholes that science studies; that is, to the constitution of entire scientific domains. As in the *Sophist*, structure will, in consequence, be no less central to the methodology of the science of such domains. I begin with the objects of science, in light of Socrates' examples of the method.

The examples that Socrates chooses to illustrate the god-given method confirm that we are dealing here with the constitution and study of scientific domains. The examples are, first, vocal or phonetic sound (beginning at 17b4–5, and returning, after the second example, in 18b5 ff.),[62] and, second, musical sound (17c1–2 ff.) Both examples concern sound (φωνή), but each concerns a different domain of sound—one, the object of phonetics,[63] the other, the object of music. Each is thus an example of a domain of science. Each is familiar from elsewhere. Both phonetics and music were used as examples in both the *Theaetetus* and *Sophist*. As we have seen, music is subsequently used as an example once again, in Socrates' twofold analysis of the constitution of mixtures. This is yet another sign of the correspondence between the two passages. I shall focus on this example in order to show this correspondence at work.

---

[62] Socrates may well have written characters (graphemes) as well as spoken sounds (phonemes) in view here; on which, see D. Frede (1997: 146–58). But the phonetic aspect of articulate sound is the driving force in the discussion here. Note in this connection that the term γράμμα (18b3) can refer to an articulate sound as well as to the symbol representing the sound (see LSJ, s.v. γράμμα II b).

[63] Or, principally of phonetics; see previous note.

First, however, consider the reason why Socrates might choose to use two examples involving what appears to be a single phenomenon, namely sound. This is the first indication of the significance of structure in the constitution of a scientific domain. Phonetics and music may appear each to be concerned with the uniform phenomenon of sound. However, each, in fact, involves rather more than simply undifferentiated sound. Even to speak of musical or phonetic sound is to imply some particular structuring of the phenomenon of sound.[64] Socrates' double use of sound highlights this fact by choosing as examples two domains that share the generic phenomenon of sound, each of which is nonetheless a distinct domain of science.

Next, then, consider what more precisely it is that makes a musical sound a *musical* sound. According to Socrates' later analysis of the constitution of mixtures, music is constituted by the imposition of limit—mathematically expressible structure—on the unlimited constituents of music, involving the paired opposing characteristics of high and low, fast and slow (26a2). But this later analysis, I have argued, is simply an elaboration of the brief ontological preface to the method, according to which the objects of the method—and thus, music included—are composed of one and many, with limit and unlimitedness naturally together within them. Now, therefore, let us see if we can elaborate on the application of this to the case of music as described in Socrates' illustration of the method. To make matters easier, I shall concentrate on the pair high and low, which are features of pitch, that is, of musical sound.[65] For Plato, I argue, musical sound in general, and notes and melodies in particular, are parasitic on structure.[66]

---

[64] So Barker (1989: 64 n. 39), commenting on 17b11–12, correctly notes that it indicates that there are two 'kinds' of sound, the subject of musical expertise and of phonetics respectively.

[65] The *Philebus* itself licenses such a separation, since, in his discussion of the example of music, Socrates treats separately, first pitch, and then rhythm and measures. See the division of topics in 17c11-d3 and 17d3–7 respectively.

[66] Nor is Plato alone in making musical sound parasitic on structure. In contemporary discussions of the psychology of music much work is done on the structures that listeners impose upon and through which they organize their perceptual experience of music. In the field of psychoacoustics a number of models have been developed to represent such musical structure. For a valuable introduction to the field, see Spender (1987), and for psychoacoustic models, see Howell *et al.* (1991, ch. 6). Pitch is

Consider the following three sounds: the sound I hear if I tap my pen on my desk; the sound I hear if I pluck a guitar string; and the sound I hear if I utter the phoneme 'æ'. What makes the second of these sounds a musical sound, where the others are not? Musical sounds, particularly if considered from the aspect of pitch, have a close connection in almost all cultures to scales. The scale divides pitch into discrete steps; pitches correspond to particular notes of the musical scale.[67] The two scales that are the tonal basis of Western music differ from the scale on which classical Greek music was based, and each scale, is, in its own way, a construction.[68] Pierce describes classical Greek music as being 'based on a mathematically derived scale'. This scale draws on a discovery, credited to Pythagoras, that there is a numerical relation between the lengths of strings and the musical intervals of which a scale is composed, a relation that is expressible in ratios between integers. For example, the interval a fifth is expressible as the ratio 2:3, since, if a stretched string is shortened by two-thirds of its length, the resulting length sounds a note a fifth above that of the original string.[69] The use of numerical ratios in the analysis of musical intervals makes music a natural example in light of the later characterization of members of the class of limit.

One key interval—the fourth, or tetrachord—is the basis of the Greek scalar system in all its species. Thus, Barker writes of the Greek musical system: 'the central octave of the most fundamental system was divided into two principal parts, each spanning a fourth, and separated ("disjoined") by a tone'.[70] The identity of this tone is itself defined in terms of musical intervals. West writes that Greek writers 'define [a tone] as the interval by which a fifth is greater than a fourth'.[71] In general, in Greek

particularly important in this context: 'Pitch has generally been regarded as the dominant structural or form-bearing dimension . . . of Western music' (1991: 201).

[67] For the close connection between pitch and scales, see Dowling and Harwood (1986: 90–2).

[68] See Pierce (1992: 74–5).   [69] Pierce (1992: 20–1).

[70] Barker (1989: 11). My debt to the work of Barker and also of M. L. West will be obvious in what follows. Thanks are due also to Andrew Lovett for guiding me to some of the relevant modern literature on music.

[71] West (1992: 167).

music, one cannot speak of a particular note, say, middle C, without reference to the intervals on which the musical scale is based. '. . . the notes of the melody are identified and named by reference to the organization of the series of intervals surrounding them, not by their absolute pitches'.[72] Thus, the notes of a melody or of a scale are, as I have put it, 'structure-laden'. They get their identity from their position in the structure as a whole.

Music is at all levels parasitic on structure, constituted by the mathematically expressible intervals which form the basis of the Greek scale. In Plato's ontology the contrasting dimensions of pitch—the high and the low—provide the undifferentiated content for music—Plato's 'unlimited': that which is to be the bearer of structure, but is, in itself, without any structure of its own. Musical sound itself is constituted only by the imposition upon such content of the relevant structure—Plato's 'limit'. The numerical ratios that constitute the intervals of the scale delineate what, by analogy with my earlier example of Platonic structure, I shall call a 'musical space', into which the tones of a piece of music fit and from which they get their identity as particular musical tones. Musical sounds are musical sounds only in relation to this musical space.[73]

The terminology of limit and unlimited is Plato's own, borrowed and adapted to his own purposes from certain of his Pythagorean predecessors.[74] But the analysis of music that it provides is in line with the work that others have done on the analysis of Greek music in general. So, Barker writes: 'The Greeks

---

[72] Barker (1989: 16). This in fact accords partly with our experience of pitch, at least when thinking in terms of whole melodies. So, Krumhansl (1991: 285): 'a melody is heard as the same melody even though it begins on a different pitch (is transposed) as long as the intervals between tones are unchanged'.

[73] Contemporary psychoacoustics in fact provides a precedent for offering topographical models of musical structure. One such—Shepard's double helix representation of the cognitive structure of musical pitch, based on experience of pitch height and chroma (pitch similarity)—is depicted and discussed in Dowling and Harwood (1986: 107–13, esp. fig. 4.13).

[74] Their use in an analysis of music no doubt makes this particularly appropriate. The 'Pythagorean' background to the ontology of the *Philebus* has been much discussed: see, in particular, Gosling (1975) and Sayre (1983). I take it, however, that Plato's use of it is meant to be such that it can be understood in its own terms, whatever its relation to the work of one or more historical Pythagoreans.

conceived their scalar systems and patterns of attunement as expressions of the divisions and organizations imposed by melody on the tonal "space" which it inhabits.'[75] This is all to the good, since music here functions primarily as an example of the ontology of science. Being an educated young man, Protarchus can be expected to understand it in light of his general understanding of music.

If this is indeed a fair sketch of the ontology that underlies the account of the method, as applied to the case of music, what of the method itself? Consider Socrates' description of what their ancestors discovered, offered as an illustration of the method.

Well, my friend, whenever you understand both how many are the intervals of sound of both high and low pitch, what kind they are, the boundaries of the intervals (διαστημάτων) and all the systems of notes (συστήματα) which are formed from them—things which those before us recognized and bequeathed to us who follow them to call scales (ἀρμονίας); and again, in the movements of the body, other affections of this kind come to be present, which, they say, being measured by numbers (δι' ἀριθμῶν μετρηθέντα), we must in turn name 'rhythms' (ῥυθμοὺς) and 'measures' (μέτρα);[76] and that, at the same time, [we must] investigate in this way regarding every one and many—for when you grasp these things in this way, then you have become wise, and when you have grasped any other one through considering it in this way, then you have become wise about that. (17c11–e3)

Barker gives the following interpretation of the four tasks involved in having sufficient understanding of the aspects of music involving pitch (high and low):[77] (i) to grasp the number of intervals is to grasp the number of distinct kinds of intervals used in music; (ii) to grasp the qualities of the intervals is to classify the intervals according to their 'character' and the contribution each makes to the music in which it occurs; (iii) to identify the boundaries of the intervals is to identify musical notes, which may be identified either as points of pitch on a continuum, as magnitudes standing in certain ratios, or by reference to named notes of

[75] Barker (1989: 11).

[76] Socrates here suggests that the etymology of the Greek names for 'rhythm' and 'measure' derives from their being the results of numerical—or, as one might rather say, arithmetical—measures, but the complete effect is hard to convey in translation.

[77] Barker (1989: 64 n. 41).

the system;[78] (iv) to identify the systems of notes is to identify the legitimate combinations of notes and intervals that form the scalar frameworks for melodies.

Compare these four tasks with my account of the way in which music, according to this analysis, is parasitic upon structure. For musical structure to be *musical* structure, it must be the structure of the relevant musical *content*: the music-bearing characteristics of the generic phenomenon of sound: high and low (for pitch), fast and slow (for rhythm and measure). But the mere highs and lows of sound have no intrinsic structure of their own. Musical sound itself is built up from a set of mathematically expressible relations between higher and lower sounds defining musical intervals (identified and characterized in tasks (i) and (ii)). These intervals are the basis of the scale, and it is only with reference to this organization of a series of intervals that one can identify musical notes as such, the notes of a melody, say (task (iii)). The framework of intervals and notes provides the scalar system on which Greek music is based (task (iv)).

What Socrates describes in the first half of the passage above is the ancestors' discovery of the mathematical basis of musical intervals and the scalar systems constituted from them. And this discovery is the discovery of limit—structure—within the unlimitedness—the mere highs and lows—of the bare phenomenon of sound. Each is necessary for the constitution of music. Their conjunction provides an analysis of the constitution of the scientific domain of musical sound.

How does this interpretation relate, first, to the ancients' description of things as made up of one and many, with limit and unlimitedness naturally together within them, and, second, to the general characterization of the method—the search for one, then two, etc.—of 16c10 ff.? Unlimitedness, on my reading, is a property of an undifferentiated phenomenon such as sound, the content of a domain of science, conceived in the absence of structure. Limit is the structure that, applied to this content, makes up a distinct domain of science from this undifferentiated

---

[78] The second way of identifying notes here suggested would clearly fit best with my interpretation of the nature of limit.

phenomenon.[79] Phonetic or musical sound—conceived as the structured unity that limit and unlimitedness jointly constitute—is the one: a unitary, systematic domain of science. Its structure-laden components—the phonetic or musical types marked out by the imposition of limit upon phonetic or musical space—are the many of which it is composed.

Unlimitedness is a property of sound if considered in abstraction from the structures that are the object of a scientific grasp of the domain whose content it provides. For this reason, it is Theuth, in the illustration provided at 18b6–d2, who begins with the unlimitedness of (here, phonetic) sound (18b9), since it is Theuth whose activity is prescientific inasmuch as his activity involves the discovery of a domain of science, and hence involves the discovery and not the application of the corresponding science, phonetics. By contrast, Theuth has often been taken to start not with what, on my interpretation, is the unlimitedness of sound, but with the unlimited number of particular phonetic tokens that each and every one of us utters.[80] Such an interpretation, however, must inevitably play down, if not altogether ignore, the fact that Theuth is the founder of the science of phonetics. To describe Theuth as beginning with phonetic tokens is anachronistic, since, when he begins with the unlimited, he is at only the first stage of his discovery of phonetics.

It is perhaps unsurprising that Theuth should be taken to begin with the unlimited number of particular phonetic tokens, for when Theuth is faced with the undifferentiated phenomenon of vocal sound, he is faced with it in the form of the phonetic tokens that each of us utters. However, in the pre-alphabetic condition in which Theuth encounters them, he is no more likely to have a grasp of particular phonetic tokens than is a monoglot

[79] Again, however, this should be thought of as an *analysis*; limit and unlimited are not, I suppose, actually separable; nor is limit actually 'applied' to something that might be described as undifferentiated sound. Here, then, I agree with McCabe (1994: 246–53) that Socrates should not be taken to be implying the literal involvement, as she puts it, of 'some "sound stuff" ' (p. 246). But that does not mean that there is no ontological story to be told here. I take it that the epistemology of the method corresponds to an underlying ontology, later elaborated in the fourfold classification.

[80] See e.g. the list of adherents to Gosling's Interpretation 2, in his (1975: 160–5).

English language speaker confronting a language from an entirely different language group. In such a situation it is hard even to distinguish separate phonemes. The important aspect of the utterances with which Theuth begins, therefore, is not the fact that there is an unlimited number of utterances of each phonetic type—since this would require a prior grasp of the phonetic types that he is as yet on his way to delineating—but is rather the, as yet undifferentiated, phenomenon of vocal sound in which he discovers a systematic pattern of relations.

The discovery of such a systematic pattern of relations is the discovery of limit, the structure that constitutes a scientific domain out of an undifferentiated phenomenon such as sound. Such structure is both an ontological limit—marking out a domain of phonetic types and relations within the undifferentiated phenomenon—and a conceptual limit—for the domain can be studied only in so far as it is structured. It need come as no surprise that Plato should be a realist about structure. The structure of science is a consequence of the way in which the domains of science are structured. So, the method is premissed on the way in which its objects are ordered or arranged (διακεκοσμημένοι, 16d1). So, too, the method is linked with scientific discovery, both at the beginning, when Socrates associates it with everything that has been *discovered* (ἀνευρίσκω, 16c2) in the realm of any skill, and in the references both to the ancestors' discovery of music (17d2–3) and to Theuth's discovery of phonetics (18b8–9). Discovery is the making known of something that previously existed, but was as yet unknown.

What makes one wise—be it in music or phonetics—is a grasp of the entire structure of the relevant domain. The expert's grasp of a scientific domain is systematic, because no one of the elements of the domain can be understood on its own, in isolation from the system as a whole. This point is made explicitly for the case of phonetics. Socrates reports that, once Theuth had distinguished each phoneme,[81]

he gave the name 'letter' (στοιχεῖον) to each one of them and to all of them. And, seeing that none of us would understand one just by itself

---

[81] And corresponding grapheme? Cf. n. 62 above.

without all of them, and considering this the link that is one and makes all of them somehow one, he pronounced the single art applied to them 'the science of letters' (γραμματικὴν τέχνην). (18c6–d2)

Why is it that one cannot understand the elements of the science of letters independently of each other? Why could I not have an understanding of the vowels, say—both how many they are and what they are like—without an understanding of the remaining letters? Could I not learn the vowels one week and the consonants the next? One might say: well, you could, but you would not *fully* understand them until you had learned them all. But one might also say something stronger than that. One might say that in fact you would not understand them at all, because, given the structure-laden nature of the various elements of the domain, to understand what they are—to have a grip on their identity—*is* to understand their structural relations with each other. Each gets its identity only in the context of the structure as a whole.

It is this 'structure-laden' character of the elements of a domain of science that can help to build a bridge between the *Sophist*'s account of science and the characterization of the method in the *Philebus*. Socrates' characterization of the method of science has often been taken as an illustration of the so-called 'method of collection and division'. And this method, in turn, has often been perceived as a method of classification, which, beginning with a genus, divides it systematically and exhaustively into specific types and sub-types, of each of which there is then an unlimited number of tokens.[82] However, if, for example, the notion of a 'consonant' is already a structure-laden term, one cannot understand what a consonant is in the absence of an understanding of the ways in which consonants combine with other elements of the domain. So, for example, a consonant is the kind of phonetic element that cannot be sounded on its own, but that, in combination with phonetic elements of another type, the vowels or sonants, can give rise to a syllable. These phonetic

---

[82] This would be a model of division. What might be involved in collection remains unclear: whether it is simply the reverse of this procedure—e.g. the activity of Theuth, considered, on the model I have rejected, as someone who begins with already individuated phonetic tokens—or something that happens at each stage of the division, gathering into one the type or sub-type in question.

elements may indeed be sorted into types—consonants and vowels—but one can do so only in the context of the structure of the
domain as a whole. In this way, what might appear to be nothing
but a method of classification—the search, first, for one, and,
after that, for two, or three, or whatever other number there may
be, continuing until one has a grasp of all the 'positions' marked
out within the relevant structured domain—can in fact be directly assimilated to what the *Sophist* described as the hallmark of
expertise: knowledge of the ways in which the elements of a
domain do and do not combine, where that means knowledge of
the (large-scale) structure of the relevant domain.

Phileban Structure

What can be said about the characteristics of structure as
described in the *Philebus*? As in the *Sophist*, structure turns out
to have a close relation to science. Structure is the proper object
of science. It is so, because structure is intrinsic to the constitution of the objects of science. The objects of science exist only in
so far as they are structured, and they can be studied only in so far
as they are structured.[83] As such, structure is essentially intelligible. It is also real. That structure that science studies is that
structure which is there to be studied. The reality of structure is
confirmed by Socrates' twofold analysis of the constitution of
mixtures: structure—that structure that is imposed through the
imposition of limit—is given a secure and irreducible place in the
Philebus' ontology. The class of limit captures the structure of
things, abstractly conceived. The unlimited, by contrast, captures the domain of content on which such structure is imposed.
Together, these are the twin ingredients of a whole—a member
of the third mixed kind; 'ingredients', not in the sense that each
is a part of a whole, but in the sense that each is required for the
analysis of a whole conceived as a contentful structure in the way
I have proposed.

---

[83] Recall that talk of the objects of science as being structured should not be taken
to imply that structure is a property that they may or may not have. In particular, one
should not assume that there are some things—the objects of science—that can be
independently identified, and that may then come to be structured in certain ways.

The analysis of structure provided by the account of limit suggests that structure, at least in the *Philebus*, is mathematical. At least, the structures of the objects of science here considered all seem to be mathematically expressible.[84] Not only that: this intelligible mathematical structure turns out to be built into the fabric of the cosmos through the operations of a guiding and providential intelligence. The role of intelligence in the production of structure emerges from the discussion of the fourth and final class in Socrates' fourfold classification of all being. Having characterized mixtures of limit and unlimited as *creations* into being, Socrates goes on to argue that such creations must have a cause. This, the cause of the mixture of limit and unlimited, is his fourth and final class.

Two premisses secure the place of intelligence—Socrates' candidate in the dialogue's contest—in the class of cause: first, the assumption that the cosmos is ordered (as indeed the Greek word κόσμος suggests[85]); and, second, the assumption that only intelligence could be responsible for this order (28d5–29a4).[86] That structure, therefore, that limit provides is the rational ordering of the cosmos, and this rational ordering is the responsibility of a governing intelligence. Only on this assumption, Protarchus admits, can one do justice to the visible order and revolutions of the heavenly bodies (28e2–6). The attribution of this role to intelligence is crucial, because the introduction of intelligence as cause is the introduction of a teleological principle. It is because the imposition of limit on the unlimited is caused by intelligence that the structures that limit provides are harmonious and commensurate.

The introduction of this teleological framework for the account of structure ties into the normative character of structure, as it is presented in the *Philebus*. Thus, the governing intelligence is said to be responsible for the nature of the finest and

---

[84] However, phonetics appears an exception in this regard. In *Categories* VI, 4^{b}22–3 and 32–5, Aristotle identifies spoken language as a quantity; but his references to long and short syllables (33–4) suggest that he is thinking of metre.

[85] See Vlastos (1975: 3–22) on κόσμος.

[86] The details of this argument will not concern me here. For two recent discussions, see D. Frede (1997: 213–21) and McCabe (2000, ch. 6).

noblest things (30b7) and of the constructive and beneficial activities of every form of science (σοφία) (30b1–4). Intelligence is a teleological principle operative in the cosmos, and structure, it is implied, is the result of its operations, the nature of the finest and noblest things. Platonic bywords for structure are thus positive terms, such as harmony, measure, and commensurability.[87] At the end of the dialogue, as we have seen, Socrates names measure and commensurability as that without which no mixture can survive (64d9–e3). They are also the sign that the nature of the good they are investigating has escaped into the nature of fineness and excellence (64e5–7). Thus, normative terms of value are concomitant upon the presence of structure. So, too, first prize in the contest for being the good of the good life goes to measure, due measure, and appropriateness.[88] All these terms are signs of structure. All are normative terms. 'Due measure' (τὸ μέτριον) and 'appropriateness' (τὸ καίριον) involve measurement according to some norm.[89]

The normativity of structure, and the role of intelligence in causing it, helps to explain the fact that all the examples of structured wholes that we are given in the *Philebus* are positive examples; limit and unlimited, when mixing together, form only the good things in life. And mixtures are either good or fail to be mixtures at all. This is undoubtedly a substantial claim; and it has sometimes been doubted that Plato makes it. Sayre, for example, has argued that it is a mistake to infer from the fact that only positive examples are offered that Plato supposes that all mixtures of limit and unlimited produce good results.[90] Sayre defends the possibility of bad mixtures on two grounds: first, the fact that a mixture is very often described as being a 'correct' or a 'good mixture' (e.g. 25e7, 61b8, 63e8–64a1), qualifications that imply in turn the possibility of an incorrect or bad mixture; second, on

---

[87] See also the plethora of positive terms surrounding Socrates' discussion of mixtures, 25e1–26c2.

[88] I have discussed this final prize-giving in greater detail in Harte (1999).

[89] Compare the distinction drawn, at *Politicus* 283d1-e11, between brute arithmetical measurement and measurement according to the norm. Like D. Frede (1997: 197–8) I suppose that the *Philebus* presupposes this distinction, rather than confusing two kinds of measurement that the *Politicus* will later distinguish.

[90] Sayre (1987, esp. pp. 57–8 with n. 10).

the grounds of the understandable intuition that 'there is no reason to think of a broken leg, or an upset stomach, as any less
determinate than the state of complete health'.[91]

Sayre, of course, is right to suppose that the fact that only positive examples of mixtures are offered does not, in itself, prove
that all mixtures are positive conditions. He is also right that to
describe a mixture as a 'correct mixture' may be taken to imply
the possibility of a mixture that is incorrect. However, this view
of the possibility of bad mixtures suffers a fatal blow from
Socrates' explicit assertion, at 64d9–e3, that a mixture without
measure and commensurability is no mixture at all—it is simply
an 'unblended disaster' (ἄκρατος συμπεφορημένη)—and from
the immediate association of having measure and commensurability with fineness and excellence (64e5–8). Where measure
goes, only good things follow.

What, then, of Sayre's apparently reasonable intuition that
there is nothing at all indeterminate about a state of ill health?
Perhaps determinacy is not to the point. Consider, once more,
my perfect bath. In order to create the perfect bath, I must
impose the perfect ratio on the unlimited ingredients of hot and
cold water; I need so many parts hot water to so many parts cold.
Too much hot water, or too much cold, and my bath is ruined.
There are an unlimited number of ways in which my bath could
be ruined; an unlimited number of ways in which it could be just
too hot or just too cold. And I could, if I wished, put numbers to
the relation between the hot and cold water in any one of them.
But it is not this positive characterization of the numerical relation between the hot and cold waters of the many failed baths that
makes each and every one of them a failure. After all, each is just
as much a failure as any of the others, but each has a different
determinate relation of hot to cold water than any of the others.
The point is not what each of these failed baths is, but what
they are *not*: what is significant about the relation of hot and
cold water in each of these failed attempts at a perfect bath is that
each of them is *not* the perfect ratio of hot to cold of the perfect
bath. So, at 64e1, a failed attempt at a mixture or blend is defined

---

[91] Sayre (1987: 57).

precisely by what is not: it is an *unblended* disaster. A failed attempt at a mixture is just that, however one comes by it.[92]

Mixture as such *is* good mixture, because mixture is caused by the teleological principle intelligence, and intelligence arranges things in such a way that things are good.[93] The fact that mixtures are described as 'fine' or 'correct' mixtures should not, therefore, be taken as an indication of the existence of incorrect or bad mixtures. Rather, it is part and parcel of the characterization of the normativity of structure. Mixtures are described as 'fine' and 'correct' as part of the association between mixture, fineness, and excellence that is developed over the course of the dialogue and that culminates in the identification of the good in the mixed life and the final prize-giving. This association between value and structure will be strengthened yet more as we turn to the *Timaeus*. The *Timaeus* takes as its subject the constitution of the most complex construction of them all: the cosmos and everything in it. And its account of the creation of the cosmos is set firmly within a teleological framework in which the creation of the cosmos is the responsibility of a governing intelligence, here personified in the form of the demiurge.

4.4 THE *TIMAEUS*: STRUCTURES WITHIN STRUCTURES

Thus far I have concentrated on examples of individual structures, be they more or less complex, treated in isolation. But structures can clearly occur within structures, and this in two senses. First is the way in which, for example, the particular phonetic sequence k-æ-t occurs within the (large-scale) structure consisting of all permissible relations between phonemes of the English language such that, in combination, they constitute a syllable. A structure that occurs within a structure in this sense might be described as a substructure of the structure in which it occurs. Second, one structure may itself occupy a position with-

---

[92] Thanks to Nick Denyer for advice on this point.

[93] Or so Socrates assumes. For the assumption, cf. *Phaedo* 97b8–c6 and also the *Timaeus*, on which see below.

in another structure, as, for example, a word, which is itself a structure of letters, occupies a position in a sentence. There may thus be structures of structures. An example of this kind of layering of structures within structures is, I shall argue, to be found in the *Timaeus*.

The *Timaeus* offers almost an embarrassment of riches for one who is interested in the constitution of complex wholes. The bulk of the work is taken up by Timaeus' extended monologue, which describes the constitution of the cosmos and of everything within it. Unlike the *Parmenides*, *Theaetetus*, and *Sophist*, however, the *Timaeus* nowhere directly reflects on the relation of part to whole. Nor does it provide anything comparable to the *Philebus'* metaphysical analysis of the constitution of mixtures in general. Its contribution to the understanding of Plato's account of composition and of structure must, therefore, be garnered from its examples of composition. I shall focus on two—the construction of the body of the cosmos and the construction of the so-called 'elements',[94] earth, air, fire, and water—and on the relation between them. To this end, I first consider the shape of Timaeus' narrative as a whole and the place of his description of these two examples within it.

Layers of Creation

At the start of the *Timaeus*, Timaeus, Critias, and Hermocrates meet with Socrates to be his hosts for a feast, not of food, but of words, in payment for that which they themselves are said to have received from Socrates on the previous day (see, for example, 17a2–3). Socrates' feast clearly stands in some relation to the conversation described in the *Republic*.[95] What he seeks in return

[94] I put 'elements' in scare quotes, because Timaeus will deny that earth, air, fire, and water are in the relevant sense elements ($\sigma\tau o\iota\chi\epsilon\hat{\iota}a$). Nonetheless, the term provides a useful way to refer to the four collectively and it is as such that I shall continue to use it. Note that, in talking of the elements, I shall be referring to phenomenal earth, air, fire, and water, and not to forms of earth, air, fire, and water, mention of which will also be made below.

[95] That the conversation here described cannot be Socrates' narration of the *Republic*'s conversation is shown by Cornford (1937: 4–5). The allusion to the *Republic*, however, is clear in Socrates' brief reprise of yesterday's talk at 17e1–19a5.

is an account of the ideal city that he has described, in action, in particular in the action of war (19b3–c8). The way in which this request is to be met is somewhat surprising. It is to begin—after several important preliminaries that I shall not here consider— with the speech of Timaeus, who is to speak not about war, nor even about cities, but 'starting from the creation of the cosmos and ending with the nature of man' (27a6). And so he does, at 29d7, in a speech that occupies the remainder of the work,[96] after yet more preliminary discussion about the ontological and epistemological framework for his speech and about the character of the account to come. Here is how his account of the creation of the cosmos begins:

Let us say, then, for what reason the one who put it together put together creation[97] and this universe. He was good, and no envy ever arises regarding anything in something good, and, being without this [sc. envy], he desired that everything come to be as like himself as possible. This most authoritative principle of creation and cosmos one would be absolutely right to accept from wise men.[98] For god, wanting everything to be good, and, so far as is possible, nothing to be bad, took over in this fashion all that was visible—not resting quietly, but moving in a disorderly fashion—and brought it out of disorder into order, thinking the latter in every way better than the former. (29d7–30a6)

Call the description of the creation of the cosmos that Timaeus here begins 'creation story 1'. In what follows he describes a series of constructive acts on the part of this god, or demiurge, as he is elsewhere described: the construction of the body of the cosmos; of the soul of the cosmos; of the lesser gods and planets; of the rational part of human soul. And he describes these acts as though happening in sequence. The idea that the events described could have happened in the sequence here described is already called into question when, after his description of the

---

[96] The unfinished *Critias* begins with Timaeus' closing remarks; Timaeus then hands the discussion over to Critias, to continue the programme announced by Critias at *Timaeus* 27a2–b6.

[97] γένεσις here appears to refer to the product of creation, rather than the process.

[98] Who are these wise men (ἄνδρες φρόνιμοι) from whom we would be right to accept this principle? We might compare *Philebus* 28c6–7, where all the wise (σόφοι) are said to agree that intelligence or reason (νοῦς) is king, and where intelligence is a principle of order in contrast to disorder.

construction of the body of the cosmos and at the start of his subsequent description of the construction of its soul, Timaeus
makes a point of saying that we should not take this order of discussion to suggest that the soul is 'younger' than the body it is to
rule (34b10–c2).[99] But the pretence of sequence is interrupted in
a far more radical way by what I shall call 'creation story 2', whose
narrative begins—at least as far as demiurgic activity goes—at
53b1, and which begins, once again, with a first demiurgic act of
creation, but one that in this case involves the creation of the components of the first item created in creation story 1.

Before this all these were without proportion or measure. When he [sc.
the demiurge] attempted to order the universe, first fire, water, earth,
and air—having certain traces of themselves, but disposed as is like for
anything when god is absent from it—these being of this nature at that
time, he first shaped by both forms and numbers. That the god put
them together in as fair and excellent a manner as possible from things
that were not thus, let this above all be the case for us, as something
always said. Now, therefore, we must attempt to reveal to you the
ordering and genesis of each of them by a *logos* uncustomary . . .
(53a7–c1)

'Before this', at the start of the passage, should be read, in context, as 'before the cosmos was put in order' (see 53a7). 'All
these', which are said to be without proportion or measure, are
the 'four kinds' of 53a3, where these appear to be pre-cosmic
traces of earth, air, fire, and water. Immediately preceding this
passage is a lengthy description of the pre-cosmos, as confirmed
by the start of our passage (53a8; cf. 52d4). 'Pre-cosmos' should
here be understood as the cosmos prior to, or considered independently of, any demiurgic activity (cf. 53b3–4 above: 'when
god is absent').[100] This description of the pre-cosmos comes at
the end of Timaeus' characterization of the receptacle, or 'nurse

[99] The question of whether or not the events described could have or are intended to be understood as having happened in the sequence so described relates to, but
is distinct from, the question of whether or not we should view the creation story as
literally intended. They are distinct, because there are ways in which one might be a
literalist about the creation story without supposing the creation described to have
happened in time, let alone both in time and in the precise sequence here described.
I am grateful here to remarks made by Myles Burnyeat in conversation.

[100] Cf. M. L. Gill (1987: 37).

of becoming' (52d4–5), a characterization to which I shall return. The description of the pre-cosmos is then followed by what is here described as yet another first demiurgic act of creation, his construction of earth, air, fire, and water. This passage thus marks the onset—in terms of demiurgic acts of creation—of creation story 2. Where creation story 1 began with the construction of the body of the cosmos out of earth, air, fire, and water, creation story 2 begins with the construction of these components of the body of the cosmos: earth, air, fire, and water.

Creation story 2 does not simply take over from creation story 1. Later in the *Timaeus* Timaeus will return to creation story 1, picking up pretty much exactly where he left off. Creation story 2 is thus contained within creation story 1. Since creation story 2 describes the creation of the components involved in the construction of all the material objects of creation story 1, one can think of the objects of these two creation stories as layers in the construction of the material cosmos as a whole. The objects of creation story 2 are embedded within the objects of creation story 1 in much the way in which, within the narrative as a whole, creation story 2 is embedded within creation story 1.

Next, then, consider the boundaries of creation story 2 and the resulting shape of the narrative as a whole. Creation story 1 breaks off at 47e2. Prior to this the demiurge has been described as constructing the body of the cosmos, its soul, and the lesser gods and planets. From 42e5 the work of construction is turned over to the lesser gods. It is they who are to have the task of creating all the mortal components of the cosmos, taking over from the demiurge only that part of human soul which is to be immortal: the rational part of soul, which is the object of the demiurge's final act of construction. The lesser gods first begin the work of constructing human body out of earth, air, fire, and water, just as the demiurge had begun his own work by constructing the body of the cosmos out of earth, air, fire, and water.

At this stage creation story 1 gets no further in its account of this work than the description of the construction of the human head (44d3 ff.), that which is the most divine part of the human body and is shaped like the body of the cosmos as a whole. Brief mention is made of the transporting body, followed by a discussion of two of the senses, each of whose organs resides in the head: sight (discussed at length, with a digression about mirrors) and hearing. The discussion of sight prompts Timaeus' distinction between contributory or auxiliary causes (συναίτια) and primary or proper causes (αἰτία) (46c7 ff.). The material constitution of the eye and the mechanics of vision are contributory causes of sight; examples of primary causes are the teleological explanations given to sight and hearing in terms of their role in contributing to the development of reason.

Creation story 2 ends and creation story 1 picks up at 69b2. Creation story 1 was interrupted at the introduction of the two kinds of causes, in the discussion of the lesser gods' construction of the head and of the organs of sight and hearing. Creation story 2 concludes with the following resumptive account of the two kinds of causes and their respective roles in the construction of the cosmos.

Among things coming to be, the demiurge of what is most fair and good took over all these things,[101] being of necessity of such a nature at that time, when he was creating the self-sufficient and most complete/perfect (τελεώτατον)[102] god. He used causes connected with these things as servants/subordinates (ὑπηρετούσαις),[103] whereas he himself fashioned the good in all the things that come to be. This is why it is necessary to distinguish two kinds of cause, the necessary and the divine, and to seek the divine in everything for the sake of the acquisition of a happy (εὐδαίμονος) life to the extent that our nature permits, but to seek the necessary for the sake of these, reckoning that, without these, those very things about which we endeavour cannot be discerned alone, nor grasped, nor got hold of in any other way. (68e1–69a5)

Prior to this, creation story 2 had made its way through the introduction and characterization of the receptacle or nurse of becoming; the account of the demiurgic 'first' act of constructing earth, air, fire, and water, beginning from the passage quoted above; an account of the interrelations between these four and their motion; an account of the phenomenal character of earth, air, fire, and water, and their compounds, including their

---

[101] The reference of 'all these things' (ταῦτα πάντα, 68e1) is unclear.
[102] The word can have both senses.   [103] Cf. 46c8–9.

perceptible and affective qualities as objects of the senses, pleasure, and pain, culminating in an account of colour, the object of vision. Creation story 1 broke off at the point of describing and explaining vision and hearing. Creation story 2 provides an account of the objects of human perception and desire, ending with an account of the objects of vision. When creation story 1 resumes once more, it embarks on an account of the constitution of the emotions and desire, followed by an account of the lesser gods' construction of the parts of the body corresponding to them. It is prefaced by yet another account of how the creation of the cosmos began, in a passage immediately following that quoted above.

Since, then, the kinds of causes from which the rest of the account must be woven together, being filtered out, now lie to hand, like wood for us as carpenters, let us again briefly go back to the starting point (ἐπ' ἀρχήν), and let us quickly journey to the same point whence we arrived here, and let us try to give our story a completion and crown/head (κεφαλήν)[104] fitting to what went before. For just as was said also at the beginning, these things being in a disorderly condition, the god produced commensurate proportions in each, both in relation to itself and in their relations to each other, as many and in the manner in which it was possible for them to be proportionate and commensurate. For, at that time, they had no share of these at all beyond the extent they had by chance, nor was there anything worthy to be named any of the things now named, such as fire and water and any of the others; but he first put in order all these [sc. fire and water, etc.], then out of these he put together this universe, a single animal having within itself all animals, both mortal and immortal. (69a6–c3)

This passage constitutes Timaeus' clearest acknowledgement of the way in which he has moved between the two different creation stories I have described. In proposing that we 'quickly journey to the same point' from which we arrived, he sets out to bring

---

[104] Timaeus' proposal to give his story a 'head' highlights the way in which his own narration may be viewed anatomically, and in comparison, directly, to the anatomy of the human body, the account of whose construction is interrupted by creation story 2, and, indirectly, to the anatomy of the cosmos as a whole. For a different, but not, I think, inconsistent approach to the construction of Timaeus' narrative, see Osborne (1996). And, for considerably more elaborate reflection on the anatomical character of Timaeus' speech, see Brague (1985).

us once again to the point where creation story 1 broke off. So, his reference to what was said 'at the beginning' is a reference to the start of creation story 1, to the first passage quoted above, 29d7–30a6. He gives a brief review of the demiurge's 'first' activity of creation story 1: the construction of the cosmos as a 'single animal having within itself all animals' (cf. 30d3–31a1). Into this review, however, he now incorporates the second of the demiurge's 'first' activities—that of creation story 2—the act of putting into order the components of the body of the cosmos, as constructed in creation story 1: earth, air, fire, and water. Here, therefore, the two creation stories are brought together. Timaeus' brief review of the demiurge's activity is followed by an equally brief review of that of the lesser gods. In this way he brings us back to the point at which creation story 1 broke off, and now resumes, with the continuation of his account of the activities of the lesser gods. The shape of Timaeus' narrative as a whole—and its repeated returns to how the construction of the cosmos began—are thus a reflection of the way in which these two distinct creation stories are embedded one within the other.

Within Timaeus' speech, the distinction between creation story 1 and creation story 2 produces three distinct accounts of a 'first' demiurgic act—the third a combination of the preceding two—and three *ab initio* accounts of creation. The first *ab initio* story (29d6 ff., the first passage quoted above) is direct and to the point. However, considerable preparatory work has been done since Timaeus began to speak at 27c1. He has invoked the gods. He has made a twofold distinction between that which is and has no becoming or creation (γένεσις) and that which becomes and never is (27d6–28a1). Corresponding to this ontological distinction he has made an epistemological distinction between grasping through reason together with an account (νοήσει μετὰ λόγου) and grasping by judgement together with perception, which is without an account (δόξῃ μετ' αἰσθήσεως ἀλόγου) (28a1–3). Since the cosmos is something created, and is therefore, Timaeus assumes, created in the likeness of some model, Timaeus has gone on to describe the appropriate character for the account he is to provide. As the cosmos is a copy or likeness (an εἰκών), the account he provides should likewise be likely (εἰκός).[105] Only once these several preliminaries are concluded does creation story 1 begin.

The first occasion on which Timaeus indicates that he is going back to the beginning once again is 48a7–b3. Once again, he invokes the gods (48d4–e1). Once again, he begins by making some distinctions. Here, however, to the twofold distinction between model and copy he adds the receptacle of all becoming, whose character he will proceed to describe at length. In due course he will add to this trio a threefold epistemological distinction; adding to the pair reason and judgement with perception that the receptacle is 'graspable through a kind of bastard reasoning with non-perception' (μετ' ἀναισθησίας ἁπτὸν λογισμῷ τινι) (52b2).[106] Once again, he emphasizes the likely character of his account (48d1–4).

In the case of this second *ab initio* account, the account of the first demiurgic activity is considerably postponed, beginning, as we have seen, only at 53b1, and preceded by the lengthy discussion of the receptacle that Timaeus' preliminaries have provoked. Discussion of the ontological and epistemological claims made in both sets of preliminaries is not my concern here.[107] (I shall, however, discuss the receptacle below.) I mention them only in order to highlight the striking symmetry between each of

[105] There has been considerable discussion in the literature on the *Timaeus* of this characterization of Timaeus' speech, in particular his subsequent description of it as a 'likely story' (εἰκός μῦθος), at 29d2. For a sample of recent discussion, see e.g. Osborne (1996); and the papers by Runia, Berti, and Santa Cruz in Calvo and Brisson (1997, pt. ii). Whatever may be the import of Timaeus' characterization of his speech as a 'story' or 'myth', it is worth noting that the characterization 'likely', in itself, given the manner of its introduction, appears to be a positive description; Timaeus' account has precisely that character it should have given the nature of the subject matter of which it is an account. The character of his account is like, that is, a likeness of, that of which it is an account. (Cf. here Vlastos 1939.) And so it is, I am suggesting, at least in so far as the anatomy of his account is comparable to the anatomy of the cosmos whose constitution it describes. For the relevance of the term 'anatomy' here, see the previous note.

[106] The term translated 'non-perception' gives us our word 'anaesthesia'. It is unclear whether we should think of this as simply denying the involvement of perception—as though equivalent to 'without perception'—or as indicating the positive engagement of non-perception, where this may be understood as perceiving values of zero for all functions of the senses.

[107] On the contrast between being and becoming, here and in general, see M. Frede (1988).

the first two *ab initio* accounts. As discussed above, the third and final return to the beginning occurs at 69a8 ff., this time in brief, with the aim of getting us back to where we left off. Here there is no repetition of these motifs.

Demiurgic Activity and the Shape of Timaeus' Narrative

Timaeus' three *ab initio* accounts of creation give somewhat different accounts of what precisely the demiurge did first. But they agree entirely on the general character and outcome of demiurgic intervention. The core component of demiurgic activity, common to each of the three accounts, is the imposition of order upon disorder (compare 53a7–b5 with 30a2–5, and again with 69b2–5). In each case, the demiurge is confronted by things that either are or are moving in a disorderly fashion (ἀτάκτως, 69b3 echoing 30a5) and that lack proportion and measure (are ἀλόγως καὶ ἀμέτρως, at 53a8, for which compare 69b5–6, as well as πλημμελῶς, literally 'discordant', at 30a4). His role is the imposition of order (τάξις, at 30a5), making the originally disordered elements proportionate and commensurate (ἀνάλογα καὶ σύμμετρα, at 69b5), in language highly reminiscent of the discussions of the constitution of structures that we have thus far considered.

The demiurge's imposition of order is governed by normative, teleological constraints: he imposes order, and order of a certain sort, on the principle that the cosmos he thereby constructs should be as fine and good as possible.[108] So, at 53b5–7, at the start of creation story 2, this governing principle of Timaeus' account is reaffirmed: 'That the god put them together in as fair and excellent a manner as possible from things that were not thus, let this above all be the case for us, as something always said.' Timaeus here echoes 29d7–e3, where the goodness of the

---

[108] I take it—to adapt a point from the *Euthyphro* (cf. 10a2–3)—that the demiurge imposes the order he does *because* it is good, not that it is good because he imposes it. Thus the value of the order so imposed is independent of the demiurge's so imposing it. This leaves it open whether or not the demiurge is a convenient fiction or whether the creation story here described should be read as literally intended. I remain neutral on this latter question.

demiurge and the impossibility of one who is good producing anything but the finest thing possible was first introduced as the governing principle and explanation of the cosmos' construction. Creation stories 1 and 2 each describes the construction of ordered wholes; creation story 2 describes the construction of ordered wholes which are themselves components of a larger ordered whole.

The teleological framework within which the demiurge works must be understood in the context of Timaeus' distinction between two kinds of causes: contributory or auxiliary causes (συναίτια, also συμμεταίτια at 46e6) and primary or proper causes (αἰτία). The distinction between these two kinds of causes clearly stands in some relation to my cartography of Timaeus' speech. Creation story 1 broke off immediately following the introduction of the distinction between these two kinds of causes and its exemplification through the account of vision. Creation story 2 concluded with a resumptive account of the distinction, now framed in terms of a contrast between the divine (τὸ θεῖον) and the necessary (τὸ ἀναγκαῖον) (68e6–7). And creation story 2 began with a clearly related distinction between 'things that have been fashioned by reason' (τὰ διὰ νοῦ δεδημιουργημένα) and 'things that come to be through necessity' (τὰ δι' ἀνάγκης γιγνόμενα).

The things that have been said thus far, except a few, have displayed the things that have been fashioned by reason; but it is necessary to place alongside them, through the account, the things that come to be through necessity. For the creation of this cosmos sprang, as having been mixed, from a combination of necessity and reason. And, since reason governs necessity by persuading it to lead to the best the majority of things coming to be, in this way and in accordance with these was this universe thus constituted from the beginning as a result of necessity being conquered by intelligent persuasion. (47e3–48a5)

The sharp distinction here made between things fashioned by reason and things coming to be through necessity, and the identification of the former as what has been displayed, for the most part, thus far has led some to see this distinction as the key to the shape of Timaeus' narrative as a whole. Thus Cornford divides his account of Timaeus' speech as follows: 'the works of reason'

(29d–47e); 'what comes about of necessity' (47e–69a); 'the co-operation of reason and necessity' (69a to the end).[109] In a variant scheme Vlastos proposes the following division: 'Triumphs of Pure Teleology' (28e–47d) and 'Compromises of Teleology with Necessity' (47e to the end).[110]

Vlastos's variant has the merits of avoiding one obvious difficulty for the schema that Cornford proposes. On any view, demiurgic activity is the activity of reason (whether or not it is an activity that also involves cooperation with necessity), and it is demiurgic activity that is responsible for the construction of earth, air, fire, and water, from 53b1, the 'first' demiurgic act of creation of creation story 2. It cannot, therefore, be the case that we are concerned solely with 'what comes about of necessity' from 47e until 69a, if we are concerned with this at all. What Vlastos shares with Cornford, however, is the assumption that the demiurgic activity described prior to 47e is of an entirely different character from that described thereafter (no matter where each takes 'thereafter' to begin). But this assumption may be questioned in light of the detail of both this and other passages.[111]

Timaeus' claim that the majority of what has been said in his speech thus far has 'displayed the things that have been fashioned by reason' does indeed suggest that he means to highlight—and subsequently depart from—some aspect of the character of what, up until now, he has *said*. However, while the claim that the things fashioned by reason are what his description of demiurgic activity has so far displayed could indicate that reason alone has been involved in the demiurgic activity described, it need not. For all Timaeus says, he may simply mean that the operation of reason is the only aspect of the demiurge's activity that his account has, in general, portrayed. This leaves open the possibility that the actual character of the demiurge's activities, in the activities described, is in fact rather more complex than Timaeus' description of them has as yet suggested.

---

[109] See e.g. the table of contents in Cornford (1937: pp. xv–xviii).

[110] Vlastos (1975: 28).

[111] Here I broadly follow the reservations of Lennox (1985, esp. 209–12) about Cornford's and Vlastos's account of the distinction between reason and necessity.

Consider what Timaeus says immediately after he draws his contrast between the things fashioned by reason and the things that come to be through necessity. Immediately he goes on to explain—as shown by the explanatory γὰρ of 47e5—that the creation of *this cosmos* resulted from a combination of reason and necessity; and that this universe was constituted *from the beginning* as a result of necessity being conquered by intelligent persuasion. There is here no suggestion that several elements of the creation of the cosmos were the works of reason alone, entirely insulated from the operations of necessity: quite the reverse.

Note, too, that, in his resumptive account of the distinction between the two kinds of causes, and of the operations of reason—the divine—and necessity, at 68e1–69a5, Timaeus says that 'when he [the demiurge] was creating the self-sufficient and most complete/perfect god'—i.e. at the point at which he was engaged in the activity described at the beginning of creation story 1, where Cornford and Vlastos find the operation of reason alone—'he used causes connected with these [things that were "of necessity" of such a nature at that time] as servants/subordinates, whereas he himself fashioned the good in all the things that come to be' (68e3–6). And Timaeus uses this account of the demiurge's activity as an explanation of why it is necessary to make a distinction between the two kinds of causes. Demiurgic reason must cooperate with necessity, then, at every stage of the construction of the cosmos.

In fact there were indications that this was the case right from the start, both in the assumption that the demiurge was faced with the existence of something prior to or independently of his creation and in the modal qualifications upon his activity. So, for example, at 30a2–3 Timaeus describes the demiurge as 'wanting everything to be good, and, so far as is possible, nothing to be bad'. At this point in his narration, however, Timaeus has provided no conceptual resources with which to understand the scope for limitation upon the demiurge's activity. Such conceptual resources await the distinction between two kinds of causes, with which creation story 1 breaks off, and the account of the creation of the cosmos in terms of reason persuading necessity, with which creation story 2 begins. These conceptual resources allow for a change in the character of Timaeus' account of creation without this implying that there is a corresponding difference in character in the *acts* of creation described before and after this change.

The modal qualifications on the demiurge's activity may be read in one of two ways. Clearly they are maximizing claims of some sort: he makes the world as good as possible and ensures, so far as is possible, that nothing is bad. But does this mean he makes the world as good as possible *tout court*, as we might say, the best of all possible worlds? Or does he simply make it as good as it can be, given the constraints within which he works? The latter seems better to reflect the way in which such qualifications are made, especially, as in 30a2–3, where the modal qualification is attached to the negative. The description of the demiurge as 'wanting everything to be good, and, so far as is possible, nothing bad' suggests that the elimination of badness entirely is not within reach. However, this need not mean that there is, within the created cosmos, an arena in which necessity operates entirely independently of the influence of reason.[112]

What is at issue here is the scope of the teleology, within whose framework the demiurge acts. The demiurge may be constrained by the limitations imposed by the materials with which he works. But, as Lennox has shown, it is these very materials that he deploys in order to bring to fruition that good order that his reasoning delivers.[113] The nature of these materials may force compromise, as it does, for example, in the lesser gods' construction of the head (75a7–c7). But these materials are not themselves outside the reach of the demiurge's intelligent activity; indeed, they are the agents of its results, the 'contributory causes' of those results.

Timaeus' distinction between the two kinds of causes and between the operations of reason and of necessity stands at

---

[112] That there is such an arena is the view that Cornford endorses (1937, esp. 162–77) and Lennox opposes (1985: 209–12).

[113] See e.g. Lennox's observation that the subject of ἄγειν (to lead) in Timaeus' assertion that reason persuades necessity 'to lead the majority of things to the best' (48a3) is necessity (1985: 210).

the juncture between creation stories 1 and 2. And the onset of creation story 2 marks the onset of a change in the character of Timaeus' account. However, the distinction between the two creation stories—the first of which, we may recall, in fact resumes at 69b2—is best seen, not in light of a contrast between the way in which the demiurge operates in each, but in light of a difference of level between them. Creation story 1 is concerned with the macro-construction of the cosmos as a whole; creation story 2 with the micro-construction of its (material) parts.

Is it significant that Timaeus' switch between levels—his move from creation story 1 to creation story 2—coincides with, and is framed by, his conceptual enrichment of his account of the teleological framework within which the demiurge acts through the distinction between two kinds of causes? It seems likely. Central to the demiurge's activity throughout, as we have seen, is the imposition of order—that is, the imposition of structure—on the pre-cosmic disorder with which he is faced. Questions about the reach of the demiurge's intelligent activity are therefore questions about the reach of that structure which his intelligent activity imposes. One of the benefits of attention to the relation between the two levels of constructive activity described in creation stories 1 and 2 is the way in which it reveals how structure goes all the way down.

My cartography of Timaeus' speech brings into focus the complex layering of the cosmos it describes and the way in which this layering is reflected in Timaeus' account of its construction. The Timaean cosmos is a whole of wholes, a structure of structures. In creation story 2 we find an account of the structure of wholes that themselves occupy positions within the larger structure whose construction is described in creation story 1. These layers of construction raise questions about the relation between the structure of the components (the objects of creation story 2) and the structure of that which they compose (the object of creation story 1). I shall approach these questions through discussion of, first, the account of the construction of the body of the cosmos, and, second, the account of the construction of earth, air, fire, and water, the 'elements' of which the body of the cosmos is composed.

The Body of the Cosmos

Creation story 1 begins, as we have seen, with a brief, first statement of the teleological framework within which the demiurge will be seen to work.

Let us say, then, for what reason the one who put it together put together creation and this universe. He was good, and no envy ever arises regarding anything in something good, and, being without this [sc. envy], he desired that everything come to be as like himself as possible. This most authoritative principle of creation and cosmos one would be absolutely right to accept from wise men. For god, wanting everything to be good, and, so far as is possible, nothing to be bad, took over in this fashion all that was visible—not resting quietly, but moving in a disorderly fashion—and brought it out of disorder into order, thinking the latter in every way better than the former. (29d7–30a6)

Working within this framework, and from the pre-cosmic condition with which he is faced—of which little is made here—the demiurge reasons out the best way for the cosmos to be in light of his desire that it be as good as possible. In particular, he reasons that the cosmos should have intelligence—on the basis of his discovery that, among naturally visible things, what has intelligence is fairer than what does not, when compared 'whole for whole' (30b1–2). Since one cannot have intelligence without soul (30b3), he thus constructs the cosmos as an ensouled animal or living thing (ζῷον ἔμψυχον, 30b8). More specifically, and in light of the nature of its model, which has within it all intelligible living things (30c7–8) and is in every respect complete (30d2), the demiurge 'constructed one visible living creature, having within itself all the things which are akin to it' (30d3–31a1).

As a living creature, the cosmos is a combination of body and soul. The demiurge's construction of the body of the cosmos is described as follows. Timaeus begins with the constraints upon the construction of body as such:

What has come to be bodily in form must be both visible and tangible; and nothing ever came to be visible in the absence of fire, nor tangible without some solidity, and not solid without earth. Hence, god, when beginning to put together the body of the universe, made it out of fire and earth. (31b4–8)

The components of the body of the cosmos must be put together in the best way possible. Timaeus thus goes on to describe the kind of 'bond' this requires:

But two alone cannot be put together in a manner that is fine without a third; for there must be some kind of bond in the middle bringing both together. And finest of bonds is whatever makes both itself and the things being bound together as one as possible; and this it is of the nature of a proportion (ἀναλογία) to accomplish in the finest manner possible. For whenever, of any three numbers—or bulks or powers[114]—the middle one is such that as the first is to it, so it itself is to the last, and, conversely, as the last is to the middle, so the middle to the first, then, since the middle becomes first and last, and the last and first both become middles, the same things will in this way, of necessity, result for all of them, and since the same things occur, they will all be one with each other. (31b8–32a7)

---

[114] I have been persuaded by the arguments of Pritchard (1990) that this is the correct translation of the disputed phrase ὁπόταν γὰρ ἀριθμῶν τριῶν εἴτε ὄγκων εἴτε δυνάμεων ὡντινωνοῦν ᾖ τὸ μέσον . . . , 31c4–32a1. By contrast, Cornford (1937: 44–7), takes ὄγκοι and δυνάμεις to refer to cube and square numbers respectively, and thus to restrict the kind of number in question. So understood, the reference to cube numbers is taken to anticipate Timaeus' subsequent reference to 'solids' (στερεά, 32b2). However, Timaeus' subsequent reference to solids precisely distinguishes them from the three-term sequences here described. Reproduction of the same kind of proportion between solids as is here illustrated by three-term sequences is said to involve the addition of two means, and produces a sequence of four. But the reference to ὄγκοι and δυνάμεις, however interpreted, clearly falls within the scope of the 'three', and thus cannot be taken to anticipate the subsequent point about solids without contradicting the very point there made. As to the need to restrict the point about numbers, the sentence in which the disputed phrase occurs is itself restricted. It does not make the (false) claim that such a proportion may be exemplified by any sequence of three numbers; rather it picks out just those sequences of three numbers—or bulks or powers—whose middle *is* such that as the first is to the middle, so is the middle to the last, and conversely. By contrast, Cornford's chosen restriction—to square and cube numbers—is, as he himself acknowledges, too narrow: three-term geometric proportions need not have a square or cube number at each extreme. I translate so as to leave open the question of the precise meanings of ὄγκος and δύναμις in this context. Pritchard offers one suggestion as to the meaning of δύναμις. Whatever precisely these terms may mean, they must refer to continuous quantities of some sort or other, such that they can be in a geometric proportion of the sort described.

Finally, therefore, Timaeus describes the demiurge's construction of the body of the cosmos in accordance with these constraints:

> If, therefore, it were necessary that the body of the universe come to be a plane, having no depth, one mean would suffice to bind both itself and the things with it. As it is, however, it should be solid in form, and solids are never fastened together with one mean, but always with two. Thus placing water and air in the middle of fire and earth, and making them proportionate to each other to the extent that is possible—such that as fire is to air, air is to water, and as air is to water, water is to earth—the god bound them together and established a heaven visible and tangible. For these reasons and out of things of this sort, four in number, the body of the cosmos was created in concord by means of proportion (δι' ἀναλογίας), and it possessed love (φιλίαν) as a result of these, so that coming together into unity with itself (εἰς ταὐτὸν αὑτῷ συνελθὸν) it became indissoluble by any but the one who bound it together. (32a7–c4)

The body of the cosmos is made out of the four elements, earth, air, fire, and water. In what follows, we are told that the formation of the cosmos exhausted these four elements, leaving nothing of them—or anything else—outside it. The body of the cosmos was made in the shape of a sphere, whose surface is smooth. And it was created so as to move in a circular motion. Each of these aspects of its construction and character has teleological warrant. The demiurge uses all of earth, air, fire, and water, first, on the grounds that the cosmos, like its model, must be as much a whole and as complete as possible; 'nothing like to what is incomplete could ever have become fine' (30c5; cf. 32d1–33a1). Not only that: the demiurge reasons that composite bodies tend to corruption through the assault of materials from without; in leaving nothing outside it, he thus ensures that the body of the cosmos may be 'ageless and without disease' (33a2).

The spherical shape of the body of the cosmos is chosen as that most appropriate for something that, being as complete as possible, is to contain within itself all other living things; the sphere being the shape 'which includes within itself all shapes' (33b3–4). The sphere is also that shape 'which is most like to itself' (33b6) or most uniform, and such likeness or uniformity is 'by far more fine' than what is unlike (33b7). The motion of the body of the cosmos is chosen as that most appropriate to its spherical body (34a1–2) and the one that attends reason and intelligence (34a2). Even in the case of those things that the body of the cosmos is said to lack—organs of sense, of nutrition, hands and feet—its lack of them has, as it were, inverse teleological justification; it lacks them for the simple reason that it has no need of them (see, for example, 33c1–d1, 34a6–7). And its lack of need is part and parcel of its self-sufficiency, itself a character of the body of the cosmos reasoned to be better than for it to be in need (33d1–3).

There is teleological justification for the use of earth, air, fire, and water in the construction of the body of the cosmos; but this justification is somewhat unevenly distributed across the four. The involvement of fire and earth is explained by the fact that the body of the cosmos, being a body, must be both visible and tangible, and by the fact that visibility requires fire and tangibility requires earth. These requirements look like material constraints under which the demiurge works, given the assumption of a created cosmos, and about which he has no real choice, nothing on which his reasoning as to what is fairest might get purchase.[115]

Clearly teleological, by contrast, is the rationale provided for the involvement, in the demiurge's construction of the body of the cosmos, of the remaining elements: air and water. At least, the addition of two further elements of some sort or other is explained by the requirement that the cosmos be put together in as fair a manner as possible, whether or not the explanation of this requirement can be tied more specifically to the character of air and water. The requirement that the cosmos be put together in as fair a manner as possible demands the inclusion of some sort of bond (δεσμός) intermediate between the two that are to be bound together. Such a bond will be fairest, Timaeus says, if it unifies both itself and the two whose job it is to bind together; and it is in the nature of a proportion, he says, to accomplish this

---

[115] Of course, the bodily aspect of the cosmos is one aspect of its construction as an ensouled living creature, and its creation as such has clear teleological warrant. But the object of the demiurge's reasoning was the construction of *soul* in body, and not the construction of body as such.

in the fairest manner possible. In the case of a solid, such a proportion is to be accomplished by the addition of two further elements, intermediate between fire and earth. In this way, the addition of air and water is a direct consequence of the demiurge's desire that the body of the cosmos be constructed in the finest way possible.

As Cornford and others have shown, the kind of proportion to which Timaeus here refers is the continued geometrical proportion, whose behaviour may be illustrated by the sequence: 2, 4, 8.[116] (i) the ratio of 2:4 is the same as the ratio of 4:8. Conversely, (ii) the ratio of 8:4 is the same as the ratio of 4:2. Given that the sequence of ratios can thus be run in either direction, the order of each pair of numbers (2, 4) and (4, 8) can be inverted thus: (i)* 4:2::8:4 and (ii)* 4:8::2:4, placing the extremes of the sequence—2 and 8—in the middle, and the middle—4—at the extremes (cf. 32a1–5).

Like Timaeus' own characterization, Cornford's example here uses a three-term sequence, with one mean. In the case of a solid, however, Timaeus says, not one, but two, means are involved in bringing it together. In light of his translation of the disputed phrase at 31c4–32a1, Cornford takes Timaeus already to have restricted his discussion to the case where the extremes of the sequences in question are either square or cube numbers.[117] But the move from two-dimensional to three-dimensional terms needs no such prior justification. Timaeus begins with three-term sequences of two-dimensional terms and uses these to illustrate the kind of proportion in question. Having thus fixed the character of the proportion, he goes on to consider how such a proportion might be realized in the case where the extremes are three-dimensional terms, a transition marked by his explicit distinction between 'plane' and 'solid' (32a7–b3). If the extremes of the sequence are solids—or cubes[118]—two means are to be

[116] Here I rely on Cornford's explanation in his (1937: 45–52).

[117] Cornford (1937: 42–7), and see n. 114 above.

[118] Here I accept Cornford's view that the reference to solids is a reference to cube numbers, or at least to three-dimensional items that can be represented by cube numbers.

used.[119] Let p^3 and q^3 be two cube numbers. A continued geometric proportion may be produced by the addition of two means as follows: $p^3: p^2q:: p^2q:pq^2::pq^2:q^3$.[120] Thus, let p be 2 and q 3, and one has the four-term sequence 8, 12, 18, 27 in continued geometric proportion, such that 8:12::12:18::18:27 and, conversely, 27:18::18:12::12:8.

The role of such geometric proportions is to bind things together so as to be one in the finest manner possible. The way in which a proportion accomplishes this binding is important. A proportion is not itself an extra element to add to those that it binds together; this despite the initial effect of Timaeus' reference to the need for a 'bond' ($\delta\epsilon\sigma\mu\acute{o}s$).[121] Such a bond is not an extra item, joining things together—like a bolt or suchlike.[122] Rather the elements to be joined are joined by means of the proportionate relations between them; and their standing in these relations exemplifies the proportion in question. It is in this way, perhaps, that a proportion is something that unifies both itself and the things it binds together (30c2–3). Against this, it might be objected that the unification here described does indeed involve the addition of something; it involves the addition of air and water. However, air and water are added only to ensure that we have sufficient terms to stand in the requisite proportions. The proportion in question requires that there be four components involved. But it is the proportion itself that constitutes these four as a unity; it is not that these extra components themselves somehow stick the four together.

The constitution of the body of the cosmos, thus described, is a good example of a structure in the sense with which I have been concerned. The four elements involved in its constitution are (an

---

[119] Timaeus' remarks might be taken to suggest that the production of a geometric proportion between two cube numbers *requires* the addition of two means. This, however, is false, as shown by the sequence 64 ($= 4^3$):216::216:729 ($=9^3$). The contrast is rather that, whereas between any two square numbers you can find one, and only one, mean such that a (three-term) geometric proportion results, there are two such means between any two cube numbers. I am grateful to Harry Harte for advice on this point.

[120] Cf. Heath (1921: 89), cited in Cornford (1937: 47).

[121] Contrast, however, the different assessment of McCabe (1994: 167–8, 184–5).

[122] Contrast the account of the lesser gods' construction of human bodies, where there is reference to what seem to be actual bolts ($\gamma\acute{o}\mu\phi o\iota$), albeit invisible ones, 43a3.

instance of) this structure, in virtue of the proportionate relations in which they stand to each other. Being so related, they are themselves structure-laden. To describe them as such is not to refer to any internal structure of their own that they may happen to have. As far as Timaeus' description here is concerned, each individual element need have no internal structure at all, although it will, in fact, turn out that they do. What is important here is rather their relations to one another. They are structure-laden in the sense that they occupy positions, both in themselves, and in relation to each other, that are determined only in the context of the structure that they themselves compose. The clearest indication of this is the fact that, as we have seen, the presence of *four*, rather than three or two, elements is a function of the requirements demanded by the nature of the structure they are to compose.

The demiurge's constructive activity begins not with the elements, but with the constraints upon the structure of the body of the cosmos of which they are to be part. He does not start by taking hold of the four elements and then seek to put them in the best relation possible. The structure he imposes is not something applied to the elements after the fact. Rather, the demiurge chooses to use (and, indeed, as we later discover, to create) four, rather than three or two, elements, because this is the number required for the realization of that unified structure that is determined by the teleological constraints upon his activity. Earth, air, fire, and water are not so much the object of the demiurge's ordering of disorder, as they are manifestations of that ordering in action. This is true of the role they play together in the construction of the body of the cosmos. It is no less true, as we later discover, of their own construction. This aspect of the demiurge's activity I shall consider below.

Several questions remain unanswered by Timaeus' characterization of the construction of the body of the cosmos. The demiurge places water and air 'in the middle of fire and earth' (32b3–4), and makes them as proportionate as possible in their relations to one another, such that 'as fire is to air, air is to water, and as air is to water, water is to earth' (32b5–7). In what sense are water and air 'in the middle' of fire and earth? The reference to what is 'in the middle' is, of course, a direct consequence of the discussion of proportions and their middle terms. But how, if at all, does this translate when applied to water and air? One might take the phrase spatially, and think of the body of the cosmos as constructed out of a nested series of rings of elements, with earth in the centre and fire at the edge; the latter since it is the stuff of which the visible heaven is made. Air and water would be placed in between these two extremes; water around the earth and air around the water and inside the fire.[123] A spatial reading of this sort would tie in with the clear Empedoclean resonances of the passage; not only in its use of Empedocles' four 'roots'—earth, air, fire, and water—but in the characterization of the body they compose as possessing 'love' ($\phi\iota\lambda\iota\alpha$) (32c2).[124] It would, however, be a somewhat subversive nod to Empedocles, since the separation of the elements from one another, in Empedocles, is a result of the agency of strife, not love.[125]

An appeal to a spatial reading of this sort may help to explain how water and air can be 'in the middle' of earth and fire. However, it does not help to explain the way in which the elements exemplify the proportion in question. In what sense is air to water as fire to air, and water to earth as air to water? The difficulty, here, as Cornford has noted, is that 'Plato has not indicated what are the quantities between which his geometrical proportion holds.'[126]

---

[123] Compare here Aristotle's account of the natural places of the elements, *de Caelo*, e.g. 287a30–3.

[124] See Empedocles fr. 6 (= 346, Kirk, Raven, and Schofield 1983) for the identification of the four roots and, e.g. fr. 17 (= 348, 349 KRS), for the role of love.

[125] I am grateful here to remarks made by Myles Burnyeat in his graduate seminar on the *Timaeus* in Cambridge 1993. That Timaeus' account of the construction of the body of the cosmos is rich in allusions to the work of the Presocratics, Empedocles included, has often been noted. For a recent discussion, see Palmer (1999, ch. 8). That such allusions may also be somewhat subversive may be seen by the way in which Timaeus concludes his deeply Parmenidean account of the uniqueness of the created cosmos: 'this heaven unique in kind ($\mu o\nu o\gamma\epsilon\nu\dot{\eta}s$) having been created, both is and will remain one' (31b3). 'Unique in kind' picks up a term now widely accepted as used in Parmenides B8. 4 (for a defence of the reading, see Owen 1975, additional note A). The subsequent sequence of past, present, and future tenses to describe the past, present, and continuing uniqueness of the created cosmos then seems a pointed contrast to Parmenides' subsequent denial of the application of past and future tenses in talk of his own unique being (B8. 5).

[126] Cornford (1937: 51).

This is so even if, as I have done, one departs from Cornford's narrowly arithmetical translation of 31c4–32a1, and sees there a reference to 'bulks' and 'powers'. This reference to 'bulks' and 'powers'—whose meaning is, in any case, less then clear—comes within the scope of the discussion of three-termed sequences. The sequence fire, air, water, earth is rather a four-term sequence of three-dimensional terms. Cornford's own suggestion is that the quantities involved are the total volumes of earth, air, fire, and water, fire being the largest and earth the smallest such quantity, whatever the figure of the quantities may be. However, it is difficult to assess such a suggestion, and for precisely the reason that Cornford himself has given: the passage provides no indication of how we are to interpret these ratios. This too may be part and parcel of the Presocratic flavour of much of the passage. Timaeus here treats earth, air, fire, and water as elements[127] in the construction of the body of the cosmos, elements whose own make-up is not subject to further analysis. This approach to the elements is subsequently corrected in creation story 2.[128]

Demiurgic Geometry: The Construction of Earth, Air, Fire and Water

Creation story 2 begins, as we have seen, with a return to the beginning (48a7–b3). Whereupon Timaeus immediately indicates the need to discuss the nature of the traditional elements 'before the genesis of the heaven':

With regard to the nature of fire and water and air and earth before the genesis of the heaven, one must behold both this and the attributes ($\pi\acute{a}\theta\eta$) before this. For no one as yet has revealed their genesis; rather we speak as though to [people who] know what fire and each of them is, [calling them] principles ($\dot{a}\rho\chi\grave{a}s$), positing them letters/elements ($\sigma\tauo\iota\chi\epsilon\hat{\iota}a$) of the universe, when it is not appropriate for them to be compared in like fashion even to types of syllable ($\dot{\omega}s$ $\dot{\epsilon}\nu$ $\sigma\upsilon\lambda\lambda\alpha\beta\hat{\eta}s$ $\epsilon\ddot{\iota}\delta\epsilon\sigma\iota\nu$) by one who has even the least sense. (48b3–c2)

---

[127] Here, as properly deserving the name; cf. n. 94 above.
[128] Cf. here Silverman (1991: 108).

Notice that Timaeus says that 'we speak' thus, including himself. And so he has, describing the body of the cosmos as a construct of earth, air, fire, and water, without providing any analysis of the 'elements' themselves. Discussion of the time 'before the genesis of the heaven' continues until the extended description of the pre-cosmos of 52d2–53a8.[129] Thereafter, the constructive work of creation story 2 begins with the demiurge's ordering of the universe and the second 'first' demiurgic act of creation, the way in which he 'shaped' (διεσχηματίσατο) earth, air, fire, and water 'by means of forms and numbers' (53b4–5).

We start with a lesson in the geometry of solids. Earth, air, fire, and water are clearly bodies (σώματα) and every body has depth (βάθος) (53c4–6). Depth is bounded by surface (ἐπίπεδον) and rectilinear surfaces are composed of triangles (53c6–8). All triangles, Timaeus says, derive from two, each having one right angle, the others acute. Of these triangles, there are two: one 'has on either side part of a right angle which is divided by equal sides' (this is the right-angled isosceles triangle) and the other 'has unequal parts [of a right angle] distributed to unequal [sides]' (this is the right-angled scalene triangle) (53d2–4). 'This', Timaeus says, we may set down as the starting point or principle (ἀρχή) of fire and the others (53d4–6), where by 'this' he appears to mean the sequence of geometrical claims he has made.

Next, Timaeus sets out the task he has set himself:

It is necessary to say which are the four fairest bodies that might have come to be, being unlike each other, but *some* of which are capable, when dissolved, of coming to be from one another. When we hit upon this we have the truth regarding the genesis of earth and fire and of those in proportion in the middle. (53d7–e4; my emphasis)

With the identification of water and air as 'those in proportion in the middle', Timaeus recalls at the start of this account of the demiurge's construction of earth, air, fire, and water the way in which the demiurge was earlier described as using them in the

---

[129] Whether or not we should take literally this reference to a time before the genesis of the heaven is, of course, a separate question. Nothing in what I say depends on a decision about this question.

construction of the body of the cosmos as a whole; placing air and water 'in the middle' (32b4) of earth and fire to create the requisite proportion. Timaeus is now to provide the analysis of their constitution that has been lacking.[130]

The task he sets himself is to identify four dissimilar bodies, which are fairest, and some of which may be transformed into one another. The need to address the intertransformation of earth, air, fire, and water into one another picks up an issue first introduced as a prelude to the introduction of the receptacle and the description of the pre-cosmos, at 49b2–c7. There Timaeus had recorded the following datum of experience:

what we have now named water, we see, when solidifying, becoming stones and earth, as we think; and this same thing in turn [namely, water],[131] when dissolving and separating, becoming wind and air; and air, burning up, becoming fire; and, conversely, fire, combining and quenching, returning into the form of air; and again air, coming together and condensing, becoming cloud and mist; and from these being condensed still further, flowing water; and from water, earth and stones once more; in this way handing on their creation into one another, as it seems, in a circle. (49b7–c7)

The circle of transformation as here described is not a perfect one. Water turns into air, which turns into fire, which can turn back into air and air back into water. Water is twice described as turning into earth and stones. But there is no mention of earth being observed to turn back into water, or to transform into anything else.

The anomalous position of earth in this description of the apparent intertransformation of earth, air, fire, and water anticipates the revision of this datum of experience that will subsequently be required by the analysis of their constitution. The results of this analysis will place earth entirely outside the cycle: it cannot transform into any of the others and none of the others

---

[130] Timaeus will describe the construction of sub-visible particles of earth, air, fire, and water. Phenomenal earth, air, fire, and water may then be explained as the result of numbers of such particles massing together.

[131] Timaeus must here start once more with water, rather than stones and earth. More on the significance of this below.

can transform into it.[132] It is a restricted-scope intertransformation, which Timaeus subsequently prefigures in setting as his
task the identification of the four fairest bodies, *some* of which
may transform into each other (53e2, cited above).

The reason for this restriction upon intertransformation is that
Timaeus identifies earth, air, fire, and water (or particles thereof)
with four of the five regular solids: fire with the pyramid; air with
the octahedron; water with the icosahedron; earth with the
cube.[133] Of these, the faces of each of the first three solids are equilateral triangles, whereas the faces of the cube are squares. And the
triangles that Timaeus selects as those used for the construction of
these respective faces differ also. The triangular faces of the first
three solids are each made up of six half-equilateral triangles,
selected as the fairest of the scalene triangles at 54a5–7. The
square faces of the cube are made up of four isosceles triangles, or
half-squares. Since the mechanism for intertransformation
involves the dissolution of one or a number of solids into its component triangles and the recombination of these same triangles
into a solid (or solids) of another kind(s), intertransformation is
possible only between those solids which share the same component triangles. Hence, cuboid earth, having different component
triangles from the others, cannot enter into such transformations.

Whether or not this restriction upon intertransformation
should be viewed as a disadvantage of the identification of earth,
air, fire, and water with the regular solids is not clear. It is a consequence of the identification which Timaeus makes a point of
noting, recalling and correcting the faulty impression which his
earlier account of our experience may have given (54b5–9). But
whether or not this constitutes it a disadvantage depends on what
we make of Timaeus' attitude to data of experience; for example,

---

[132] One might also notice that, at least on the first occasion of describing the apparent transformation of water into earth, Timaeus describes this as something we see
'as we think', a qualification he does not include in the descriptions of the other
observed transformations, returning only for the resumptive conclusion that they
hand on their creation into each other 'as it seems', where this, of course, would
include transformations involving earth.

[133] The fifth regular solid, the dodecahedron, is mentioned, indirectly, only once,
at 55c4–6, where it is said, somewhat obscurely, to have been used 'for the all' (ἐπὶ τὸ
πᾶν), 'embroidering figures on it', in Zeyl's felicitous translation (in Cooper 1997). It
plays no role in the construction of the elements.

whether or not he views such data as acting as a control on his account. I do not propose to pursue this question here. Whatever his attitude to data of experience, the principal influence upon his choice of the regular solids must be the necessity of identifying the fairest bodies. And, of course, to identify the fairest bodies is to identify the bodies the demiurge chose to construct. The demiurge acts, as always, in such a way as to produce the fairest result.

What makes the four regular solids—the pyramid, the octahedron, the icosahedron, and the cube—the fairest of bodies? As Cornford suggests, it must be their very regularity that holds the key.[134] Each of the four is regular; each, if circumscribed within a sphere, divides the whole sphere into equal and like parts (55a3–4).[135] And the faces of each—the equilateral triangle (pyramid, octahedron, and icosahedron) and the square (cube)— are also regular, having sides of the same length. And such regularity may naturally be associated with fairness. Notice, however, that the way in which Timaeus describes the construction of the solids disrupts the maintenance of regularity. In describing the construction of the solids, he does not take as elements in their construction their regular faces: the equilateral triangle in the case of the pyramid, octahedron, and icosahedron; the square in the case of the cube. Rather, he treats as elements the triangles of which these faces are said to be composed: the half-equilateral and the half-square. As has often been noted, this raises several questions about the rationale behind his procedure.

The first question is: why have triangles at all? The mechanism for intertransformation between those solids that can so transform involves their dissolution into component elements and the recombination of those same elements in a different form. But it is not obvious why this need involve recourse to elementary triangles, as opposed to the faces of the solids concerned. Second,

---

[134] Cornford (1937: 213).

[135] Cf. Artmann and Schäfer (1993). I am greatly indebted to Artmann and Schäfer's discussion of this passage, and to that of Cornford (1937). In what follows, I shall be taking over aspects of the discussion of each. With regard to the fairness of the regular solids, I am, however, rather less persuaded by Artmann and Schäfer's explanation than I am of their explanation of his choice of elementary triangles.

why have these two triangles in particular? Timaeus has claimed that all triangles originate from two triangles: the isosceles and right-angled scalene. Of these two triangles, he says, the isosceles has a single nature, whereas the scalene is unlimited in number (54a1–2). From this unlimited number, he selects the half-equilateral as being the fairest (54a5–7). But what makes this triangle the fairest? Why use these two triangles in the construction of the faces of the solids?

Finally, there is a question regarding the way in which Timaeus builds up the faces of the solids from their respective triangles. The triangles he has chosen—the half-equilateral and the half-square—are such that two of each would suffice to form the face required for the solids in question: two half-equilaterals could make up the equilateral face of the pyramid, octahedron, and icosahedron; two half-squares could make up the square face of the cube. But, in describing the construction of the faces of the solids, Timaeus chooses to use not two, but six half-equilaterals in the construction of the equilateral, and not two, but four half-squares in the construction of the square. Again, the question is: why do it this way?

In response to these questions, we may note, first, that, while the use of triangles as elements in the construction of the solids disrupts the maintenance of regularity, the choice of triangles does preserve symmetry. Each of the triangles chosen divides the respective faces of the solids—the equilateral and square—into two like triangles. (This, of course, is precisely why the third of our questions arises at all.) Not only that: both the half-equilateral and the half-square can themselves be divided into parts that are themselves half-equilaterals or half-squares, and this division can continue without limit.[136] The half-square subdivides into two half-squares; the half-equilateral subdivides into three half-equilaterals, as shown in Figure 1.[137]

As Cornford has noted,[138] the elaborate procedure that Timaeus chooses to use for the construction of the equilateral and square faces of the solids—which gives rise to our third question—

---

[136] So, Cornford (1937: 233–4), who suggests that this property of subdividing into parts of the same type as itself might be considered characteristic of an element.

[137] Taken from Cornford (1937: 233–4).   [138] Cornford (1937: 233–4).

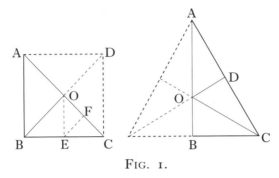

itself highlights this feature of the triangles chosen. In constructing the square faces of the cube from not two, but four half-squares, he constructs a figure containing two half-squares, each subdivided into two further half-squares. Likewise, in constructing the equilateral faces of the pyramid and others out of not two, but six half-equilaterals, he constructs a figure containing two half-equilaterals, each subdivided into three further half-equilaterals.

This feature of the triangles chosen provides the first instance of the way in which structure may here be said to go all the way down. The geometrical structure of the triangles chosen may be replicated internally without limit.[139] As Morrow notes, this means that we should be cautious in thinking of these elementary triangles as atoms.[140] While nothing other than such a triangle results from their division, such triangles are divisible without limit. In contrast to what we might dub a 'billiard ball' conception of atoms, this feature of the elementary triangles chosen places (geometrical) structures at the bottom-most level of material analysis.

In this self-replicating character of the triangles, Cornford finds the answer to all three of our questions: the explanation of

[139] Structure here does not just mean shape. The fact that the triangles chosen may be replicated internally without limit means that, within any one such triangle, one can endlessly reproduce the same internal geometrical relations as obtain between the sides and interior angles of the triangle. More on the significance of these internal relations below.

[140] Morrow (1968: 23).

the use of triangles, of the choice of these particular triangles, and of the over-elaborate way in which Timaeus uses them in the construction of the faces of the solids.[141] Since the triangles sub-divide into triangles of the same type, there are a number of different ways in which one might construct the faces of the solids, using different numbers of elementary triangles of the same type and size. This allows for different grades of each solid, whose faces are made up of different numbers of elementary triangles of the same size. So, for example, three grades of pyramid might have as faces equilateral triangles composed, respectively, of two, six, or eight half-equilateral triangles of the same size. Likewise, three grades of cube might have as faces squares composed, respectively, of two, four, or eight half-squares of the same size.[142]

Different grades of solid are required by Timaeus' later commitment to explaining the different varieties of earth, air, fire, and water in terms of a difference in the size of the triangle from which the faces of the solids are in each case composed. Here is Cornford's translation of the passage in question:

The reason why there are several varieties within their [the primary bodies'] kinds lies in the construction of each of the two elements: the construction in each case originally produced its triangle not of one size only, but some smaller, some larger, the number of these differences being the same as that of the varieties in the kinds. (57c8–d3)[143]

In this passage Cornford takes the 'construction' (σύστασις) of each of the elements, that is, the elementary triangles, to refer not to their own internal constitution, but to the way in which they are used in the construction of the faces of the solids. And he takes 'the triangle' produced by this construction in each case to be the half-equilateral and half-square; this because the reference cannot be to the triangle that forms the face of the solid, since only three of the four solids have triangular faces. He takes the reference to different sizes of half-equilateral and half-square as a reference not to different sizes of elementary triangles as such, but to the different sizes of half-square and half-equilateral triangles

[141] Cornford (1937: 234–9).   [142] Cf. Cornford (1937: 236, 238).
[143] Cornford (1937: 230).

that may be produced by combining different numbers of elementary such triangles of the same size, as described above.

The advantage of Cornford's interpretation is to allow for different sizes of solids without compromising the possibility of intertransformation between solids of different grades. Different-size solids have different-size faces, because they are made up of a greater or lesser number of elementary triangles. But the possibility of intertransformation is preserved because the elementary triangles used in greater or lesser numbers to make up the faces of the solids are all of the same size. As Cornford notes, if instead we took this passage to indicate that there were different sizes of elementary triangles *tout court*, it would be hard to see how different varieties of, say, fire, could transform into one another, or how there could be transformation between one (large) grade of air and a (small) grade of fire. Thus, when Timaeus chooses to use six half-equilaterals in the construction of the equilateral faces of the pyramid and others, and four half-squares in the construction of the square faces of the cube, he does so, Cornford supposes, in illustration of the construction not of the smallest grade of each, but of a grade of intermediate size. And his mode of construction highlights precisely that feature of his choice of triangles that allows for the construction of different sizes of solids from elementary triangles of the same size.

Cornford's interpretation of 57c8–d3 does indeed have the merit of providing a model for the construction of solids of different sizes that preserves the possibility of intertransformation between different grades of solids of the same or different type. But his interpretation suffers from the following difficulty. There were, recall, three questions to ask about the way in which Timaeus describes the construction of the regular solids: (i) why use triangles at all? (ii) why use these triangles? (iii) why put the triangles together in this particular way? Once triangles are involved, Cornford's interpretation responds to questions (ii) and (iii). But it does not explain why we need use triangles at all. For one could accomplish exactly the same result as that of Cornford's proposed interpretation by constructing the faces of the solids out of different numbers of equilateral triangles and squares, as appropriate, of the same size.

So, for example, if each face of the smallest grade of pyramid is one equilateral triangle, two further grades might have as faces equilateral triangles composed of four and nine equilateral triangles of the same size. Likewise, if each face of the smallest grade of cube is one square, two further grades might have as faces squares composed of four and nine squares of the same size. Cornford is, of course, aware of this possibility. He notes, however, that the intervals of size between the various grades of solid would be considerably larger, on this proposal; too large, he claims, to retain the claim that particles of the various varieties would remain below the level of vision. Thus: 'The three varieties of fire, for instance, would be too far apart; and if (as seems to be the case) there are considerably more than three varieties of water, it would be hard to suppose that the icosahedra could all be microscopic.'[144] But this claim is without obvious warrant.[145] Without it Cornford has no real explanation of the use of triangles.

An alternative explanation of Timaeus' choice and use of triangles comes from Artmann and Schäfer.[146] Their explanation also exploits the feature of the two elementary triangles remarked on above; that each subdivides into itself: the half-square into two further half-squares; the half-equilateral into three further half-equilaterals. But Artmann and Schäfer's explanation concentrates on the mathematical properties of these triangles, which are revealed in the manner in which Timaeus chooses to put them together to form the faces of the solids. Since Timaeus uses not two, but four half-squares for the construction of the square faces of the cube, the resulting square is double in area to the square of which the elementary triangle used is half. His chosen procedure for putting the faces of the cube together thus represents the method for doubling the square. For the construction of the equilateral faces of the pyramid and others, Timaeus uses not two, but six half-equilaterals; the resulting equilateral triangle is therefore triple in area to the equilateral triangle of which the elementary triangle used is half. The procedure used for putting the faces of the pyramid and others together thus represents the method for tripling the triangle.

---

[144] Cornford (1937: 238).   [145] Cf. Artmann and Schäfer (1993: 258).
[146] Artmann and Schäfer (1993: 258).

What Artmann and Schäfer go on to show is that, when the square and equilateral triangle faces of the solids are so constructed, they display the same kind of continued geometric proportion as was praised in the earlier account of the construction of the body of the cosmos. This is shown in Figure 2.[147]

When the face of the cube is composed of four elementary half-squares in the manner proposed, then a:b::b:2a. And when the face of the pyramid and others is composed of six elementary half-equilaterals in the manner proposed, then a:b::b:3a. Only by choosing to construct the faces of the solids out of triangles, and out of these triangles in particular, put together in just this way, would the faces of the solids display such geometric proportions.

Artmann and Schäfer's elegant mathematical explanation of the way in which Timaeus constructs the faces of the solids is preferable to Cornford's on a number of counts. First, it identifies a feature of this construction that could not be replicated by resting content with constructing the solids from their respective faces. Second, it gives a mathematical construal of the fairness ascribed to the particular right-angled scalene triangle chosen from the unlimited number available, at 54a5–7.[148] The description of this

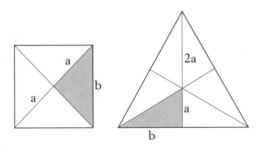

FIG. 2.

---

[147] Taken from Artmann and Schäfer (1993: 260).

[148] Artmann and Schäfer themselves write as if both elementary triangles are explicitly identified as the 'fairest' triangles (1993, *passim*). In fact, the description 'fairest' is applied only to the half-square, for it is in the case of this triangle that a choice is made. But, of course, the overall construction is designed to produce the fairest of bodies, and thus the half-equilateral must itself be fair, in this regard.

triangle as 'fairest' (κάλλιστος) ties in with the earlier characterization of the geometrical proportion that the use of the triangle displays as being the 'fairest' (κάλλιστος) of bonds (31c2). Indeed,
Artmann and Schäfer's explanation allows that, throughout this
passage, the criterion for fairness in the construction of the solids is
mathematical: fairness being found in the regularity of the solids
themselves, which is, of course, a mathematical regularity; in the
regularity of the faces of the solids, each having sides of equal
length and equal angles; and in the symmetry of these faces owing
to the manner of their construction out of the elementary triangles,
displaying in two dimensions the same geometrical proportion as
was constructed in three dimensions between the components of
the body of the cosmos whose own construction is here being
described.[149]

Adopting Artmann and Schäfer's explanation of Timaeus'
choice of these triangles allows for a second account of the way in
which structure, in the Timaean cosmos, may be said to go all the
way down. Consider once more the relation between the constructive activities of creation stories 1 and 2, as far as the construction of material bodies is concerned. Creation story 1
described the construction of the body of the cosmos out of
earth, air, fire, and water. It made the body of the cosmos a structure, exemplifying a continuous geometric proportion, instantiated, in a way that was left unclear, by the relations between its
components, earth, air, fire, and water. Creation story 2 describes
the construction of these components of the body of the cosmos—construction that is of sub-visible particles thereof.
Particles of earth, air, fire, and water are identified as geometrical
structures—the four regular solids—whose construction is such
that it exemplifies in the faces of the solids the same kind of proportionate relations. Geometrical proportion of the fairest sort

---

[149] Cornford's interpretation by contrast would be, at best, utilitarian: the triangles chosen are such as to enable the maximum number of grades of faces, and so
solids, with the least escalation in size. Even if Cornford were right that this is the best
way to account for intertransformation between solids of different grades, the 'fairness' of the triangles would then appear to reside in their ability to account for the
phenomena of intertransformation. But it is not clear how concerned Timaeus is to
account for phenomena, nor that he judges it grounds for an ascription of 'fairness' to
have done so.

thus appears both at the macro-level in the constitution of the body of the cosmos and at the micro-level in the constitution of the components of the body of the cosmos.

Notice that the reappearance of continuous geometric proportion in the constitution of the components of the body of the cosmos is not here offered as an explanation, in retrospect, of how the relations between earth, air, fire, and water exemplify such a proportion in the body of the cosmos as a whole. For such an explanation one would have to look to relations between the regular solids themselves, as opposed to the triangles involved in the construction of their faces. And I agree with Cornford that there is no obvious way in which the quantities involved in the construction of the regular solids (such as the number of faces or of elementary triangles of which each is composed) can shed light on the earlier passage.[150] Rather, there is a parallel between the macro- and micro-structure of the body of the cosmos, such that the same geometrical structure is found between the elements of the body of the cosmos—instantiated in the relations between earth, air, fire, and water—and the elements of the regular solids—instantiated in the relations between the elementary triangles and the faces of the solids, or sides thereof. And this latter is, of course, the bottom-most level in the construction of the material of which the cosmos is made, for the triangles are the elements of the solids.[151] It is in this way that structure may be said to go all the way down, and the same kind of structure at that.

Timaean Structure and the Nature of the Receptacle

Earth, air, fire, and water—or sub-visible particles thereof—have each been identified as a regular solid. These regular solids are clearly geometrical structures. But what are they structures of?

---

[150] Cornford (1937: 51).

[151] This is not to say that the triangles are the ultimate principles (ἀρχαί) of fire and the others. Timaeus makes explicit that his derivation of principles stops at this level, but that principles beyond these may be known to god and those god-loved among men (53d6–7). Nor does it threaten to make fire and the others syllables, even if not letters, that is components with only one layer of parts. The triangles compose the faces of the solids and the faces of the solids compose the solids, and even yet one does not have phenomenal fire, but only sub-visible particles thereof.

And how are we to understand such structures? Answers to these questions require consideration of the preceding discussion of the receptacle and the pre-cosmic condition of earth, air, fire, and water, and of the relation between this description of the pre-cosmos and the subsequent account of the construction of earth, air, fire, and water as regular solids.

Pre-cosmos, recall, may be understood as the condition of the cosmos prior to or considered independently of any demiurgic activity; independently, that is, of the imposition of structure. I take the preceding description of the receptacle and of the pre-cosmic condition of earth, air, fire, and water to provide an account of the material constitution of the cosmos conceived in the absence of that structure which the demiurge imposes. The subsequent account of the construction of earth, air, fire, and water as regular solids provides an account of the structure imposed by the demiurge upon this pre-cosmos.[152] Just this relation is indicated by the transition between the two passages, where, having described conditions prior to the creation of the heaven (52d4–53a7), Timaeus declares his intention to go on to describe the demiurge's imposition of order upon the pre-cosmic, unordered condition he has just described.

Before this all these were without proportion or measure. When he [sc. the demiurge] attempted to order the universe, first fire, water, earth, and air—having certain traces of themselves, but disposed as is like for anything when god is absent from it—these being of this nature at that time, he first shaped by both forms and numbers. That the god put them together in as fair and excellent a manner as possible from things that were not thus, let this above all be the case for us, as something always said. Now, therefore, we must attempt to reveal to you the ordering and genesis of each of them by a *logos* uncustomary . . . (53a7–c1)

Recall, too, the task that Timaeus set himself at the beginning of creation story 2: to describe the nature of earth, air, fire, and water before the creation of the heaven:

[152] This need not imply that there ever was a time at which the universe lacked structure and was as described in the receptacle passage; the description may be an abstraction from the ordered state of the cosmos; this despite the fact that Timaeus' manner of exposition suggests a time 'before the heaven came into being' (52d4) at which things were in the pre-cosmic condition described.

With regard to the nature of fire and water and air and earth before the genesis of the heaven, one must behold both this and the attributes (πάθη) before this. For no one as yet has revealed their genesis; rather we speak as though to [people who] know what fire and each of them is, [calling them] principles (ἀρχάς), positing them letters/elements (στοιχεῖα) of the universe, when it is not appropriate for them to be compared in like fashion even to types of syllable (ὡς ἐν συλλαβῆς εἴδεσιν) by one who has even the least sense. (48b3–c2)

The reason he gives for this task is that 'no one as yet has revealed' the genesis of earth, air, fire, and water.[153] And this, in turn, implies that Timaeus himself intends to do so. But to describe the nature of earth, air, fire, and water before the creation of the heaven is not in and of itself to describe their genesis. Rather, it is a necessary preliminary to so doing; necessary, because, if, unlike those who suppose that earth, air, fire, and water are permanent elements, we suppose that earth, air, fire, and water are constructions, there must be something to be said about their condition prior to or independently of that construction. This preliminary—the description of the pre-cosmic condition of earth, air, fire, and water—has been completed by 53a7.[154] Only thereafter does Timaeus set about the description of the genesis of each: so, in 53b7–c1, Timaeus proposes to reveal 'the ordering (διάταξιν) and *genesis* (γένεσιν) of each of them by a *logos* uncustomary' (my emphasis).

The description of the pre-cosmos and the subsequent account of the construction of earth, air, fire, and water as regular solids are thus related in ways that complement each other.[155] The description of the pre-cosmos describes the material condition of the cosmos in abstraction from that structure which the demiurge imposes; the account of the construction of earth, air, fire, and water describes the material structures the demiurge

---

[153] I take the γάρ at 48b5 to be explanatory.

[154] Notice that, at this stage, we have only 'traces' (ἴχνη) of earth, air, fire and water, on which more below. Whatever precisely this may mean, it suggests, once again, that we have not as yet completed the account of the genesis of the four.

[155] Contrast here Lee (1966) and Algra (1995, ch. 3), each of whom treats the discussion of the receptacle as a relatively detachable piece, available to be read in isolation from its surroundings.

creates—or at least the lowest-level such structures, the structure of the material components of all else bodily. As regards the understanding of these material structures, the two passages may, therefore, be interpreted together. However, the interpretation of Timaeus' description of the pre-cosmos—in particular, his introduction and characterization of the receptacle—is extremely vexed. I propose, therefore, to begin by reflecting on the nature of the regular solids with which earth, air, fire, and water are identified, and to work back to the receptacle from this standpoint.

The regular solids are geometrical structures; configurations of space (in three dimensions). They are, note, configurations *of* space, and not configurations *in* space—at least not if we think of the space they are in as a separate container. They are configurations of space because the three dimensions of which they are configurations are space. The regular solids could be configurations *in* space, like objects in a container, if they were made of some (other?) material, as if made of paper, say. However, nothing in what Timaeus says suggests that the regular solids are made of any material, unless space itself be that material (on which more below). Further, since the regular solids are to be identified with particles of earth, air, fire, and water, and since these latter are the material constituents of all else bodily, it is hard to see what (other) material the regular solids could be made of.

Since the solids are configurations of space, space as such—the three dimensions considered in abstraction from any specific configuration—might be viewed as the matter of such configurations. However, if we do so view it, we must not be misled by talk of 'matter' into thinking of bodily stuff.[156] A comparison with Aristotle may be instructive. Aristotle supposes that geometrical objects have matter (ὕλη), what he calls 'intelligible matter' (ἡ

---

[156] The receptacle cannot be *bodily* stuff, since it is not made of some combination of some or all of earth, air, fire, and water; but, according to the *Timaeus*, these are the constituents of all else bodily. Keeping the notions of stuff and matter separate will be important in what follows. Cf. here Algra (1995: 82–3), for the point that matter need not be viewed as corporeal stuff.

ὕλη νοητή);[157] and one persuasive interpretation of what he means by this identifies it as spatial dimension.[158]

These considerations allow a first approach to Timaeus' description of the pre-cosmos. Earth, air, fire, and water, ident-ified as four of the five regular solids, are specific geometrical configurations of space, where space, or spatial dimension, may be viewed as the matter of these configurations, providing we do not think of matter as stuff. If we then abstract from this account of the construction of earth, air, fire, and water that structure which the demiurge imposes, what we are left with is simply: space. Timaeus' description of the pre-cosmos is, I have sup-posed, precisely a description of the material constitution of the cosmos in abstraction from that structure which the demiurge imposes. Central to this description is an account of the recept-acle, which, notoriously, is explicitly identified as space (χώρα), at 52a8 (cf. 52d3), but which is described in ways that might make one think of it as matter.[159]

The 'receptacle of all becoming' (49a5–6) is introduced in response to a problem that arises in light of the datum of experi-ence, considered above, according to which earth, air, fire, and water appear to transform into one another (49b5–c7). The pre-cise nature of the problem that arises from the phenomenon of apparent intertransformation is unclear. It has something to do with the difficulty of securing identifying references to earth, air,

[157] Aristotle mentions intelligible matter by name on only three occasions: *Metaphysics* 1036ᵃ9–10, 1037ᵃ4, and 1045ᵃ34. In the first two cases there is no dispute as to the identification of intelligible matter as the matter of geometrical objects. The context of the third occurrence has given rise to dispute; for a defence of the parity between this passage and the others, see Harte (1996, esp. pp. 287–9).

[158] See the illuminating discussion of Detel (1993: i. 211–14).

[159] See Algra (1995: 72) for the identification of these (apparently) competing characterizations of the receptacle as one of the central interpretative issues for the passage as a whole. Algra himself identifies the dominant conception of the recepta-cle as being both matter and space, although he finds the passage inconsistent over-all. As Algra emphasizes, as important as the choice between the receptacle as matter and the receptacle as space is one's conception of matter and/or space. In particular, matter need not be stuff; and space need not be viewed as an absolute container (1995: 82–4). For a representative sample of views on the receptacle, see Cornford (1937: 177–210); M. L. Gill (1987); McCabe (1994, ch. 6); Silverman (1991); Sorabji (1988, ch. 3).

fire, and water. So, for example, 49b2–3: 'respecting each of these [earth, air, fire, and water], it is difficult [to say] which one must call really water rather than fire'.[160] And this difficulty, in turn, seems a consequence of a problem as regards the individuation of the four that arises in light of their apparent intertransformation: 'Since these each never present the same appearance, which would one not shame oneself in affirming without reservation that it is this—whichever one you like—and not another?' (49c7–d3).[161]

One can see how problems regarding individuation might arise here, especially in light of the fact that earth, air, fire, and water, viewed as elements, in the way which Timaeus proposes to correct, are, by tradition, the leading candidates for being the things that persist through change.[162] Suppose that one is faced with the apparent intertransformation of phenomenal earth, air, fire, and water into one another, but wishes to preserve the claim that these four persist through change. Water, one may say, persists through the transformation of the wet stuff of our acquaintance into stuff with the characteristics of earth, or of air, then fire. And so, of course, do earth, air, and fire. Each stage of the cycle is a stage of water, and of earth, air, and fire.[163]

---

[160] ὄντως, 49b2, appears to go with ὕδωρ, rather than with λέγειν, as Cornford (1937, ad loc.). Alternatively, the question is which one must really call water.

[161] The translation of this passage has given rise to dispute. My translation broadly follows that of Cornford (1937, ad loc.).

[162] Cf. here Zeyl (1975: 128–9), for a construal of the problem resulting from the apparent intertransformation of the elements broadly similar to mine. Zeyl, however, shares the widespread assumption that this problem is posed simply as an example of a more widespread phenomenal flux, often in turn compared to the radical flux discussed in the *Theaetetus*. However, if, as I suppose, the problem here posed is indeed closely tied to the role of earth, air, fire, and water, as candidate elements in the traditional sense, it is not clear to me that the problem must generalize, nor that the 'flux' on offer is anywhere near as radical as that of the *Theaetetus'* discussion. For examples of this widespread assumption, see Gulley (1960); Lee (1967); M. L. Gill (1987). For doubts, cf. McCabe (1994: 177–9).

[163] One might suppose that only one of the traditional elements persists and view the successive stages in the cycle as producing transformations of just one persisting element. However, in this case, too, this single element would not maintain a constant appearance over the course of the cycle. And, since there seems no reason to privilege any one of the elements over the others as the unique persister, it would again be hard to see why, at each stage of the cycle, one should identify it as a stage of fire, say, as opposed to one of earth, air, or water.

This being the case, no one of earth, air, fire, and water maintains a constant (phenomenal) appearance: each is at one time
wet and cold, at another cold and dry, and so on. But each gives
rise to the same sequence of (phenomenal) appearances as all
the others. How, then, is each to be individuated from the
others? At what stage in the cycle could one be sure to identify
one of earth, air, fire, and water, as distinct from any of the
others? And what exactly would one be identifying as earth, air,
fire, or water?

This problem regarding the individuation of earth, air, fire,
and water—however exactly it should be understood—is followed by legislation as to how we should speak (49c7–50b5, in
particular, 49d3–50a4). The precise force of this legislation has
been the subject of much dispute.[164] In brief, disagreement arises over whether Timaeus legislates for how we should speak
about fire—that we should call it not 'this', but 'suchlike'; not
'fire', but 'firelike'[165]—or legislates for what we should take ourselves to speak of when we speak of fire—phenomenal fire or
something else.[166] I do not propose to attempt to adjudicate this
long-standing interpretative dispute here.

There are, however, some relatively non-controversial things
one can say in light of the 'much misread' passage[167] and what follows. First is that, during the course of the passage, the receptacle
is identified as that in which earth, air, fire, and water come to be
present, and, in doing so, make their appearance therein, and from
which they in turn perish or disappear (49e7–50a1). The receptacle is thus a vehicle, in a manner yet to be explained, for appearances of earth, air, fire, and water. These phenomenal appearings
of earth, air, fire, and water are subsequently identified as imitations (50c5), imitations of the intelligible forms of earth, air, fire,
and water, for whose existence Timaeus 'votes' (see 51d3), at

---

[164] See e.g. the various discussions of Cherniss (1954); Gulley (1960); Lee (1967);
Mills (1968); Zeyl (1975); M. L. Gill (1987); Silverman (1991).

[165] So, Cornford (1937); Gulley (1960); Zeyl (1975); and M. L. Gill (1987).

[166] So Cherniss (1954), Lee (1967), Mills (1968), and Silverman (1981). What we
should take ourselves to speak of, when we say 'fire', is not agreed by all who take this
line. Cherniss takes it that we speak of certain recurring characteristics.

[167] After the title of Cherniss (1954).

51d2–52d1.[168] Discussion of the means by which this imitation is effected is explicitly postponed, at 50c6; I shall return to it. In all, then, Timaeus' description of the pre-cosmos somehow involves three kinds of entity (cf. 51e6–52b5): (i) forms; (ii) imitations of forms—phenomenal appearances of fire and the like;[169] and (iii) the receptacle, only now identified as space (52a8).

The identification of the receptacle as space comes relatively late in the order of Timaeus' discussion. Prior to that, and in addition to the comparison of the receptacle to a nurse (49a6) and, later, a mother (50d3), Timaeus has used three different images in describing the character and role of the receptacle.[170] He has used an analogy involving gold; he has described the receptacle as an impress or mould; and he has likened the receptacle in his characterization of it to the odourless base of perfumed ointments. I shall consider each image in turn.

[168] Timaeus uses the language of forms—εἴδη, 51d5—and of the characteristics of forms as 'themselves by themselves' (αὐτὰ καθ᾽ αὑτὰ, 51c1), reminiscent of his characterizations of forms in the *Phaedo* and *Republic*. But these terms, in themselves, tell us little about the nature of such forms; still less, therefore, could they be used to determine questions of the relative dating of the *Timaeus* and other works that talk of forms in ways that might appear to distance them from earlier characterizations.

[169] Both Cherniss and Lee divide this into two, distinguishing phenomenal appearances of earth, air, fire, and water from imitations of forms, which they identify as certain recurring self-identical characteristics. See Cherniss (1954: 129–30) and Lee (1966: 367).

[170] Timaeus is often also taken to compare the receptacle to a winnowing basket; and it is often supposed that this image quite clearly indicates that the receptacle is space, in the manner of a container, whatever else may be supposed to be the conception elsewhere in the passage; see e.g. Mohr (1980: 145). I myself find this image extremely opaque. First, the primary purpose of the appeal to a winnowing basket is to claim an analogy between the separation it effects in corn and the separation effected in the 'things'—whatever they may be—'in' the receptacle in its pre-cosmic condition as a result of its motion and theirs, each of which appears to cause the other. The primary comparanda, then, are, in each case, the things moved and separated—the corn and the 'things' in the receptacle—and not the things doing the separating—the basket and the receptacle. Second, if these latter—instruments for separating and the receptacle—are to be compared, it is not clear whether the comparison is to tell us something about what the receptacle is like, or simply about what it does. If the former, the information conveyed is less than specific, for the motion of the 'things' in the receptacle is compared to the motion of things shaken by 'winnowing baskets and other instruments for the purification of grain' (52e6–7), and the motion of the receptacle to 'an instrument for shaking' (53a4). Neither of these suggests that careful attention to the nature of a winnowing basket on its own should act as a significant control on our interpretation of the receptacle.

In the first, gold analogy (50a5–b5) Timaeus invites us to imagine someone who forms all the shapes (triangle, square, etc.) from gold, and who never ceases forming different shapes, one after the other (50a5–7). The image is followed by yet more legislation as to how we should speak, whose interpretation is again controversial. My concern is with the image and its significance. Within the image the gold stands in for the receptacle; the shapes for the appearance of fire, etc., within it; the ceaseless replacement of one shape by another for the continuing cycle of intertransformation of fire, etc., from which Timaeus began.[171] Since the shapes are here described as formed 'out of' or 'from' gold (ἐκ χρυσοῦ, 50a6), it is natural to think of the gold—and so, the receptacle—as the matter from which the shapes are made. And it is tempting to think of such matter as pliable stuff, something like plasticene, that can be moulded, by hand, into different shapes. But there is need to be cautious here.

The verb that I have translated as 'form' is πλάσσω, a verb that is indeed generally used for the activity of someone who works in soft materials such as clay.[172] But the material involved here is gold and gold is a metal, albeit a soft one. How exactly would a Greek of this period form shapes from gold?[173] Is this something that could be done by hand? Or should one think of a process involving heating the gold and pouring it into a mould or marking the shape upon it?[174] Notice, in this regard, that the things to be formed are shapes—the triangle and others—and that these

---

[171] Cf. here, for example, Zeyl (1975: 142).   [172] See LSJ, s.v. πλάσσω.

[173] This may be the question Lee had in mind when he asked, parenthetically, 'why *gold*?' (Lee 1971: 231). Mohr answers: because 'Gold is malleable . . . can receive and hold all shapes, unlike, say, a liquid, yet it offers no resistance . . . [and] can constantly be molded and remolded, unlike, say, stone' (Mohr 1978: 248). But the question is surely why gold rather than, say, clay, not than water or stone.

[174] Whatever procedure Plato has in mind in this image, it cannot, I think, involve rapid manipulation of gold by hand. Cook (1972: 160) lists the following techniques for Greek metalwork in general: 'hammering, stamping and impressing, repoussé, chasing (or ingraving), inlay, gilding and silver-plating, solid and hollow casting, and—for jewellery only—filigree and granulation'. (The latter apply to gold whose most common use was in jewellery.) So far as I have been able to discover, none of these are techniques of manual manipulation. For more on these techniques and their application to gold, see the entries under 'gold' and 'metal' in Turner (1996: xii and xxi respectively).

are two-dimensional figures.[175] How does one form a two-dimensional figure, the triangle, in three-dimensional gold? By making it as flat as possible in the shape of a triangle? Or by putting the shape of a triangle in it? Notice too that Timaeus does not persist in his 'stuffy' language; he goes on to describe the triangle and others as 'having come to be present in' (ἐνεγίγνετο) the gold (50b3).[176]

It seems, therefore, at best unclear whether or not the first image is an image for stuff, whether or not the receptacle may in some sense be considered to be matter in light of this image. The gold may instead be meant to be seen as the medium in which the shapes occur. This is certainly the tenor of the second image. Here Timaeus describes the receptacle as 'lying by nature as an impress/mould (ἐκμαγεῖον) for everything' (50c2). For ἐκμαγεῖον, LSJ have 'that on or in which an impression is made'.[177] This is the term used by Plato in the *Theaetetus* (191c9) for the wax block or tablet that provides the model for memory, on which sensory impressions are imprinted. The image is reinforced by Timaeus' description of the receptacle as 'being changed (κινούμενον)[178] and shaped (διασχηματιζόμενον) by the things which enter into it' (50c2–3). The term here translated 'shaped' is, we may note, the same verb later used to describe the demiurge's activity in imposing order on earth, air, fire, and water in their pre-cosmic condition: he 'shaped (διεσχηματίσατο) [them] by means of forms and numbers' (53b4–5). Shape and the process of being shaped thus feature in both the first and second analogies. In the first, shapes are formed from gold and come to be present in it. In the second,

---

[175] As noted by McCabe (1994: 182).

[176] See Algra (1995: 90–1) for one careful proposal as to how to construe the 'in' and 'out of' language in such a way as to respect both.

[177] LSJ, s.v. ἐκμαγεῖον II.

[178] I translate κινούμενον as 'changed' rather than 'moved' since, if the receptacle is to be identified as space, it is hard to see how it could itself move (as opposed to have things move within it). The description of things 'entering into' and 'departing from' it (50c4–5) is consistent with the receptacle's identification as space, providing their so entering into and departing from it coincides with their coming to be and perishing; and so it must, for the things that enter into and depart from the receptacle are phenomenal appearings of fire, etc., that can have no (individual) existence beyond their occurrence in the receptacle.

the receptacle, as impress or mould, is shaped by the things that enter it.

The third and final image begins with a departure from talk of shapes and shaping. But it continues to represent the receptacle as a kind of medium, analogous to the odourless base of perfumed ointments. The point of the analogy is to show that a medium must itself be free from the characteristics for which it is to act as medium, in order to do so effectively; if a perfume base were itself scented, its own scent would obtrude and destroy, or at best disrupt, the effect of the perfume. Timaeus provides a second example, which returns to the core example of shapes: 'those who set out to take impressions of shapes in soft materials, do not', he says, 'allow any shape to be apparent therein, but by levelling [the materials] out make them as smooth as possible' (50e8–51a1). Here, unlike the first analogy, we appeal to those who work in soft materials such as clay. But the shapes to be formed are not formed by moulding the material; they are impressed within it. Again, the image is of a medium in which the shapes are formed, not of a stuff from which they are made.

Taken together, then, the images used for the receptacle characterize it as a medium in which imitations of forms occur.[179] While there is much that remains unclear about the manner of their occurrence within it, the images used suggest the following points. The occurrence of imitations of forms within the receptacle may be thought of in a manner analogous to the way in which an impress occurs in wax or other soft materials. This may be viewed in contrast to the way in which an object may be 'in' a container.[180] An impress, unlike a container, does, in some sense, take on and display the impressions it receives, but it does so without altering its own character. Indeed, as in the first analogy, an impression made upon wax—or softened gold—may be said to be formed 'from' the gold, for it is the configuring of the wax or gold as a result of the impression made that produces an observable triangular shape. But the triangle thus displayed is

---

[179] Cf. Mohr (1980, esp. pt II), who also takes the image of the receptacle as a medium to be the dominant conception arising from Timaeus' various images.

[180] For a similar contrast, see Algra (1995: 92).

not, note, a waxen or golden triangle.[181] It is not made out of wax or gold; the wax or gold is the medium that is informed by the impression it receives. One may think of this medium as the matter for the impression; but, if one does, one should not think of it as the stuff of which the impression is made. In all three analogies the lead example of this process of being impressed is a medium that takes on, or in some sense displays, shape by being itself shaped.

When the receptacle, viewed as such a medium, is subsequently identified as space, this provides us with a characterization of the medium of the sort we should expect in light of reflection on the subsequent identification of earth, air, fire, and water with the regular solids. These, as I have said, are configurations of space. And space, abstractly conceived, may indeed be viewed as the (unstructured) medium, which takes on and is informed by the geometrical structure of a regular solid—precisely by taking on (specific) shape, now in three dimensions—and in which such geometrical structure occurs. Thus far, whatever else remains unclear, the two passages—the characterization of the receptacle in the description of the pre-cosmos and the subsequent identification of earth, air, fire, and water with the regular solids—do indeed complement one another.

Return once more, then, to the regular solids, conceived as configurations of space, now identified as the receptacle. One might be tempted to ask whether these configurations are empty, are configurations of empty space? The question, though natural, is, I think, mistaken. It is tempting to provide oneself with a visual image for the regular solids, at least in one mind's eye. One might imagine the solids made using pipe cleaners or straws for their edges, or sheets of paper for their faces. Imagined thus, the solids are hollow; they seem to be empty. And thus the question of their content—or lack of it—arises. But models of the regular solids, thus imagined, are configurations *in* space, where space is, if you like, their container; they are not configurations *of* space or configurations in space where space—rather than pipe cleaners

---

[181] Cf. M. L. Gill (1987: 46), although Gill takes it to follow from this that the receptacle is not matter.

or paper—is what takes on and displays the shape. Viewed as configurations *of* space the regular solids are not empty, not empty of space, that is, for they are three-dimensional.

But, while the full–empty question seems mistaken, there is another question that might be supposed to lie behind it. This is the question of whether the space, so configured, has features or is without features. Considered as configured in the form of one of the regular solids, the space so configured is clearly intended to be viewed as having features, the features, as it may be, of fire, or of earth, air, or water. Timaeus ties these features to the geometrical character of the solid in question. So, for example, particles of fire are both mobile and light, the lightest and most mobile of the four elements. It is most mobile through having the least number of faces and hence the sharpest, or most acute, edges and points; it is lightest through having the least number of like parts (it is made of the smallest number of elementary triangles, and has the least number of faces) (56a6–b2). The relative mobility and lightness of the other three may be similarly explained, *mutatis mutandis*. For each solid, their respective mobility and lightness is explained in terms of the geometrical character of the relevant solid; indeed, the specific configuration of space involved is, we might say, constitutive of the features in question.

Timaeus later goes on to explain the perceptual features of earth, air, fire, and water, and varieties and compounds thereof, by appeal to the geometrical character of (masses of) the regular solids (in combination with the sensory organs of the body).[182] Consider, for example, his explanation of the (felt) heat of fire:

First, let us say how it is we call fire 'hot'. We may see this by considering as follows: having in mind the separating and cutting effect it has on our body. We all at least perceive that the affection is something sharp; the extreme fineness of sides, acuteness of the angles, smallness of the

---

[182] Timaeus stresses that, in fact, a full account of sensory qualities cannot be given without reference both to the character of the objects of the senses and to that of the sensory organs of the body and the relevant (mortal) parts of soul (61c6–d2). Since it is not possible to talk of both at once (d2), the first task is accomplished by the final stages of what I have labelled creation story 2; the second is the task that creation story 1 takes up first, immediately upon resuming.

parts and swiftness of movement, as a result of all of which it is violent and sharp and cuts whatever it encounters, must be reckoned (λογιστέον)[183] by our recalling the creation of its shape [or: figure] (σχήματος); [recalling] that this and no other nature most especially divides and cuts up bodies into small pieces and provides that affection which we just now called hot, in like fashion, and the name.[184] (61d5–62a5)

The affective qualities of heat are here directly traced to the geometrical character of the shape with which fire has been identified.

At least when configured in the form of the regular solids, then, space, so configured, does indeed have features, including perceptible features; the latter at least when such solids accumulate together in sufficient numbers for their effects to be observable. And the specific configuration of space involved and its geometrical character are constitutive of the features in question. This being the case, it need come as no surprise if space, considered in abstraction from such specific configurations, should itself be lacking in features. In the earlier passage Timaeus has indeed portrayed the receptacle as being entirely without features. It has no form (μορφή) like to any of the things that enter into it (50c1–2). It is 'invisible (ἀνόρατον) and formless (ἄμορφον)' (51a7). Indeed, it is, quite literally, 'without *shape*', 'shape' being one possible translation of μορφή (twice translated as 'form').[185]

This cannot be all of the story, however. Even in its pre-cosmic condition, as described in the passage preceding the account of the regular solids, the receptacle does take on certain impressions and gives the appearance of certain features. 'The part of it which is made fiery appears on each occasion as fire; the part which is moistened appears as water; and [it appears] as earth and air

---

[183] These latter features cannot, of course, be *perceived*, since the particles of fire—and of earth, air, and water—are (individually) imperceptible, and what can be perceived when such particles accumulate en masse is just their perceptible qualities, an example of which is here being illustrated.

[184] Cornford (1937: 260 with n. 1) must be right to suppose that Timaeus is here suggesting an etymology for θερμός (hot), although the details of the proposed etymology are unclear.

[185] See LSJ, s.v. μορφή.

throughout however much of it[186] receives imitations of these' (51b4–6). Notice that it is a part or region of the receptacle that is made fiery and thus appears as fire. The identification of specific parts or regions of space is parasitic upon that (portion) of space being somehow configured.[187] We may, therefore, suppose that, even in its pre-cosmic condition, in the absence of that structure the demiurge imposes, the receptacle is somehow configured.

This supposition will help to answer two key questions. First, how are we to understand the claim that in the pre-cosmic condition here described earth, air, fire, and water have 'certain traces of themselves', despite 'being disposed in the manner likely for everything when god is absent' (53b2–4)? Second, how are we to understand the role played by forms in these appearances within (regions of) the receptacle? Timaeus is explicit that the portions of the receptacle that appear as earth or air receive 'imitations' ($\mu\iota\mu\dot{\eta}\mu\alpha\tau\alpha$) of these (51b6), that is, of forms. But how does this work? And what is the relation between the reception of imitations of forms and the later identification of particles of earth, air, fire, and water with the regular solids?

If we are allowed to suppose that, in its pre-cosmic condition, the receptacle is somehow configured, as we must, it seems, given the reference to parts or regions thereof, there are two ways in which the first question might be answered. In both cases we may continue to assume that, as in the subsequent account of the regular solids, having the features of—and thus appearing as— earth, air, fire, or water is tied to the way in which (a portion of) the receptacle is configured. The alternatives are: (i) to suppose that, by some cosmic accident, portions of the receptacle take on precisely those configurations which the demiurge sub- sequently imposes, but do so only fleetingly, or in some other

---

[186] My translation takes $\kappa\alpha\theta'$ $\ddot{o}\sigma ov$ $\ddot{\alpha}v$ . . . on the model of $\kappa\alpha\tau\dot{\alpha}$ $\pi\hat{\alpha}v$, in 51a2, 'throughout all', and in a way comparable to the identification of parts of the recepta- cle in the case of its appearance as fire and as water. Alternatively, it may simply be read as saying that it appears 'as earth and air to the extent that it receives imitations of these', where the reception of these imitations by a part of the receptacle in each case will simply be left implied.

[187] Silverman (1991: 93) rightly stresses that the regionalization of the receptacle requires something further than the receptacle itself, even when the receptacle is viewed, as does Silverman also, as space.

unstable fashion; or (ii) to suppose that, in the pre-cosmic condition, portions of the receptacle are configured in ways that closely resemble, but do not precisely correspond to, the configuration of the regular solids. For my purposes, the important point is common to these two alternatives: that the presence of phenomenal fire, rather than earth, is tied to the specific configuration of the relevant portion of the receptacle. Of the alternatives, I myself favour the second, for, on the first, it seems to me hard to see why we have only 'traces' of fire or earth, as opposed to the phenomena themselves.[188]

What makes an (irregular, but pyramid-like) configuration of a portion of the receptacle a trace of fire, as opposed to a trace of water? The short answer is: by being an imitation of fire. But what makes this an imitation of fire, rather than of water? If the configuration of the portion of the receptacle in question is responsible for its appearance as fire and its fire-like qualities, then its being so configured must be what constitutes it an imitation of fire. This then allows the following answer as regards the relation between the reception of forms by the receptacle and the demiurge's construction of the regular solids. The regular geometrical configurations that the demiurge imposes upon the receptacle are the means by which the demiurge instantiates the forms of earth, air, fire, and water.[189] The account of the geometrical construction is what gives content to the manner of the receptacle's (eventual, ordered, stable) reception of forms, content the requirement for which was flagged and postponed, at 50c6. Particles of earth, air, fire, and water, as constructed by the

---

[188] One might, however, take the references to 'traces' to be another way of distinguishing the phenomena from forms.

[189] My interpretation, which is, in a number of respects, broadly in sympathy with that of Silverman (1991), departs from his interpretation here. On his interpretation, the configuration of the receptacle merely provides a locus for the occurrence of instances of fire, earth, etc. (see esp. 1991: 109–10). On my interpretation, the configuration of the receptacle thus and so itself constitutes the occurrence of an instance of fire or earth; this without suggesting that the forms of fire and earth are themselves (the type) regular solids. This rather simpler model has the advantages of avoiding the ad hoc quality of the co-occurrence of (i) a geometrical configuration of the appropriate sort and (ii) the presence of form-copies of the corresponding sort, which Silverman himself identifies as a consequence of his position.

demiurge, imitate forms through their geometrical construction; they are structures of space, whose properties, perceptible and other, are parasitic upon their geometrical structure.[190]

This, I contend, is, at least, a permissible interpretation of Timaeus' discussion of the receptacle and his account of the regular solids and of their relation, although it is not without difficulties.[191] But it is, clearly, an interpretation. Timaeus does not say all of this. In particular, he does not tell us that the configuration of space—pre- or post creation—accounts for the imitations therein of forms. But then he does not tell us anything directly about how this works (unless the geometrical account does so). Of course, the geometrical account does not tell us why one specific geometrical configuration—the pyramid, for example—should constitute an instance of fire. That, in part, is because Timaeus tells us nothing very much about the nature of the form of fire. He does, however, make a concerted effort to tie the properties of fire etc. to the geometrical character of the particles thereof.

Is the account of earth, air, fire, and water as here reconstructed at all plausible? In one sense, clearly not. I do not suppose that we will embrace the physics of the *Timaeus*. But is it so implausible that it casts doubt upon the interpretation? What may seem odd to us is the idea that something as 'physical' as fire should be identified with a geometrical structure, a configuration of (a

[190] Is the space the subject of these properties or their location? I do not think that my interpretation has as yet forced a decision on this issue, a resolution of which appears to depend upon resolving the disagreement as to how Timaeus legislates for speech. I do not propose to attempt to resolve this question here.

[191] One among them concerns motion: that of the receptacle and of the 'things' within it, each of which appears to be said to move—each in consequence of the other's motion—in the pre-cosmic condition described in 52e1–53a7, on which see also n. 170 above. But this interpretation is not obviously worse off than an interpretation according to which the receptacle is space, viewed as a container. While it might then be easier to see how the 'things' within it might move, it is not easy to see why this should result in the receptacle moving, nor how the receptacle could move at all, unless it too is in a (further) container. On the other hand, if we may think of change here—rather than motion in space—it is rather easier to see why the change of a configuration of something would change that which is configured and vice versa than to see why the change of an object in a container should change the container. Two nice objections of a different kind to a configuration interpretation like my own are outlined in A. Gregory (2000, ch. 8, §5).

region of) space.[192] In the context of the *Timaeus*, however, there
is rather less reason to find this odd. Throughout the *Timaeus*
that structure which it is the business of the demiurge to impose
is characterized, broadly speaking, as mathematical in nature.
This is true of examples I have not considered: the construction
of the world soul, for example.[193] And it is true of the examples I
have considered. In identifying particles of earth, air, fire, and
water with geometrical structures, Timaeus demonstrates that
here, at the lowest level of the material constitution of the cosmos, as in its macro-constitution, the demiurge imposes structure which, first and foremost, is geometrical in character.

Timaean and Phileban Structure

The geometrical character of the structure the demiurge imposes may be compared with the *Philebus'* characterization of the
members of the class of limit—where members of the class of
limit, recall, constitute structure. Members of the class of limit
are mathematically expressible relations—ratios and proportions—instantiated by the paired opposing members of the
unlimited class—this latter class constituting the domain of content upon which such structure is imposed. This mathematiciza-
tion of structure is especially pronounced in the *Timaeus*. In
identifying particles of earth, air, fire, and water—themselves the
material components of all else bodily—as the regular solids, the
Timaeus, at least in some sense, makes these mathematical, or
geometrical, entities. In both the *Philebus* and the *Timaeus* mathematical structure is associated with value. In the *Timaeus* it is by
the imposition of such mathematical structure on the pre-cosmic

---

[192] This is no less odd, I submit, than the association, often identified in works
such as the *Republic* or indeed the *Philebus*, between mathematical properties and
properties of value, present in the *Timaeus* also in the normative characterizations of
the (mathematical) structure imposed by the demiurge. For a defence of the substantive nature of such associations, see Burnyeat (2000). Indeed, it may seem less odd
than such associations, given the close relation between 20th-century physics and
mathematics.

[193] See 35a1–36b6 with Cornford (1937, ad loc.). Here again, the imposition of
mathematical proportions is important, and the structure mathematical, and, indeed,
musical, in nature.

condition with which he is faced that the demiurge makes the world as good as possible.

Both the *Philebus* and the *Timaeus* support a twofold analysis of the constitution of structured wholes. The *Philebus* does so directly, in its analysis of mixtures in terms of limit and unlimited. The *Timaeus* does so indirectly, if, as I have suggested, one identifies the respective, complementary roles played by the characterization of the receptacle and the pre-cosmic condition of earth, air, fire, and water and the characterization of the demiurgic ordering thereof. In each work, the twin aspects of the analysis, broadly stated, are: (i) mathematical structure and (ii) that on which such structure is imposed. In the *Philebus* the twin components of its twofold analysis appeared separable only in analysis. In the *Timaeus* the separation between that on which order is imposed and the order imposed thereon seems sharper. In large part, however, this is a function of the *Timaeus'* talk of a creator and of a creation in time. It is less clear how separable the twin components of the analysis would seem, except in abstraction, were these features of Timaeus' description to be suppressed or construed atemporally.

Like the unlimited of the *Philebus*, the receptacle is described in negative terms. Here, though, this negative characterization is taken to an extreme not found in the *Philebus*. Thus, in the *Philebus*, members of the unlimited—paired components, such as hot and cold—have some positive characteristics of their own. In the *Timaeus*, by contrast, although the receptacle is not without features, in its pre-cosmic condition, having traces of earth, air, fire, and water, the receptacle, in itself, is characterized as being entirely lacking in (positive) features. *A fortiori*, there is no sign, in the *Timaeus*, of the opposition between pairs of features—such as hot and cold—that is central to the characterization of the unlimited in the *Philebus*. In the *Timaeus* the receptacle's lack of any positive characteristics is, I suggest, a corollary of the proposal that, here, structure is seen to go all the way down. In the Timaean cosmos there is nothing that can be characterized positively that is not in some way the product of structure. The receptacle—being, as it were, the matrix for such structure, at least in the material realm—is thus without positive features of its own.

This contrast between the *Timaeus* and the *Philebus* has consequences for the division of labour in their respective twofold analyses between content and structure. In the analysis of the *Philebus* the unlimited provides the domain of content; limit the structure imposed thereon. In the *Timaeus*, by contrast, characterful content is itself a product of structure; the receptacle is the characterless medium upon which such contentful structure is imposed.[194] In both, however, if in somewhat different ways, structured wholes may be characterized as contentful structures in the way I have proposed.

It need come as no surprise that there should be differences regarding the analysis of wholes between the *Philebus* and the *Timaeus*. For one thing, they are concerned to give an account of the constitution of rather different wholes: with the constitution of those complex abstract objects that are the objects of scientific expertise, in the *Philebus*; with the macro- and micro-constitution of the body of the cosmos, in those passages of the *Timaeus* on which I have focused. And there is, in any case, no reason to suppose that Plato has a single, fully determinate positive theory about the constitution of complex wholes that he must put to work on every occasion. What is, perhaps, surprising is the number of points of convergence and related ideas one finds in these disparate positive discussions of composition in the *Sophist*, *Philebus*, and *Timaeus*. Bringing these together allows for some final consideration of what we might, with due provisos, call 'Plato's metaphysics of structure'.

---

[194] At least this seems to be the model for the analysis of the *created* cosmos. The *Timaeus* does, however, have an account of what the cosmos would be like in the absence of that structure which the demiurge imposes in its account of the pre-cosmic condition of the receptacle. In this condition, the receptacle is not without features. Thus, one might rather suggest that this—the pre-cosmic condition of the receptacle—is analogous to the unlimited of the *Philebus*. In the *Philebus*, however, the unlimited is presented as one of the ingredients in the metaphysical analysis of mixtures. In the *Timaeus*, by contrast, the pre-cosmic condition of the receptacle is an alternative to the created cosmos and not an ingredient in the analysis thereof.

CHAPTER 5

Plato's Metaphysics of Structure

My examination of Plato's discussions of composition has focused on his exploration of two different models of composition. In the *Theaetetus*, in the discussion of the monists in the *Sophist*, and, above all, in the negative movement of the mereological undercurrent to the *Parmenides*, we have seen Plato create puzzles from the view that a whole is identical to its parts; that is, that composition is identity. This model of composition, I have argued, is one that Plato rejects. His concern with this model is rather to expose the problems that its adoption creates. It is the Eleatics who are identified as being guilty of this inadequate model, at least by association. Whatever the historical justification for this association, its philosophical basis is found in Plato's portrayal of the Eleatics' desire for ontological innocence. The problem with innocence is that it fails to provide an account of a whole as a complex individual that is composed of, and does not simply collapse into, many.

Against the backdrop of these discussions of the innocent, but inadequate, model of composition Plato has been seen to offer his own, alternative model of composition. This alternative model departs not only from the extreme position on the relation between composition and identity of the innocent model, but also from the more moderate, but more pervasive, strategy of

interlinking composition and identity, which is found in Mereological discussions and in metaphysics based upon them. We saw
this, in particular, in the *Parmenides*, in the way in which the relations of parthood and of being a whole for were entirely divorced
from the relation of distinctness and from that of identity.

The outlines of Plato's alternative model emerge from the
positive movement of the mereological undercurrent to the
Parmenides. According to this alternative model, composition is
restricted; it is ontologically committed or creative; and it centrally involves the existence of certain structural relations
between the parts of a whole. The meat of the theory is then
found, not in direct discussion of part and whole, but in Plato's
recurring interest in certain composing relations; in the widespread discussions of combining, of mixing, and of fitting things
together, in the *Sophist*, *Philebus*, and *Timaeus*.

Plato's discussions of these composing relations provide myri-
ad diverse examples of composition: the composition of syllables; of sentences; of melodies; of entire scientific domains; and
of the whole material cosmos. But what these discussions provide is not particular theories about the examples as such: for
example, a theory about the composition of sentences or about
the composition of syllables. Rather, the sheer range of examples—and the common features that emerge from their consideration—show Plato at work on a general theory of composition,
which is partly illustrated through its application to certain
examples. That this is so is only confirmed by the general theorizing of relations such as mixing and combining that is found
both in the *Sophist* and, above all, in the *Philebus*, in its general
analysis of the constitution of mixtures.

What emerges from this general theorizing and from the illustrative examples of combining and of mixing, I have argued, is a
conception of wholes as contentful structures. Structure, according to this conception, is essential to the constitution of a whole.
Indeed, wholes, I have argued, are here best thought of as being
(instances) of structures and not as things that 'have' structure in
a way that makes structure seem more or less detachable from the
whole and its parts. In Plato's conception of wholes, structure is
no less essential to the parts of such a whole than to the whole

itself. The parts of such a whole are structure-laden; that is, the identity of the parts is determined only in the context of the whole they compose.

In concluding this book, I shall briefly consider, first, what one might say about the place of this conception of wholes in the broader context of Plato's (late) philosophical work; and, second, the questions that arise from reflection on this model of composition, considered as such.

5.1 THE PLATONIC CONTEXT

Plato's works provide us with numerous examples of wholes conceived as structures in the way I have proposed. (I have by no means considered them all.) In the main, such examples appear to be types, rather than tokens or particulars. For example, the complex domains of science that dominate the *Philebus'* examples are complex types; so too is the linguistic example that I extrapolated from the *Sophist*. However, the *Timaeus* has provided a comparable example of the (material) constitution of one—albeit rather special—particular, the cosmos, and of the material basis of all other particulars, at least according to the *Timaeus*.

The fact that the *Timaeus* applies this model of composition to a particular is interesting. For one might suppose that Plato is rather dismissive of the problem of composition as applied to particulars. Twice, certainly, he has Socrates give voice to such apparent lack of concern, in the *Parmenides* (129c4–d1) and in the *Philebus* (14d4–e4), where Socrates is keen to move the discussion on to talk of forms or types. And one might take such lack of concern at face value, and suppose that the innocent conception of composition will do just as well when it comes to particulars.[1]

Alternatively, however, one might suppose that, while the solution to Plato's problem of composition is sought at the level of types, and types are the principal focus of Plato's interest, the

---

[1] I am grateful here to discussion with Eric Lewis.

solution is expected to be applied in addition to tokens thereafter. Consideration of the *Timaeus* lends support to this alternative, as does the apparent ease with which one could move from an account of the composition of a type to an account of the composition of a token of the type. For example, the analysis of the constitution of a (type) sentence could surely be readily transferred to all tokens of that type.

Since Plato's analysis of wholes does, nonetheless, give pride of place to an analysis of complex types, it is tempting to seek from this analysis some answer to the question of what happens to forms, those intelligible, imperishable entities that play such a prominent role in the discussions of the *Phaedo* and *Republic*, and in the first part of the *Parmenides*. However, it is not at all clear to me how one should approach the kind of questions this would raise. Should one identify the kind of complex structures whose constitution I have been concerned to describe as being forms? Or would forms correspond to the structure of such wholes, abstractly conceived? Or to the structure-laden parts of such structures, as well or instead? And would this account for all the things one might describe as forms in Plato's later works? I do not know how to answer such questions, nor what criteria one would use as guides in attempting to do so.

The question of forms aside, there are, however, a number of general things that may be said about Plato's model of composition and its place in the context of his (late) philosophical work. Wholes, according to this model, are contentful structures. And structure—the structure of such wholes, abstractly conceived— turns out to be a basic and irreducible item in Plato's (late) ontology. This can be seen, for example, by the place given to structure in the *Philebus'* general analysis of the constitution of mixtures. Structure and the domain of content on which structure is imposed are the twin ingredients of this twofold analysis. (But they are not, as such, the ingredients of a mixture or whole; structure and content are separable only in analysis.)

Such structure is, pre-eminently, something intelligible. Indeed, it is the proper object of Platonic science, or so the analyses of science in both the *Sophist* and *Philebus* would suggest. Further, in both the *Philebus* and the *Timaeus*, if perhaps in different ways, this intelligible structure is portrayed as being built into the very fabric of things by the operations of a guiding and providential intelligence or of the equally providential demiurge. As such, structure is normative; a good thing that good things—and only good things—have. Thus, as we have seen, normative terms of value—such as harmony, proportion, and (due) measure—are bywords for structure, in Plato. The presence of such normative characteristics are conditions on structures. Thus, in the *Philebus*, mixtures are either good or fail to be mixtures at all.

The irreducibility, intelligibility, and normativity of structure might be identified as the core components of Plato's metaphysics of structure. And they can be seen to be closely connected, in various ways, with other recurring aspects of his (later) thought, to which others have drawn attention. The role of structure as the proper object of Platonic science may be placed within the context of the exploration of, broadly speaking, holistic models of knowledge or understanding, which has often been identified as a central feature of Plato's later works.[2] Indeed, his account of wholes might be viewed as a 'holist ontology' corresponding to such a holist epistemology. The normativity of structure may be placed within the context of the project of offering a teleological explanation of the cosmos and of the things within it. This project was first canvassed in the *Phaedo*, where Socrates found himself disappointed in Anaxagoras' failure to live up to the promise of providing such an account (97b8–99c8). It is carried out, in brief, in a passage of the *Philebus*, and, above all, in the *Timaeus*.[3]

The normativity of structure may also be seen to have an ethical dimension, although this has played no role in my discussion. Perhaps the best way to illustrate this dimension is to pick up on the wider resonances of Plato's talk of harmony in describing the nature of wholes and in his frequent use of musical structure as an

---

[2] See e.g. Burnyeat (1990: 209–18); G. Fine (1979); McCabe (2000); and Nehamas (1984).

[3] For the history of this project in Plato and discussion of the way in which it is carried out, see e.g. Lennox (1985); McCabe (2000, esp. ch. 6); and Sedley (1991).

example. Consider the role that (musical) harmony is accorded, in the *Timaeus*, in the teleological explanation of the organs of hearing.

> As much of music as is useful with respect to the hearing of sound[4] has been given for the sake of harmony (ἁρμονίας).[5] And harmony, which has motions akin to the revolutions of the soul within us, has been given by the Muses to one who avails himself of the Muses with intelligence not with a view to irrational pleasure—for which it is now thought to be useful—but as an ally in relation to the discordant revolution of the soul which has come to be within us towards its [coming to be] ordered and in harmony with itself. (47c7–d7)

As we learn from the end of the *Timaeus*, the goal of human life is to seek to bring the revolutions of the human soul into line with the harmonious revolutions of the universe. And to bring the revolutions of one's soul into line with those of the universe is to bring them into line with the revolutions of the world soul, whose constituents were mixed according to the proportions of the musical scale (for which, see *Timaeus* 35a–36b). The proportionate structure of the musical scale is here presented as the proportionate structure of the soul of the world and that structure which a human soul should itself aspire to attain. To attain this structure is to bring one's own (human) reason into line with the objects of reason, and so to gain fulfilment of the best human life (cf. *Timaeus* 90b6-d7).[6] It is thus fitting that music should be so frequent an example in the *Philebus* also, since the *Philebus* is a dialogue whose overall aim is to identify that psychic order (ἕξιν ψυχῆς καὶ διάθεσιν, *Phlb.* 11d4) which is responsible for the good human life.

Such ethical and epistemological concerns are, no doubt, but an example of the broader contexts in which Plato's metaphysics of structure is found. Detailed discussion of such broader concerns has, however, been outside the scope of this book. Instead, I have focused on trying to make sense of Plato's discussions of

---

[4] Reading φωνῆς, rather than φωνῇ, following Cornford (1937: 158 n. 4).

[5] Literally: the proportionate relations of the scale.

[6] Compare also the teleological explanation of vision, at *Timaeus* 47a1–c4. For a recent, valuable discussion of this ethical dimension of the *Timaeus* and its relation to the ethical goal of becoming like god (ὁμοίωσις θεῷ), see Sedley (1999).

composition considered on their own. In addition, I have sought to locate Plato's discussions of composition within the context of (some of the) dominant trends in modern discussions of composition. Thus, setting these specifically Platonic contexts aside, it remains to say something about the issues raised by reflection on the model of composition that Plato develops, considered as such.

5.2 PLATO'S MODEL OF COMPOSITION

Plato's model of composition is presented against the background of his exploration of what he takes to be an inadequate conception of composition. Central to this inadequate conception is the thesis that composition is identity. This—and the desire for ontological innocence that lies behind it—marked the principal point of contact between ancient and modern discussions of composition that I identified at the start of this book. The problem with innocence, I argued, is that it threatens to undermine the status of a whole as an individual, rather than a collection of many.[7] And the problem, I argued, that Plato sets out to solve is the problem of how to give an account of composition in such a way as to allow that a whole is an individual, rather than a collection.

The model of composition that Plato develops in response to this problem is not as yet a fully developed theory of composition. It is better described as an attempt to say what a whole of parts must be like. However, the model does have certain key characteristics that suffice to contrast it with those of others. According to this model, wholes of parts are contentful structures, whose parts get their identity only in the context of the whole they compose. Thus, unlike Lewis, Plato makes structure essential to the constitution of a whole. But, unlike Van Inwagen, he takes such structure to be no less essential to the parts than to the whole.[8]

---

[7] As in Ch. 1, I use the term 'collection' here simply as a convenient way of referring to many.

[8] Cf. my discussion in §4.1.

Plato presents the structure of such wholes, abstractly conceived, as something essentially intelligible. It is also normative in character. In reflecting on his conception of wholes, I shall consider the kinds of questions one would need to address if one were to attempt to develop a 'neo-Platonic' conception of composition for the modern age. However, I do not myself propose to attempt to develop such a conception; I shall do no more than indicate the directions in which one might look for an answer to the questions raised.

One very striking feature of Plato's characterization of wholes is their normative character. Wholes are either good things or fail to be wholes at all. This, I suspect, is a feature of the account that one might wish to detach. And it raises a number of questions. In particular, what should one say about apparently composite things that fail to meet the normative criteria for wholes? This is one aspect of a more general question as to what one should say about apparently composite things that fail to meet any one of Plato's conditions on wholes.

Consider, for example, the *Sophist*'s illustrative example: the composition of sentences. A sentence is something woven together from name and verb, in contrast to a string of names or a string of verbs. What, then, should we say about a string of names? Is it something—a string? And, if so, how is it composed? Borrowing from Aristotle, one might think of this as the question of heaps. In a number of places Aristotle distinguishes between wholes—things that are put together in such a way as to constitute a unity—and heaps.[9] The question is: what should we say about heaps?

There are, I think, three possible strategies of response, which are not necessarily exclusive. First, one might return to the thought that there might be more than one kind of composition. Thus, although a string of names fails Plato's criteria for the kind of whole he has been keen to describe, it may nonetheless be a composite of a different sort. (Plato's silence on the matter of other kinds of wholes suggests that this is not his own view, but it is a possible view.)

---

[9] See e.g. *Metaphysics* VII. 17, 1041^{b}11–12.

Second, one might try to weaken Plato's constraints upon wholes in order to accommodate (at least some) heaps.[10] This is related to a question I raised earlier (§4.1). If wholes are structures, then the question arises: what structures are there? Plato has placed both normative and what one might call 'rational' constraints upon structures: structures are the proper objects of science. If the normative constraints seem problematic, we might stick with the rational constraints. Thus we might, as I suggested, leave the question of what structures there are to be answered by science.[11]

No doubt, any such weakening of Plato's constraints will still leave some candidate wholes—some heaps—out of the account. And this is only to be expected, given the restricted character of Plato's conception of wholes (on which more below). The third possible strategy is then simply to deny that these are wholes at all. Taking our cue from Van Inwagen, we may rather think of these as things arranged 'heapwise', where nothing follows about the existence of a thing so arranged.[12]

Perhaps the most striking feature of Plato's model of composition is the view that the parts of a whole are structure-laden; that is, the parts of a whole get their identity only in the context of the structure of which they are part. And this view has some interesting consequences when it comes to considering the restricted character of Plato's conception of composition. Recall once more Lewis's claim that 'whenever there are some things, then there exists a fusion of those things': his Axiom of Unrestricted Composition.[13] At the start of this book I identified this as the principal assumption that Plato would reject (§1.2). And Plato has indeed proposed a restricted conception of composition.

[10] Or perhaps one might think of wholeness as something that comes in degrees, according as things approximate to the criteria in question.

[11] Cf. §4.1.

[12] Cf. Van Inwagen's account of artefacts in his (1990, §13). Notice, however, that whereas Van Inwagen's commitment to the claim that some things only compose something when they are caught up in the activity of a life commits him to denying the existence of any non-biological composite, the version the proposal here envisaged would rule out only candidate composites about which there were no scientific generalizations to be made.

[13] Lewis (1991: 74).

This can be seen, both in the outlines of the positive theory that emerged from the *Parmenides*; in the *Sophist*'s direct argument for the restricted character of combination; and in the fact that Plato's requirements upon wholes are clearly such that it is not the case that any and every collection of things will meet them.

However, the way in which Plato's conception of composition constitutes a rejection of Unrestricted Composition requires some thought. In particular, it should not be assumed that we might express such a rejection by a simple negation of the axiom as stated: that it is not the case that whenever there are some things, then there exists a fusion of those things; that is, that there are some things for which it is not the case that there is a fusion of those things, at least not if this is taken to suggest that we could identify some subset of 'things', such that there exist fusions (or, rather, wholes) of (only) those things.[14] Rather, the structure-laden character of parts, on Plato's model, suggests that he should instead be taken to challenge an assumption that may be seen to underlie Lewis's axiom: the assumption that there are some things that may readily be turned into parts. What is at issue, I suggest, is a contrast between two different approaches to composition.

Lewis has what one might call an 'atomistic' approach to composition. By this I do not mean that Lewis is committed to the existence of atoms.[15] What I mean is that Lewis approaches composition from the bottom up. One starts with things, which are candidate parts, as the building blocks of composition. And one builds up to composites from these things by taking various sets of things, which are more or less related to each other in various ways. But the various ways in which the things in question are related (including their composing something) seem somehow secondary to the things themselves. As an image for this conception, one might look to one of Lewis's own images,[16] as follows:

[14] A rejection of this sort is exemplified by Van Inwagen (1990).

[15] Lewis himself is explicit that his position is neutral as to the existence of atoms and/or atomless gunk, given Mereology and prior to the introduction of set theory, where (some) atoms are presupposed in the form of singletons. See Lewis (1991: 21, 74), and cf. Simons (1987, §I.6) on the general neutrality of systems of classical extensional mereology on the question of whether or not there are atoms.

[16] I am grateful to Chris Hughes for drawing this image to my attention.

Imagine a grid of a million tiny spots—pixels—each of which can be made light or dark. When some are light and some are dark, they form a picture, replete with interesting intrinsic gestalt properties. The case evokes reductionist comments. Yes, the picture really does exist. Yes, it really does have those gestalt properties. However, the picture and the properties reduce to the arrangement of light and dark pixels. They are nothing over and above the pixels. They make nothing true that is not made true already by the pixels. They could go unmentioned in an inventory of what there is without thereby rendering that inventory incomplete. And so on.[17]

This image is not offered in the context of a discussion of composition. But it uses language similar to that one finds in Lewis's discussions of composition.[18] And it nicely illustrates what I call Lewis's 'atomistic' approach.

In contrast to such an 'atomistic' approach to composition, the alternative model of composition that I have attributed to Plato might rather be described as a 'holist' conception. Rather than working from the bottom up, it proceeds, as it were, from the top down. The identity of a part is determined only in the context of the whole of which it is part. Thus, whether or not there is something such that it is a part of something else is determined only in the context of the whole in question. Wholes come first; and parts—and the things that are parts—only thereafter.[19]

The contrast between these two approaches to composition has consequences for the evaluation of Lewis's argument against the imposition of any restrictions upon composition.[20] Lewis's 'things' are all candidate parts. Indeed, by the Axiom of Unrestricted Composition, they will all in fact be parts, and, in almost all cases, parts of very many fusions indeed. But each such thing has perfectly good identity conditions independently of the fusion(s) of which each is part. Such an assumption is necessary, if,

[17] Lewis (1999: 294).

[18] Compare e.g. his talk of fusions as being 'nothing over and above' the parts that compose them, and thus as having no need of inclusion in an inventory of reality (Lewis 1991: 81).

[19] Cf. here K. Fine (1994), who calls into question the assumption that parts are prior to wholes, although in the context of a discussion in which structural modes of composition have been set to one side.

[20] For the argument, see Lewis (1986c: 211–13; 1991: 80–1), with my discussion in §1.3 above. I here redeem the promissory note there issued.

in arguing against restrictions upon composition, Lewis is to argue that any attempt to impose restrictions on which 'classes of things'[21] compose something must perforce result in vagueness, since, Lewis supposes, it will be 'a vague matter whether a given class satisfies our intuitive *desiderata* for composition'.[22] But, Lewis argues, 'The question . . . whether a given class does or does not have a mereological sum . . . cannot have a vague answer.'[23] If this argument is to get purchase, things must come first. If, alternatively, parts are to be found only in the context of the whole they compose, Lewis's argument appears to be blocked at the first move.

This characterization of parts as being, as I have put it, 'structure-laden' raises a number of questions of its own. The first is one to which I have already alluded in passing.[24] If the identity of the parts of a whole is determined only in the context of the whole they compose, then the parts will exist only for so long as the whole exists. Distinguish two versions of this: one trivial, one not. If parts as such are parts of a whole, then the parts will exist *as parts* only for so long as the whole exists. But the view that parts are structure-laden claims something stronger than this: that the parts in question are what they are—and not just are parts—only in the context of the whole they compose. It is the stronger claim that creates difficulties. For example, we are often inclined to talk of one thing that has at one time been part of one thing coming to be part of another. But such talk would need considerable refinement on the model proposed.

A second question concerns the nature of the dependence here claimed between part and whole. The claim that parts are structure-laden ties the identity of the parts (and not just as parts) to the whole of which they are part. Such a claim is very strong, especially as applied to perishable objects. One might preserve much of the spirit of the claim, while nonetheless weakening it to a modal claim, by tying the identity of the parts to a whole of which they are or *could be* part. An artefact example may then help to illustrate the nature of the claim at work.[25]

[21] The language is Lewis's (1986c: 211–12). Note, once again, how 'things' come first.
[22] Lewis (1986c: 212).   [23] Lewis (1986c: 212).   [24] §4.1 and §4.3 n. 51.
[25] I am grateful here to advice from Kathrin Koslicki.

Suppose that you are walking along a beach and discover a shaped wooden object, which you identify as a chair leg. The claim that parts get their identity only in the context of the whole of which they are or could be part is the claim that the identification of this wooden object as a chair leg is in some way dependent on the role it could play in the constitution of a chair. Note that we are not here concerned with an epistemological claim—the grounds on which you identify this wooden object as a chair leg. What is at issue is, rather, a metaphysical claim—the grounds on which it is true to say of it that it *is* a chair leg. The thought would be this: that in a world in which there are shaped wooden objects of precisely this sort, but no chairs, such shaped wooden objects would not be chair legs at all. The claim that parts are structure-laden is thus the claim that there is some sort of metaphysical dependence of the parts on the whole. Quite how such dependence should be understood would then need to be made clear.[26]

The view that parts are structure-laden also raises a question about the scope of this dependence of the parts on the whole, however understood. Consider the kind of layering of structures within structures of which the *Timaeus* has provided an example. One structure may occupy a position in—may be part of—another such structure, as, for example, a word, which is a structure of letters, may occupy a position in a sentence, which is a structure of words. If parthood is transitive, then the parts of the word—the letters—are parts of two different wholes: the word and the sentence. Is the identity of these parts—the letters—dependent on both of these wholes? Or should we instead say only that the identity of a part is determined in the context of some, but not every, whole of which it is part? The second seems preferable, being weaker than the first. Regarding Plato, it is not clear to me how one would determine which of these might be Plato's position; nor, indeed, whether Plato himself accepts the assumption of transitivity on which the question depends.[27]

---

[26] Discussions of dependence relations that may be of relevance here are found in K. Fine (1995); Lowe (1994); and Simons (1987, ch. 8).

[27] It is worthy of note that the kind of layering of structures that the *Timaeus* illustrates provides an example of precisely the kind of situation in which Rescher, for one, rather denies transitivity: thus he denies that a part of a cell is part of the organ of which that cell is part (Rescher 1955: 10).

These are (at least some of) the questions raised by reflection on Plato's model of composition, considered as such. Perhaps the most general question, however, is about the plausibility or otherwise of the kind of ontology it suggests. Plato's model of composition places structures (among) the fundamental items in his ontology,[28] and it resists the supposition that one can perfectly well identify the parts of such structures outside the context of the structure in which they are found. But an ontology of this sort may seem somewhat alien. Structures, it might be thought, are just not the right sort of entity to be at the base of one's ontology; there must be structure-independent 'objects' underlying them somewhere.

The attitude we take to such an ontology may differ, according as we think of it as an ontology for types or for tokens. It may fare better when viewed as an ontology for (complex) types, and this, as I have noted, is certainly Plato's own predominant focus. Certainly, in general, this has been the context in which I have been able to find comparable modern interest in structure: in the work of mathematical structuralists; and in their use of analogues from language and music. The ontological model may fare less well when viewed as an ontology for concrete tokens or material particulars. Perhaps, however, this is an Aristotelian prejudice[29]—structure is a relational item and relations are dependent items—or a Newtonian prejudice, based on a billiard-ball conception of the fundamental items of physics. If it is the latter, we might bear in mind that twentieth-century physics might well be thought to put this kind of assumption in doubt.[30]

---

[28] I say 'among', since there is nothing to prevent Plato from believing, in addition, in mereological atoms.

[29] If so, this may well be an Aristotelian prejudice from which Aristotle himself does not suffer. Of course, Aristotle's own views on composition would require extensive treatment of their own; but my own view is that they are in a number of respects in keeping with those of Plato.

[30] In this connection I have been interested to discover that, in contemporary philosophy of science, it has been suggested that one way in which to pursue the adoption of structural realism is to take it as a metaphysical thesis. Structural realism emphasizes that what is retained in the case of theory change is the structural content of scientific theories. One way in which to adopt a realist position that gives due weight to such continuity of structure has been described as '[entailing] a corresponding shift from a metaphysics of objects, properties and relations, to one that

Plato, of course, had no eye on twentieth-century physics. But the model of composition that he develops may be contrasted with what I have called an 'atomistic' approach to composition. Plato's approach to composition does not begin with independently identifiable things as the basic building blocks of composition. Rather, composites are contentful structures whose parts exist and may be identified only in the context of (some) whole of which they are (or could be) part. Such contentful structures are not subject to further ontological analysis except in abstraction.

takes structure as primitive' (Ladyman 1998: 418). Thanks are due here to James Ladyman for an introduction to this area of philosophy of science.

REFERENCES

ALGRA, K. (1995), *Concepts of Space in Greek Thought* (Leiden: Brill).

ALLEN, R. E. (ed.) (1965), *Studies in Plato's Metaphysics* (London: Routledge & Kegan Paul).

—— (1970), 'The Generation of Numbers in Plato's *Parmenides*', *Classical Philology*, 65: 30–4.

—— (1974), 'Unity and Infinity: *Parmenides* 142b–145a', *Review of Metaphysics*, 27: 697–725.

—— (1983), *Plato's Parmenides*, trans. with comment (Minneapolis: University of Minnesota Press).

ANSCOMBE, G. E. M. (1966), 'The New Theory of Forms', *The Monist*, 50: 403–20.

ANTON, J. P., and KUSTAS, G. L. (eds.) (1971), *Essays in Ancient Greek Philosophy* (New York: Albany).

ARMSTRONG, D. M. (1978), *Universals and Scientific Realism*, 2 vols. (Cambridge: Cambridge University Press).

—— (1989), *A Combinatorial Theory of Possibility* (Cambridge: Cambridge University Press).

—— (1991), 'Classes are States of Affairs', *Mind*, 100: 189–200.

ARTMANN, B., and SCHÄFER, L. (1993), 'On Plato's "Fairest Triangles" (*Timaeus* 54a)', *Historia Mathematica*, 20: 255–64.

BAKER, L. R. (1997), 'Why Constitution is not Identity', *Journal of Philosophy*, 94: 599–621.

BALTUSSEN, H. (2002), 'Philology or Philosophy? Simplicius on the Use of Quotation', in Worthington and Foley (2002).

—— (forthcoming), 'Wehrli's Edition of Eudemus of Rhodes: The Physical Fragments from Simplicius' Commentary on Aristotle's *Physics*', in Fortenbaugh and Bodnár (forthcoming).

BARKER, A. (1989), *Greek Musical Writings*, ii: *Harmonic and Acoustic Theory* (Cambridge: Cambridge University Press).

BARNES, J. (1988), 'Bits and Pieces', in Barnes and Mignucci (1988: 225–94).

—— and MIGNUCCI, M. (eds.) (1988), *Matter and Metaphysics*, Proceedings of the Fourth Symposium Hellenisticum, *Elenchos*, 14 (Naples: Bibliopolis).

BAXTER, D. (1988*a*), 'Identity in the Loose and Popular Sense', *Mind*, 97: 575–82.

—— (1988*b*), 'Many–One Identity', *Philosophical Papers*, 17: 193–216.

BLANCHETTE, P. (1999), 'Relative Identity and Cardinality', *Canadian Journal of Philosophy*, 29: 209–24.

BLUCK, R. S. (1975), *Plato's Sophist*, ed. G. C. Neal (Manchester: Manchester University Press).

BOGAARD, P. (1979), 'Heaps or Wholes: Aristotle's Explanation of Compound Bodies', *Isis*, 70: 11–29.

BOSTOCK, D. (1979), *Logic and Arithmetic*, ii: *Rational and Irrational Numbers* (Oxford: Clarendon Press).

—— (1988), *Plato's Theaetetus* (Oxford: Clarendon Press).

—— (1994), *Aristotle Metaphysics book Z and H* (Oxford: Clarendon Press).

BRAGUE, R. (1985), 'The Body of the Speech: A New Hypothesis on the Compositional Structure of Timaeus' Monologue', in O' Meara (1985: 53–83).

BROWN, L. (1986), 'Being in the *Sophist*: A Syntactical Inquiry', *Oxford Studies in Ancient Philosophy*, 4: 49–70.

BRUMBAUGH, R. S. (1961), *Plato on the One: The Hypotheses in the Parmenides* (New Haven: Yale University Press).

BURNYEAT, M. F. (1990), *The Theaetetus of Plato*, with trans. by M. J. Levett, rev. Burnyeat (Indianapolis: Hackett).

—— (2000), 'Plato on Why Mathematics is Good for the Soul', in Smiley (2000: 1–81).

—— *et al.* (1979), *Notes on Book Zeta of Aristotle's Metaphysics*, Study Aids Monograph no. 1 (Oxford: Sub-Faculty of Philosophy).

CALVO, T., and BRISSON, L. (eds.) (1997), *Interpreting the Timaeus–Critias*, Proceedings of the IV Symposium Platonicum, International Plato Studies, 9 (Sankt Augustin: Academia Verlag).

CHERNISS, H. (1954), 'A Much Misread Passage of the *Timaeus* (*Timaeus* 49c7–50b5)', *American Journal of Philology*, 75: 113–30.

—— (1957), 'The Relation of the *Timaeus* to Plato's Later Dialogues', *American Journal of Philology*, 78: 225–66.

COOK, R. M. (1972), *Greek Art: Its Development, Character and Influence* (London: Penguin).

COOPER, J. M. (ed.) (1997), *Plato: Complete Works* (Indianapolis: Hackett).

CORNFORD, F. M. (1935), *Plato's Theory of Knowledge*, The *Theaetetus* and *Sophist* of Plato trans. with running commentary (London: Routledge & Kegan Paul).

—— (1937), *Plato's Cosmology*, The *Timaeus* of Plato trans. with running commentary (London: Routledge & Kegan Paul).

—— (1939), *Plato and Parmenides: Parmenides' Way of Truth and Plato's Parmenides* (London: Routledge & Kegan Paul).

CURD, P. (1990), '*Parmenides* 142b5–144e7: The "Unity is Many" Arguments', *Southern Journal of Philosophy*, 28: 19–35.

DENYER, N. C. (1983), 'Plato's Theory of Stuffs', *Philosophy*, 58: 315–27.

—— (1991), *Language, Thought and Falsehood* (London: Routledge).

DETEL, W. (1993), *Aristoteles Analytica Posteriora*, 2 vols. (Berlin: Akademie Verlag).

DIELS, H. (ed.) (1882), *Simplicii in Aristotelis Physicorum Libros Quattuor Priores Commentaria, Comm. in Arist. Graeca*, ix (Berlin).

DIXSAUT, M. (ed.) (1999), *La Fêlure du plaisir: Études sur le Philèbe de Platon*, 1, commentaires (Paris: Vrin).

DOWLING, W. J., and HARWOOD, D. L. (1986), *Music Cognition* (Orlando, Fla.: Academic Press).

FINE, G. (1979), 'Knowledge and *Logos* in the *Theaetetus*', *Philosophical Review*, 88: 366–97.

—— (1986), 'Immanence', *Oxford Studies in Ancient Philosophy*, 4: 71–97.

—— (ed.) (1999), *Plato 2: Ethics, Politics, Religion and the Soul* (Oxford: Oxford University Press).

FINE, K. (1994), 'Compounds and Aggregates', *Noûs*, 28: 137–58.

—— (1995), 'Ontological Dependence', *Proceedings of the Aristotelian Society*, 95: 269–90.

FORTENBAUGH, W. W. and BODNÁR, I. (eds.) (forthcoming), *Eudemus of Rhodes*, Rutgers University Studies in Classics and Humanities, 11 (New Brunswick, NJ: Transaction).

FOWLER, H. N. (1921), *Plato: Theaetetus and Sophist*, Loeb Classical Library (London: William Heinemann).

FREDE, D. (1993), *Plato: Philebus*, trans. with introduction and notes (Indianapolis: Hackett).

—— (1997), *Platon: Philebos*, Übersetzung und Kommentar (Göttingen: Vandenhoek & Ruprecht).

FREDE, M. (1980), 'The Original Notion of Cause', in Schofield *et al.* (1980: 217–49).

—— (1988), 'Being and Becoming in Plato', in J. Annas and R. H. Grimm (eds.), *Oxford Studies in Ancient Philosophy*, suppl. vol., 37–52.

—— and PATZIG, G. (1988), *Aristoteles Metaphysik Z*, Text, Übersetzung, und Kommentar, 2 vols. (Munich: C. H. Beck).

FREGE, G. (1953), *The Foundations of Arithmetic: A Logico-Mathematical Enquiry into the Concept of Number*, trans. J. L. Austin, 2nd edn. (Oxford: Blackwell).

FURLEY, D. J., and ALLEN, R. E. (eds.) (1975), *Studies in Presocratic Philosophy*, ii (London: Routledge & Kegan Paul).

GALLOP, D. (1963), 'Plato and the Alphabet', *Philosophical Review*, 62: 364–76.

GENTZLER, J. (ed.) (1998), *Method in Ancient Philosophy* (Oxford: Clarendon Press).

GILL, C., and McCABE, M. M. (eds.) (1996), *Form and Argument in Late Plato* (Oxford: Clarendon Press).

GILL, M. L. (1987), 'Matter and Flux in the *Timaeus*', *Phronesis*, 32: 34–53.

—— (1996), *Plato Parmenides*, trans. Mary Louise Gill and Paul Ryan, introd. by Mary Louise Gill (Indianapolis: Hackett).

GÓMEZ-LOBO, A. (1977), 'Plato's Description of Dialectic in the *Sophist* 253d1–e2', *Phronesis* 22: 29–47.

GOSLING, J. C. B. (1975), *Plato Philebus*, trans. with notes and commentary (Oxford: Clarendon Press).

GREGORY, A. (2000), *Plato's Philosophy of Science* (London: Duckworth).

GREGORY, R. L. (ed.) (1987), *The Oxford Companion to the Mind* (Oxford: Oxford University Press).

GULLEY, N. (1960), 'The Interpretation of Plato, *Timaeus* 49D–E', *American Journal of Philology*, 81: 53–64.

HARTE, V. A. (1996), 'Aristotle: *Metaphysics* H6: A Dialectic with Platonism', *Phronesis*, 41: 276–304.

—— (1999), 'Quel prix pour la vérité? (64a7–66d3)', in Dixsaut (1999: 385–401).

HEATH, T. L. (1921), *A History of Greek Mathematics*, i (Oxford: Clarendon Press).

—— (1956), *The Thirteen Books of Euclid's Elements*, with introd. and comm., 3 vols., 2nd edn. (Cambridge: Cambridge University Press).

HEINAMAN, R. E. (1983), 'Communion of Forms', *Proceedings of the Aristotelian Society*, 83: 175–90.

HOSSACK, K. (2000), 'Plurals and Complexes', *British Journal for the Philosophy of Science*, 51: 411–43.

HOWELL, P., CROSS, I., and WEST, R. (eds.) (1991), *Representing Musical Structure* (London: Academic Press).

IRWIN, T. H. (1977), 'Plato's Heracleiteanism', *Philosophical Quarterly*, 27: 1–13.

JOHNSTON, M. (1992), 'Constitution is not Identity', *Mind*, 101: 89–105.

JORDAN, W. (1983), *Plato's Arguments for Forms*, Proceedings of the Cambridge Philological Society, suppl. vol. 9.

KIRK, G. S., RAVEN, J. E., and SCHOFIELD, M. (1983), *The PreSocratic Philosophers*, 2nd edn. (Cambridge: Cambridge University Press).

KRUMHANSL, C. L. (1991), 'Music Psychology: Tonal Structures in Perception and Memory', *Annual Review of Psychology*, 42: 277–303.

KUTSCHERA, F. von (1995), *Platons Parmenides* (Berlin: Walter de Gruyter).

LADYMAN, J. (1998), 'What is Structural Realism?', *Studies in History and Philosophy of Science*, 29: 409–24.

LEE, E. N. (1966), 'On the Metaphysics of the Image in Plato's *Timaeus*', *The Monist*, 50: 341–68.

—— (1967), 'On Plato's *Timaeus* 49D4–E7', *American Journal of Philology*, 88: 1–28.

—— (1971), 'On the "Gold-Example" in Plato's *Timaeus* (50A5–B5)', in Anton and Kustas (1971: 219–235).

LENNOX, J. (1985), 'Plato's Unnatural Teleology', in O' Meara (1985: 195–218).

LEWIS, D. (1986*a*), 'Against Structural Universals', *Australasian Journal of Philosophy*, 64: 25–46.

—— (1986*b*), 'Comment on Armstrong and Forrest', *Australasian Journal of Philosophy*, 64: 92–3.

—— (1986*c*), *On the Plurality of Worlds* (Oxford: Blackwell).

—— (1991), *Parts of Classes* (Oxford: Blackwell).

—— (1999), *Papers in Metaphysics and Epistemology* (Cambridge: Cambridge University Press).

LOCKE, J. (1894), *An Essay concerning Human Understanding*, ed. A. C. Fraser, 2 vols. (Oxford: Clarendon Press).

LOWE, E. J. (1989), *Kinds of Being: A Study of Individuation, Identity and the Logic of Sortal Terms* (Oxford: Blackwell).

—— (1994), 'Ontological Dependency', *Philosophical Papers*, 23: 31–48.

MCCABE, M. M. (1994), *Plato's Individuals* (Princeton: Princeton University Press).

—— (1996), 'Unity in the *Parmenides*: The Unity of the *Parmenides*', in Gill and McCabe (1996: 5–47).

—— (2000), *Plato and his Predecessors* (Cambridge: Cambridge University Press).

MANSION, S. (ed.) (1961), *Aristote et les problèmes de méthode*, Papers of the Second Symposium Aristotelicum (Louvain: Publications Universitaires de Louvain).

MEINWALD, C. (1991), *Plato's Parmenides* (Oxford: Oxford University Press).

—— (1996), 'One/Many Problems: *Philebus* 14c1–15c3', *Phronesis* 41: 95–103.

MEINWALD, C. (1998), 'Prometheus's Bounds: *Peras* and *Apeiron* in Plato's *Philebus*', in Gentzler (1998: 165–80).

MILLS, K. W. (1968), 'Some Aspects of Plato's Theory of Forms: *Timaeus* 49c ff.', *Phronesis*, 13: 145–70.

MOHR, R. D. (1978), 'The Gold Analogy in Plato's *Timaeus* (50a4–b5)', *Phronesis*, 23: 243–52.

—— (1980), 'Image, Flux and Space in Plato's *Timaeus*', *Phoenix*, 34: 138–52.

MORAVCSIK, J. (1962), 'Being and Meaning in the *Sophist*', *Acta Philosophica Fennica*, 14: 23–78.

—— (1982), 'Forms and Dialectic in the Second half of the *Parmenides*', in Schofield and Nussbaum (1982: 135–53).

—— (1992), *Plato and Platonism* (Oxford: Blackwell).

MORROW, G. (1968), 'Plato's Theory of the Primary Bodies in the *Timaeus* and the Later Doctrine of Forms', *Archiv für Geschichte der Philosophie*, 50: 12–28.

—— and DILLON, J. M. (1987), *Proclus' Commentary on Plato's Parmenides* (Princeton: Princeton University Press).

NAGEL, E. (1952), 'Wholes, Sums, and Organic Unities', *Philosophical Studies*, 3: 17–32.

NEHAMAS, A. (1984), '*Episteme* and *Logos* in Plato's Later Thought', *Archiv für Geschichte der Philosophie*, 66: 11–36.

NOONAN, H. W. (1993), 'Constitution is Identity', *Mind*, 102: 133–46.

OLIVER, A. (1994), 'Are Subclasses Parts of Classes?', *Analysis*, 54: 215–23.

O'MEARA, D. J. (ed.) (1985), *Platonic Investigations* (Washington: Catholic University Press of America).

OSBORNE, C. (1996), 'Space, Time, Shape and Direction: Creative Discourse in the *Timaeus*', in Gill and McCabe (1996: 179–211).

OWEN, G. E. L. (1953), 'The Place of the *Timaeus* in Plato's Dialogues', *Classical Quarterly*, NS 3: 79–95; repr. in Owen (1986: 65–84).

—— (1957), 'A Proof in the *Peri Ideôn*', *Journal of Hellenistic Studies*, 77: 103–11; repr. in Owen (1986: 165–79).

—— (1961), '*Tithenai ta phainomena*', in Mansion (1961: 83–103); repr. in Owen (1986: 239–51).

—— (1970), 'Notes on Ryle's Plato', in Wood and Pitcher (1970: 341–72); repr. in Owen (1986: 85–103).

—— (1971), 'Plato on Not-Being', in Vlastos (1971: 223–67); repr. in Owen (1986: 104–37).

—— (1975), 'Eleatic Questions', in Furley and Allen (1975: ii. 48–81); repr. in Owen (1986: 3–26).

—— (1986), *Logic, Science and Dialectic: Collected Papers in Greek Philosophy, G. E. L. Owen*, ed. Martha Nussbaum (London: Duckworth).

PALMER, J. A. (1999), *Plato's Reception of Parmenides* (Oxford: Clarendon Press).

PIERCE, J. R. (1992), *The Science of Musical Sound*, rev. edn. (New York: Freeman).

PRITCHARD, P. (1990), 'The Meaning of Δύναμις at *Timaeus* 31c', *Phronesis*, 35: 182–93.

—— (1995), *Plato's Philosophy of Mathematics* (Sankt Augustin: Akademia Verlag).

QUINE, W. V. O. (1953), *From a Logical Point of View*, Nine Logico-Philosophical Essays, 2nd edn. (Cambridge, Mass.: Harvard University Press).

RESCHER, N. (1955), 'Axioms for the Part Relation', *Philosophical Studies*, 6: 8–11.

—— and OPPENHEIM, P. (1955), 'Logical Analysis of Gestalt Concepts', *British Journal for the Philosophy of Science*, 6: 89–106.

RESNIK, M. D. (1975), 'Mathematical Knowledge and Pattern Cognition', *Canadian Journal of Philosophy*, 5: 25–39.

—— (1981), 'Mathematics as a Science of Patterns: Ontology and Reference', *Noûs*, 15: 529–50.

—— (1982), 'Mathematics as a Science of Patterns: Epistemology', *Noûs*, 16: 95–105.

—— (1988), 'Mathematics from the Structural Point of View', *Revue Internationale de Philosophie*, 42: 400–24.

RYLE, G. (1939), 'Plato's *Parmenides*', *Mind*, 48: 129–51, 302–25; repr. with Afterword in Allen (1965: 97–147).

—— (1960), 'Letters and Syllables in Plato', *Philosophical Review*, 69: 431–51.

SAYRE, K. M. (1983), *Plato's Late Ontology: A Riddle Resolved* (Princeton: Princeton University Press).

—— (1987), 'The *Philebus* and the Good: The Unity of the Dialogue in which the Good is Unity', *Proceedings of the Boston Area Colloquium in Ancient Philosophy*, 2 (ed. J. J. Cleary), 45–71.

—— (1996), *Parmenides' Lesson: Translation and Explication of Plato's Parmenides* (Notre Dame, Ind.: University of Notre Dame Press).

SCALTSAS, T. (1985), 'Substratum, Subject and Substance', *Ancient Philosophy*, 5: 215–40.

—— (1990), 'Is a Whole Identical to its Parts?', *Mind*, 99: 583–98.

SCHOFIELD, M. (1972), 'The Dissection of Unity in Plato's *Parmenides*', *Classical Philology*, 68: 102–9.

SCHOFIELD, M. (1973*a*), 'A Neglected Regress Argument in the *Parmenides*', *Classical Quarterly*, NS 23: 29–44.

—— (1973*b*), 'Eudoxus in the *Parmenides*', *Museum Helveticum*, 30: 1–19.

—— and NUSSBAUM, M. C. (eds.) (1982), *Language and Logos: Studies in Ancient Greek Philosophy Presented to G. E. L. Owen* (Cambridge: Cambridge University Press).

—— BURNYEAT, M. F., and BARNES, J. (eds.) (1980), *Doubt and Dogmatism: Studies in Hellenistic Epistemology* (Oxford: Clarendon Press).

SEDLEY, D. N. (1982), 'The Stoic Criterion of Identity', *Phronesis*, 27: 255–75.

—— (1991), 'Teleology and Myth in the *Phaedo*', *Proceedings of the Boston Area Colloquium in Ancient Philosophy*, 5 (ed. J. J. Cleary and D. C. Shartin), 359–83.

—— (1999), 'The Ideal of Godlikeness', in G. Fine (1999: 309–28).

SHAPIRO, S. (1983), 'Mathematics and Reality', *Philosophy of Science*, 50: 523–48.

—— (1989), 'Structure and Ontology', *Philosophical Topics*, 17: 145–71.

SILVERMAN, A. (1991), 'Timaean Particulars', *Classical Quarterly*, NS 42: 87–113.

SIMONS, P. (1982), 'Three Essays in Formal Ontology', in Smith (1982: 111–260).

—— (1987), *Parts: A Study in Ontology* (Oxford: Clarendon Press).

SMILEY, T. (ed.) (2000), *Mathematics and Necessity: Essays in the History of Philosophy*, Proceedings of the British Academy, 103 (Oxford: Oxford University Press).

SMITH, B. (ed.) (1982), *Parts and Moments: Studies in Logic and Formal Ontology* (Munich: Philosophia Verlag).

SORABJI, R. K. (1988), *Matter, Space and Motion* (London: Duckworth).

SPENDER, N. (1987), 'Music, Psychology of', in Gregory (1987: 499–505).

STRIKER, G. (1970), *Peras und Apeiron. Das Problem der Formen in Platons Philebos* (Göttingen: Vandenhoeck & Ruprecht).

TAYLOR, A. E. (1934), *The Parmenides of Plato* (Oxford: Clarendon Press).

TREVASKIS, J. R. (1966), 'The μέγιστα γένη and the Vowel Analogy of Plato, *Sophist*, 253', *Phronesis* 11: 99–116.

TURNER, J. (ed.) (1996), *The Dictionary of Art*, 34 vols. (New York: Grove; London: Macmillan).

VAN INWAGEN, P. (1990), *Material Beings* (Ithaca, NY: Cornell University Press).

—— (1994), 'Composition as Identity', *Philosophical Perspectives*, 8 (*Logic and Language*), 207–20.

VLASTOS, G. (1939), 'The Disorderly Motion in the Timaios', *Classical Quarterly*, 33: 71–83.

—— (ed.) (1971), *Plato: A Collection of Critical Essays*, i: *Metaphysics and Epistemology* (Garden City, NY: Doubleday).

—— (1975), *Plato's Universe* (Oxford: Clarendon Press).

WALKER, G. (2000), 'Creation and Destruction', Ph.D. thesis, London University.

WATERFIELD, R. A. H. (1980), 'The Place of the *Philebus* in Plato's Dialogues', *Phronesis*, 25: 270–305.

WEST, M. L. (1992), *Greek Music* (Oxford: Clarendon Press).

WIGGINS, D. (1980), *Sameness and Substance* (Oxford: Blackwell).

WOOD, O. P., and PITCHER, G. (eds.) (1970), *Ryle* (New York: Doubleday).

WORTHINGTON, I., and FOLEY, J. (eds.) (2002), *Epea and Grammata: Oral and Written Communication in Ancient Greece*, Orality and Literacy, 4 (Leiden: Brill).

ZEYL, D. (1975), 'Plato and Talk of a World in Flux: *Timaeus* 49a6–50b5', *Harvard Studies in Classical Philology*, 79: 125–48.

GENERAL INDEX

INDEX OF NAMES

INDEX LOCORUM